SMART SCIENCE

Explore • Investigate • Inspire

D1322324

SMART LEARNING

SMART **SCIENCE**

Smart Learning Limited
39 Parkside
Cambridge CB1 1PN
Tel: 01223 477550
Fax: 01223 477551
Website: www.smart-learning.co.uk

© Smart Learning Limited 2013
First published 2013

Acknowledgements
Authors: Karen Bysouth, Aidan Gill, David Sang and Gary Skinner
Series Editor: Aidan Gill
Cover design: Red Graphic Cambridge Ltd and Sharpe Graphic Design: Andrew Sharpe
Inside design: Sharpe Graphic Design: Andrew Sharpe

(Key: l-left; r-right; t-top; c-centre; b-bottom)

Illustrations: All original artwork is courtesy of **Sharpe Graphic Design: Andrew Sharpe**, with the exception of the following by **Claudia Hahn**, www.heliocyan.com: 90c, 98b.

Data: Swift migration courtesy of the **British Trust for Ornithology**: 93tr.

Photographs: The Advertising Archives 50tr; **Andrew Davis and Sue Bunnewell, with thanks to Professor Cathie Martin and the John Innes Centre** 30b; **epa european pressphoto agency b.v. / Alamy** 219r; **Aidan Gill** 176cr; © **Gordon Stillman Photography** 58bl; **NASA** 248br; **Noise Killer**, for the use of their photograph on which to base artwork 277tr; **Science Photo Library Ltd:** 78cr, 136b, 174tr, 220tr, 254tr, 257b, 264b, 285r; 3D4medical.com 70r; AJ Photo 274t; Steve Allen 270tr; Andrew Lambert Photography 118t, 122bl, 122br, 132bl, 132br, 149r, 151b, 153tr, 163r, 171r, 173cr, 220br, 223t, 270cr; Henry Arden 28b; Bill Barksdale, AGStock USA 176b; Adrian Bicker 21tl, 21tc; Ian Boddy 79tr; Martin Bond 187br; Dr John Brackenbury 35t; Massimo Brega 9tr; Massimo Brega, The Lighthouse 232t; Rolf Brenner 138tr; Robert Brook 105b, 162c, 172tr; Andrew Brookes, National Physical Laboratory 237t; Will Brown, Chemical Heritage Foundation 141r; BSIP, Alexandre 114r; BSIP, Chassenet 292tr; Dr Jeremy Burgess 319tr; Tony Camacho 57r; Alex Cherney, Terrastro.com 5b, 210–211c; Martyn F. Chillmaid 41c, 122c, 162cl, 179cr, 265tr; Christian Jegou Publiphoto Diffusion 292br; John Chumack 307tr, 315cr; David C Clegg 104r; Clouds Hill Imaging Ltd 87b; CMS Experiment, CERN 211br; Corbin O'Grady Studio 8cr; Gerald & Buff Corsi, Visuals Unlimited 33cr, 37l; Nick Daly 21tr; DB2Stock 269r; Mark De Fraeye 197tr; Victor De Schwanberg 293br; Garry Delong 12tl; Alan & Linda Detrick 21cl; Michael Donne 29b, 246cr; A.B. Dowsett 46b, 77bl; John Durham 185t; Wally Eberhart, Visuals Unlimited 204cr; Jim Edds 214tr; Emilio Segre Visual Archive, American Institute of Physics 110cr; William Ervin 92tr; Robert J. Erwin 169t; European Space Agency 302c; John A EY III 257t; Don W. Fawcett 67tr; Jock Fistick, Reporters 111b; David Fleetham, Visuals Unlimited 16b, 33tr; Fletcher & Baylis 21c, 37r; Frank and Helena 301tr; Simon Fraser 187tr, 206br, 209tr; Gordon Garradd 203b; G.F. Gennaro 53t; GIPhotostock 227r, 260tr, 286tr; Steve Gschmeissner 3b, 4b, 8–9bl, 48t, 58bc, 110–111bl; Gustoimages 39br; Adam Hart-Davis 200tr; John Heseltine 172cr; Phil Hill 155t; Tim Holt 96t; J.C.Hurni, Publiphoto Diffusion 153br; Ralph Hutchings 49b, 55b; Hybrid Images 231b; IPMB/European Space Agency 306r; Carlyn Iversson 63c; Ashley Jouhar 259r; Joyce Photographics 204 tr; James King-Holmes 80cr; Stephen J. Kraseman 102cr; Lawrence Lawry 113cr; Tom & Pat Leeson 21b; G. Brad Lewis 193br; LTH NHS Trust 211tr; Dr P. Marazzi 55t, 77cr, 172br; Michael Marten 109cr; Doug Martin 253r; Maximilian Stock Ltd 39tr, 214br; Tony McConnell 193tr, 296tr, 297br, 301br; Astrid & Hanns-Frieder Michler 11t; Cordelia Molloy 249tl, 284t; Glennis Moore 41tr; Hank Morgan 210cr; NASA 191t, 310c, 317t; Natural History Museum, London 21bl; NIBSC 77cl; Susumu Nishinaga 12bl; Ria Novosti 45r, 168br; NSIL/Dick Roberts, Visuals Unlimited 204br; David Nunuk 37r, 187cc, 291b, 314br, 318br; Stephan & Donna O'Meara 195r; David Parker 288br; Pasieka 77br, 318b; Pegasus, Visuals Limited 116r; David M. Phillips 178r; Photostock-Israel 311b; Philippe Plailly 279r, 281b, 314cr; Maria Platt-Evans 233b; Power and Syred 21cr, 36b; Monty Rakusen 84r, 111tr; Paul Rapson 187cr; Hans Reinhard 92tl; Rosal 192bl; Alexis Rosenfeld 9br, 89r, 95r, 236t; John Sanford 316r; Science Source 273b; Sciepro 51r; 10r Scimat; Alexander Semenov 21br; Millard H. Sharp 62r, 93b; Duncan Shaw 271cr; Martin Shields 58tr, 72c; Paul Shoesmith 41tc; Springer Medizin 271br; St Mary's Hospital Medical School 80tr; Paul D. Stewart 28c; Bjorn Svensson 212r, 27b; Tek Image 183r, 299r; Mark Thomas 25b; Tim Vernon LTH NHS Trust 79br; Rachel Warne 107cl; F.S. Westmorland 239b; Dirk Wiersma 71b, 166r; Mark Williamson 278tr; Charles D. Winters 127r, 142c, 152br, 156r, 180t; Kent Wood 275b; Ed Young, AGstock USA 172tc; Walter Zerla 295b; Jim Zipp 102cl; **Shutterstock:** 16cl, 32r, 43b, 66cr, 75b, 76r, 91t, 93tr, 108b, 119br, 121r, 123t, 135b, 142tr, 145bl, 145br, 146tr, 146cr, 146br, 147tr, 147cr, 153bl, 164c, 179tr, 181tr, 181br, 189b, 192br, 196c, 197c, 198tr, 200cr, 250tr, 252t; **Gary Skinner** 85tr.

Front cover: **Shutterstock**

The publishers have made every effort to trace the copyright holders, but if they have inadvertently overlooked any they will be pleased to make the necessary arrangements at the first opportunity.

All our rights reserved. No part of this book may be reproduced, stored in a retrieval system, or transmitted, in any form or by any means, electronic, mechanical, photocopying, recording or otherwise, without prior permission of Smart Learning Limited.

British Library Cataloguing-in-Publication Data
A CIP record for this book is available from the British Library

ISBN 978-1-84276-256-1

Printed in the UK by Bell & Bain Limited, Glasgow

Contents

How to use this book

This book is organised into the three main sciences: Biology, Chemistry and Physics. The Chemistry section also contains Earth Sciences, showing how our planet works.

Each subject has an introduction, and then a set of Units.

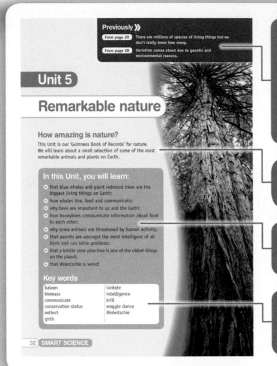

Each Unit starts with a 'Previously' box that shows what you need to have understood before the Unit starts:

▶ **'Remember' means you will have learnt about this in primary school.**

▶ **'From page …' points you to where you can find this information in this book.**

The opening text introduces the science ideas contained in the Unit.

There is a summary of all the things you will learn in this Unit on the introduction page.

There is a Key Words list for every Unit. Each Key Word is highlighted in the main text, and there is a full Glossary of all Key Words at the back of the book.

Each new science idea is explained in its own box. The heading is usually a question you might want to think about as you read the text.

There are some icons that appear next to science ideas or questions. This one means that this idea will help you with using data.

There is also a special section at the back of the book all about handling data.

Often, there will be a question or two with each science idea. You can use these to test yourself – if you can answer them, it means you have understood the science idea.

Sometimes the question will ask you to do some online research or find out more.

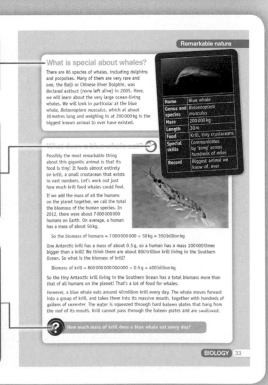

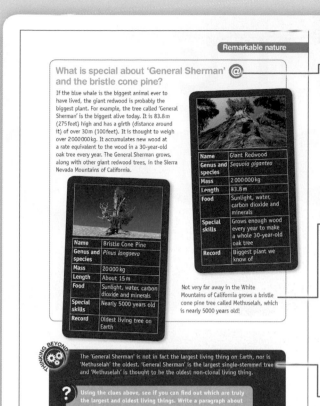

Remarkable nature

What is special about 'General Sherman' and the bristle cone pine? @

If the blue whale is the biggest animal ever to have lived, the giant redwood is probably the biggest plant. For example, the tree called 'General Sherman' is the biggest alive today. It is 83.8m (275 feet) high and has a girth (distance around it) of over 30m (100 feet). It is thought to weigh over 2 000 000 kg. It accumulates new wood at a rate equivalent to the wood in a 30-year-old oak tree every year. The General Sherman grows, along with other giant redwood trees, in the Sierra Nevada Mountains of California.

Name	Giant Redwood
Genus and species	*Sequoia gigantea*
Mass	2 000 000 kg
Length	83.8 m
Food	Sunlight, water, carbon dioxide and minerals
Special skills	Grows enough wood every year to make a whole 30-year-old oak tree
Record	Biggest plant we know of

Name	Bristle Cone Pine
Genus and species	*Pinus longaeva*
Mass	20 000 kg
Length	About 15 m
Food	Sunlight, water, carbon dioxide and minerals
Special skills	Nearly 5000 years old
Record	Oldest living tree on Earth

Not very far away in the White Mountains of California grows a bristle cone pine tree called Methuselah, which is nearly 5000 years old!

THINKING BEYOND

The 'General Sherman' is not in fact the largest living thing on Earth, nor is 'Methuselah' the oldest. 'General Sherman' is the largest single-stemmed tree and 'Methuselah' is thought to be the oldest non-clonal living thing.

? Using the clues above, see if you can find out which are truly the largest and oldest living things. Write a paragraph about each of them.

BIOLOGY 37

This icon means this science idea talks about how science works in the real world around us, and why science is important.

Throughout the book you will find all sorts of interesting facts and stories about scientists and about the world around you – keep an eye out for them!

Sometimes you will see 'Thinking Beyond' sections. These will tell you more about science and scientists, and get you to think about big ideas. These are great for learning more, and if you like a challenge!

This icon means this science idea also helps explain ideas from other subjects, like maths, geography or history.

There are many facts in this book that the rest of your family and even your teachers might not know – see if you can spot them!

Every Unit has a 'You need to remember that' section near the end. These are to help you check what you have learnt, and can be really useful for revision too.

Every Unit ends with a 'Next time' box, which points you to parts of the book that build on the ideas you have just learnt.

Unit 5

Why is Welwitschia truly special

Welwitschia has been given a number of different descriptions; the world's ugliest, weirdest, strangest, most wonderful and most bizarre plant.

Welwitschia is the only species in its genus, the only genus in its family and the only family in its order. There is no other species of living thing even remotely like it!

It lives on the coast of Namibia and Angola in South West Africa. This region is a dry desert but water is available in early morning mists. *Welwitschia* consists of a long taproot, a short trunk and just two leaves. The leaves grow throughout the life of the plant, which can be as long as 2000 years. The leaves curve downwards, so that they collect the mist into water droplets. These droplets run into the soil and to the roots.

Growing plants have leaves about 2m long, but the wind blowing them against the sand wears away the growth. If they weren't constantly worn away like this it is thought each leaf would be well over 100m long!

Name	Welwitschia
Genus and species	*Welwitschia mirabilis*
Mass	100 kg
Length	About 2 m
Food	Sunlight, water, carbon dioxide and minerals
Special skills	Lives in very harsh conditions
Record	Very, very unique

You need to remember that:

- The world is full of amazing living things.
- Blue whales are the biggest animals that have ever lived.
- Whales feed off some of the smallest animals on the Earth.
- Whales communicate with each other by 'singing' under water.
- Honey bees communicate information about food to each other through 'waggle dances'.
- Whales and bees are threatened by human activity.
- Parrots are amongst the most intelligent of all birds and can solve problems.
- The biggest giant redwood trees are some of the largest living things on the planet.
- Bristle cone pine trees can live to be some of the oldest things on the planet.
- *Welwitschia* is weird!

Next time »

Unit 15 Each living thing is adapted to the place it lives, its habitat (page 95).
Unit 16 There are over 7 billion people on Earth, which puts a big strain on the environment (page 104).

Introducing Biology

The science of biology is the investigation of living things. Those living things can be as small as cold viruses or as big as a Giant Redwood tree! Scientists have explained a great deal of how life works, but there is a huge amount we still don't know. One recent achievement has been the complete mapping of the human genome. This is the 'code' made of over 3 300 000 000 chemical pieces that tells our bodies how to work and grow. The way this map was built was invented by Fred Sanger, who has a research lab named after him in Cambridge.

What makes a thing a living thing?

The usual answer is that a living thing does ALL of the following 'functions':

Nutrition – it requires food
Respiration – it releases energy from food
Excretion – it gets rid of wastes left behind after energy is released from food
Movement – it uses energy to move
Growth – it uses energy and materials from food to grow
Reproduction – it uses energy and materials from food to create more versions of itself
Sensitivity – it can sense and respond to its environment

The first letters of the seven functions can be used to help you remember them. Many people remember 'MRS GREN' but you can make up your own if you prefer.

In addition, all living things are made of *cells*, tiny 'building blocks' that we can only see if we view them through a microscope. To give you an idea of how small they are, a human is made up from around 100 000 000 000 000 cells!

What do biologists do?

A knowledge of biology is important for all sorts of jobs.

- ▶ Doctors, nurses, vets and pharmacists all use biology every day to care for people and choose the right medicines.

- ▶ Ecologists, botanists, farmers, plant growers and researchers all depend upon biology to understand how living things grow and reproduce.

- ▶ Plant scientists, geneticists, toxicologists and molecular biologists are developing new crops that resist pests and diseases, and are healthier for us to eat.

- ▶ Sport scientists need biology to help athletes perform at their best.

What will you see?

In this book, we will explore and investigate the functions of life, and how they work together. We will look at:

- ▶ What cells look like and what they are made of.

- ▶ How chemicals like DNA control how living things look, behave and grow.

- ▶ How we can catalogue all the living things we know about, showing how they are related to each other.

- ▶ How the human body works and how to look after it.

- ▶ How living things interact with their environment, and how humans are changing the environment.

Humans are changing the environment in many ways. Here, an underwater ecologist is inspecting a reef created by people as a nature reserve.

Previously »

Remember Life processes common to animals include nutrition, movement, growth and reproduction.

Remember Life processes common to plants include nutrition, growth and reproduction.

Unit 1

Cells

What is a cell?

In the ancient ocean, hundreds of millions of years ago, we think small spheres of fat (lipid) formed. Inside these spheres were chemicals that had formed in the ocean water. These spheres with chemicals inside were the first cells.

So, at its simplest, a cell is a sphere with chemicals in it.

In this Unit, you will learn:

- ⊙ how cells formed;
- ⊙ what unicells and multicells are;
- ⊙ how we can examine cells using microscopes;
- ⊙ that cells can be specialised;
- ⊙ that cells form tissues, tissues form organs and organs form systems;
- ⊙ some differences between animal cells and plant cells;
- ⊙ the features present in most cells.

Key words

cell	nucleus
cell wall	organ
chloroplasts	specialised cells
electron microscope	system
granular cytoplasm	tissues
light microscope	unicell
membrane	vacuole
multicells	

What are unicells?

Some modern-day living things are made of just one **cell**. They are called **unicells**. Even though they are tiny single cells, they show the seven characteristics of living things we listed on page 8. A well-known example of a unicell is *Amoeba*.

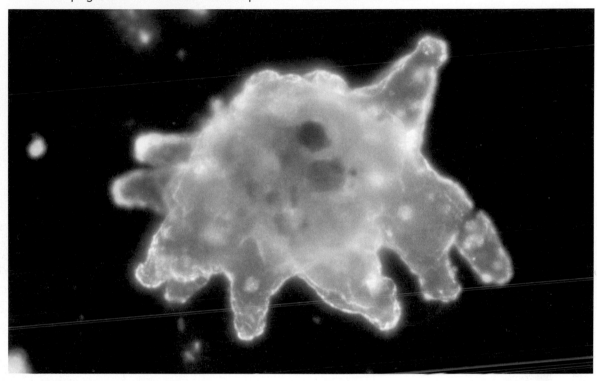

The unicells all belong to a Kingdom (see page 18) called the Protoctists. These unicells can be found everywhere around us, but they are usually too small to see without a microscope. That is, they are smaller than 0.1 mm across.

 Draw a scale diagram of the Amoeba in the photograph. Set the scale so that 1 cm on the drawing equals 0.1 mm in real life. (A typical *Amoeba proteus* is about 500 micrometres in length. A thousand micrometres is 1 mm.)

 The most well-known unicells are probably members of the genus *Amoeba* and other so-called amoeoboids. *Chaos carolinensis* is one of the biggest unicells known in this genus, with specimens reaching up to 5 mm in length. However, there are single cells much bigger than this.

 See if you can find out what is the biggest single cell alive today, and what might have been the biggest in the past. (Hint: eggs are technically single cells.)

What do we use microscopes for? ⇄

A **light microscope** combines two lenses to magnify what we can see up to a thousand times. We need to prepare the objects we view to make them quite thin, so that light can be shone through them.

A bee leg seen through a light microscope.

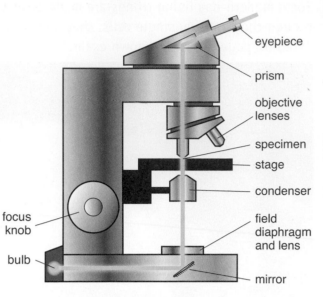

Light microscope labels: eyepiece, prism, objective lenses, specimen, stage, condenser, field diaphragm and lens, mirror, bulb, focus knob

Light microscope.

If we need to see more detail, we use an **electron microscope**. This uses beams of electrons instead of light, and can magnify millions of times.

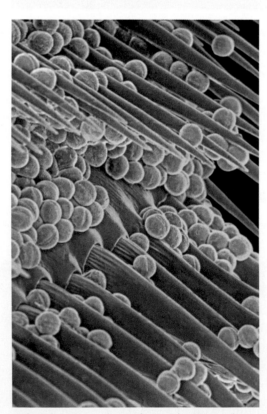

A bee leg seen through an electron microscope, with pollen grains stuck to the hairs.

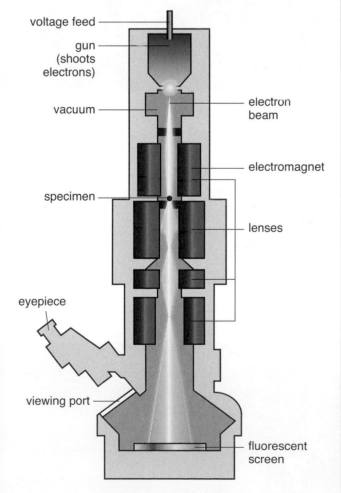

Electron microscope labels: voltage feed, gun (shoots electrons), vacuum, specimen, eyepiece, viewing port, electron beam, electromagnet, lenses, fluorescent screen

Electron microscope.

How much can we magnify images?

We multiply the magnification of the first lens by that of the second lens to get the total magnification. For example, a 10× eyepiece and a 50× objective lens will give a total magnification of 500×.

 Work out the total magnification given by a microscope which has the following eyepiece/objective combinations.

Eyepiece	Objective	Magnification
10	10	
15	100	
5	20	
10	40	

How are bigger living things made from cells?

Cells cannot be very big because materials would not be able to move in and out, or reach the middle, quickly enough. The cell would not be able to get oxygen into its centre or get waste materials out quickly. Bigger living things are made from more than one cell: they are **multicells**. That is, all animals and plants, and most types of fungi.

What are specialised cells?

As we examine bigger living things, we find some cells get good at just one job. These cells become **specialised cells**. Groups of specialised cells work together to form **tissues**. For example, muscle cells make muscle tissue and nerve cells make nervous tissue. These tissues can then work together to form an **organ**, for example the heart. A heart contains muscles and nerves, together with other tissues, working together to pump blood round the body and to the lungs (page 55).

 List five specialised cells in the human body and three in a flowering plant.

How do organs make systems?

When a number of different organs work together this makes a **system**. For example, the heart works with arteries, veins and capillaries to make the circulatory system (see Unit 8, pages 51 to 56).

 Using the example of the circulatory system as a guide, suggest what organs make up your excretory, nervous and digestive systems.

What are cells like?

This is not such an easy question as it may seem. This is because there are many different types of cells. It is possible to look at some features that nearly all cells have in common.

All cells (except bacteria) have:

▶ A **nucleus** – where all the instructions to run the life of the cell are stored.

▶ A **granular cytoplasm** – where most of the chemical reactions happen.

▶ A **membrane** – which controls the movement of things in and out of the cell.

In addition, plant cells have:

▶ A cellulose **cell wall** – this gives them (and the plant they make up) support and shape.

▶ **Chloroplasts** – where plants make food from carbon dioxide and water using energy from sunlight (see page 40).

▶ A **vacuole** – full of watery sap that stores minerals and also helps to support the plant.

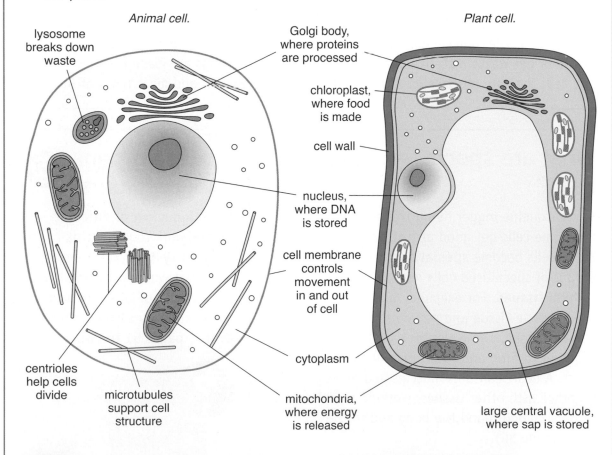

Animal cell.

lysosome breaks down waste

Golgi body, where proteins are processed

Plant cell.

chloroplast, where food is made

cell wall

nucleus, where DNA is stored

cell membrane controls movement in and out of cell

cytoplasm

centrioles help cells divide

microtubules support cell structure

mitochondria, where energy is released

large central vacuole, where sap is stored

Draw your own simpler diagrams of an animal cell and a plant cell. Only show the cell membrane, cell wall, nucleus and vacuole.

What is special about bacterial cells?

Bacterial cells are very different to animal and plant cells. They have no nucleus but they do have a cell wall, although it is not made of cellulose as it is in plants.

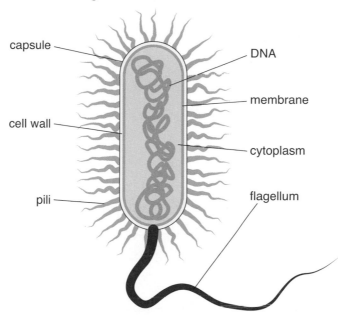

capsule — DNA

— membrane

cell wall — cytoplasm

pili — flagellum

You need to remember that:

▷ We think the first cells formed in ancient oceans from spheres of fat containing chemicals.

▷ Unicells are living things formed from just one cell.

▷ Multicells are bigger living things made from collections of cells.

▷ We can examine cells using light microscopes.

▷ We can examine cells in more detail using electron microscopes.

▷ Cells can specialise and then work together to form tissues.

▷ Tissues of different types work together to form organs.

▷ Different organs can work together to form systems.

▷ Nearly all cells contain a nucleus, granular cytoplasm and a membrane.

▷ Plant cells also contain a cell wall, chloroplasts and a vacuole.

▷ Bacterial cells are very simple and have no nucleus or other specialist structures inside them.

Next time »

Unit 2 As a living thing gets bigger, its surface area to volume ratio gets smaller (page 17).

Unit 7 Energy is released from food in respiration (page 46).

Previously »

| Remember | Life processes common to animals include nutrition, movement, growth and reproduction. |

| From page 13 | Multicells are bigger living things made from collections of cells. |

Unit 2

Size matters

Why does size matter?

Living organisms range from very small, like bacteria, to very big, like the blue whale. A blue whale, the biggest organism that has *ever* lived, weighs about 150 000 000 000 000 000 000 000 000 times as much as a typical bacterium! How does this affect the biology of large and small organisms?

In this Unit, you will learn:

▶ how to calculate the surface area (SA), volume (V) and surface area to volume ratio $\left(\frac{SA}{V}\right)$ of a cube;

▶ that as an object (including animals and plants) gets bigger, its $\frac{SA}{V}$ gets smaller;

▶ why the reduction of $\frac{SA}{V}$ with increase in size matters for living things;

▶ that brain size matters too, but the evidence is not so clear.

Key words

surface area (SA)
volume (V)
surface area to volume ratio $\left(\frac{SA}{V}\right)$
brain size
intelligence

What is the surface area to volume ratio?

Look at the picture of the two fish.

The one on the right is clearly much bigger. A large fish will have a larger volume and a larger surface area. The **surface area** is the total area of all the outer skin of the animal. The **volume** is the amount of space the animal takes up.

For living things, the important thing is the surface area (SA) to volume (V) ratio, SA/V. It is not easy to calculate the surface area or volume of a fish, so let's have a look at some cubes instead.

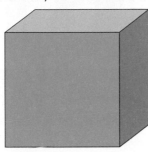

The cube on the left has a side of 3 cm (check it with your ruler!), the one on the right is 6 cm. So, the area of the cube on the left is:

   area of each side × number of sides

Each side is a square so:

   Surface area of each square = 3 cm × 3 cm = 9 cm²

   Total surface area of cube = 9 × 6 = 54 cm²

   Volume of cube = 3 × 3 × 3 = 27 cm³

so, the **surface area to volume ratio** $\frac{SA}{V} = \frac{54}{27} = 2$

Now for the cube on the right. Each side is a square with area 6 cm × 6 cm = 36 cm²

   Total surface area of cube = 36 × 6 = 216 cm²

   Volume of cube = 6 × 6 × 6 = 216 cm³

   so, $\frac{SA}{V} = \frac{216}{216} = 1$

Although the cube on the right has a bigger surface area and a bigger volume, its surface area to volume ratio is smaller!

Try this out on your calculator with other bigger and smaller cubes. For example, a cube with a side length of 12 cm has a surface area to volume ratio of 0.5.

 Work out the surface area to volume ratio for a cube with a side length of 4 cm. Show all the steps!

Why is the surface area to volume ratio important for living things?

Animals and plants lose heat energy through their surface. Materials important for life, like the gases oxygen and carbon dioxide, are gained and lost through their surface too.

Thinking about the surface area to volume ratio, a small mouse will lose much more heat relative to its body size than a large elephant. So a mouse spends much of its waking time eating and taking in energy to replace the heat it loses.

 What other differences between a mouse and an elephant can you think of that helps the mouse avoid losing heat?

Why do larger animals have organs?

An *Amoeba* (see page 11) can get all the oxygen it needs by absorbing it through its relatively large surface area. A human has to have special organs called lungs to do the same.

Much of the biology of large animals and plants comes about because of their small surface area to volume ratio, so size really does matter!

 Which features of the biology of large organisms (apart from getting gases) are affected by their size? How are the organisms adapted to this?

Smaller animals are generally more active than larger animals, partly because of the surface area to volume ratio and the need for the animal to spend more time finding food. Smaller animals have smaller organs, too.

Smaller animals have evolved many different ways to reduce the amount of energy they 'lose' as heat.

 Choose three different kinds of small animals (such as a bird, a mammal and a reptile). Research where they live, how they move around and what is different about them (such as skin covered in feathers, scales or fur). What links can you draw between their size, where they live and how they behave?

How does brain size affect animals?

There is some disagreement among scientists about whether the size of the brain is related to intelligence. The human brain has increased in size over the last few million years, which suggests there is a connection between **brain size** and **intelligence**. When we look at other animals, though, the pattern is not so clear.

We cannot measure the brain sizes of animals that lived many millions of years ago, because the living tissue of the brain decays over time. But we can estimate their brain sizes by measuring the volume of the insides of fossil skulls. The graph shows some results.

When we look at animals alive today, brains vary a great deal in size. Some of the most intelligent animals, such as parrots and crows, actually have quite small brains – many times smaller than human brains.

So with brains, size matters again, but we are not so sure just how!

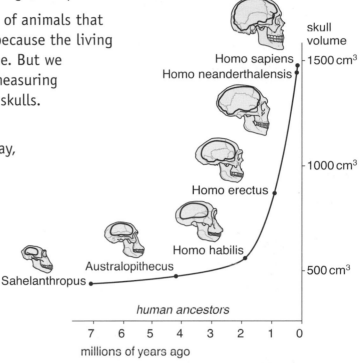

 How big is a blue whale's brain? Do you think that means they are very intelligent?

You need to remember that:

- Living things vary enormously in size.
- As an object (including a living thing) gets bigger, its surface area to volume ratio gets smaller.
- Small animals with a large surface area to volume ratio lose heat and materials rapidly through their skin.
- Large animals cannot absorb all the materials they need through their skin, so they have developed organs such as lungs.
- A bigger brain suggests greater intelligence, but there are exceptions to this rule.

Next time »

Unit 7 — Energy is released from food in respiration (page 46).

Unit 7 — Your thorax (chest) contains muscles that move your ribs and thorax when you breathe (page 47).

Previously »

| Remember | We can identify animals and plants and group them based on their common features. |
| Remember | We can make and use keys. |

Unit 3

Variety and classification

How much life is there?

No-one knows how many types (species) of living things there are on planet Earth. The *variety* of life we already know about is amazing. The latest estimate suggests there are between 6 million and 10 million species, without counting bacteria! We have only named about 1.2 million; that is just over 10% of the living things we think are out there!

However many it is, when we have so many it is necessary to classify and name them properly.

In addition, even within a species or kind, there are differences. Look at other members of your class. Nobody looks exactly the same as you (unless you have an identical twin!). They may be taller, shorter, have different hair and eye colour and differ in many other ways too. This is called variation. We are beginning to understand what causes this variation.

In this Unit, you will learn:

- ▶ how many species of living things we know of;
- ▶ that there are many living things still to be discovered, described and named;
- ▶ how living things are classified;
- ▶ the main features of different Kingdoms;
- ▶ the main features of some major groups of plants and animals;
- ▶ the use of keys to name things;
- ▶ the causes of variation.

Key words

Angiosperms	environmental	keys	Protoctista
Animals	Families	Kingdoms	Pteridophytes
Bryophytes	Fungi	Marchantiophytes	Species
characteristics	gene	Orders	variation
Chordates	genetic	Phylum	
Class	Genus	Plants	
Coniferophytes	inherited	Prokaryotes	

How do we classify living things?

The 1.2 million living things described so far are grouped into five **Kingdoms**. This table gives a very brief introduction to the Kingdoms.

Kingdom	Types of living things	Main features	Characteristics
Prokaryotes	bacteria and some algae	all made of one cell; cells grow in size; most reproduce asexually	some swim, some cannot move; some make their own food; most sense light and chemicals
Protoctista	single-celled organisms such as *Amoeba* and seaweeds (although they look multicellular the cells are not really arranged into tissues and organs)	all made of one cell; cells grow in size; most reproduce asexually	most can swim or creep; some make their own food, some feed on other living things; most can sense light, sound and chemicals
Fungi	mushrooms, toadstools and moulds	some made of one cell, some of many cells (multicelled); cells grow in size and number; most reproduce sexually	some can creep across a surface; most feed on dead organisms; most can sense light, gravity and water
Plants	non-flowering plants like mosses and ferns, and flowering plants like dandelions and daisies	multicelled; cells grow in size and number; most plants reproduce sexually	most plants make their own food from carbon dioxide, water and minerals; they contain chlorophyll; they sense light, gravity and water
Animals	worms, insects, birds, reptiles, fish, humans and so on	multicelled, often containing organs; cells grow in size and number; most animals reproduce sexually	most animals can move around; they feed on other living things; most can sense light, sound and chemicals

We know much more about animals and plants than the other three Kingdoms, so we will concentrate on them. Animals and plants are sometimes thought of as the two main Kingdoms, but some people believe that there at least a further 10 million species of bacteria and that they far outnumber all other kinds of life put together!

All the food we eat comes from living things. List all the food you eat in a day and then put each item that is in your list into a Kingdom. (You may need to research what goes into some processed foods.)

How do we classify animals?

One simple way to divide the Animal Kingdom is into vertebrates (animals with a backbone) and invertebrates (animals with no backbone). However, there are so many different types of invertebrates compared to vertebrates that we need a better way to classify them all.

One level down from a Kingdom is the category called a **Phylum**. Animals are classified into 36 Phyla. All animals with a backbone belong in a single Phylum called the **Chordates**. There are so many kinds of invertebrates, they are classified into 35 other Phyla.

Next, one level down from a Phylum, we have a category called a **Class**.

The Chordates (vertebrates) have five Classes: fish, amphibians, reptiles, birds and mammals. The table shows their main features.

After this, Classes are split into **Orders** (like the Primates in which humans are located), then **Families** (humans are Hominids), then the **Genus** (humans are in Homo) and then the **Species** (humans are sapiens). The scientific name of a species is made up of its Genus and Species, so humans are *Homo sapiens*, written with a capital 'H' and a small 's' and printed in italics (underlined in handwriting).

Out of the 35 Phyla of invertebrates, the Arthropods (including insects and spiders), Molluscs (slugs and snails), Annelids (segmented worms like earthworms) and Echinoderms (starfish and sea urchins) are probably the best known.

Class	Examples	Characteristics
fish	sharks, salmon, tuna, trout	scales on skin, breathe through gills, move using tail
amphibians	frogs, toads, newts	moist skin that can let water through, many can live on land and in water
reptiles	snakes, crocodiles, lizards	dry scales on skin, lay eggs with a soft shell
birds	emu, gulls, finches, geese, parrots, eagles	feathers and beak, lay eggs with a hard shell, most can fly
mammals	humans, cats, elephants, mice, sloths, whales	fur or hair on skin, most have eggs that grow to babies inside the body, most live on land

THINKING BEYOND...

The best place in the UK to see the widest variety of animal Phyla is on the seashore.

? The next time you are by the sea, especially if it is a rocky shore, take the 'Phylum Challenge'. Use your digital camera or mobile phone camera to take pictures of examples of as many different Phyla as you can.

How do we classify plants?

The Plant Kingdom is split into ten Phyla. The best known are **Bryophytes** (mosses), **Marchantiophytes** (liverworts), **Pteridophytes** (ferns), **Coniferophytes** (Conifers) and **Angiosperms** (plants that flower).

Phylum	Examples	Characteristics
Bryophytes	mosses	simple roots, reproduce by spores
Marchantiophytes	liverworts	simple roots, reproduce by spores
Pteridophytes	ferns	complex roots and tubes, reproduce by spores
Coniferophytes	fir trees, pine trees	mostly trees, bear cones with seeds
Angiosperms	flowering plants	flowers, roots and stems, all produce seeds

 Make a mini herbarium to show samples of a few of each plant Phyla in the table. Collect a good specimen from the garden and then press it between sheets of blotting paper for a few weeks. Mount on good quality card with invisible glue or tape.

How do we name living things?

The best way to work out what species a living thing belongs to, is to use a key. **Keys** consist of a series of questions that can be answered with a 'yes' or a 'no'.

A question might be: 'Does it have wings or not?'

If you are looking at a bird you will answer 'yes', if a tortoise, 'no'. Then you move on to the next question. Eventually, after several such questions you are left with one option and that is the species.

The key in the table below is for some ants:

	Question	Answer	Species or go to question ...
1	Large notch on top of head?	Yes	*Formica exsecta*
		No	Go to 2
2	Clypeus (shield-like plate on front of head) notched?	Yes	*Formica sanguinea*
		No	Go to 3
3	Hairs on top and sides of head extend down to lower part of eyes?	Yes	*Formica lugubris*
		No	Go to 4
4	Hairs on top or sides of head?	Yes	*Formica aquilonia*
		No	*Formica rufa*

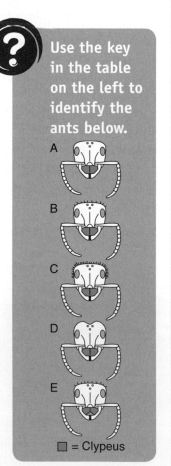 Use the key in the table on the left to identify the ants below.

A

B

C

D

E

□ = Clypeus

What is variation?

As well as all the millions of different species in the world, each species shows **variation** between different individuals. (Just like you see in the humans in your class.) This variation is due to what an individual has **inherited** from its parents (**genetic** variation) and the environment it has grown up in (**environmental** variation). The two sources of variation are combined to make the living thing what it is. This includes how we humans are all different.

What is genetic variation? @

People with the same parents are not usually exactly the same as each other. This is because they inherit different **characteristics** (controlled by **genes**) and do so randomly. For example, if your father has blue eyes and your mother has brown eyes, there is a chance you might have blue eyes or brown eyes. But if you have a brother, he might have a different eye colour to you.

What is environmental variation?

The environment consists of everything around you, both before and after birth. Even identical twins (who inherit the same characteristics) will often be different as adults in many ways due to growing up in different environments.

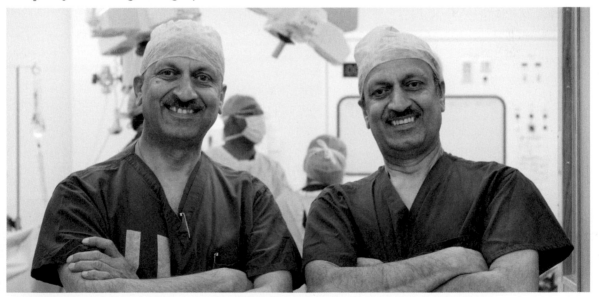

? List three varying features in humans (like eye colour) that you think are mainly genetic, and three which are mainly environmental. How could you check if you are right (apart from looking it up in a book or website!)?

You need to remember that:

- There are millions of species of living things but we don't really know how many.
- Living things are classified into five Kingdoms.
- Each Kingdom is further divided into Phyla.
- The next levels of classification are Class, Order, Family, Genus and finally Species.
- Humans have the Genus *Homo* and the Species *sapiens*.
- Living things in particular Phyla and Classes share similar characteristics, such as how they live and how they reproduce.
- Keys are questions that help us work out how to classify living things.
- Individual living things of the same species can still be different – they show variation.
- Variation comes about due to genetic (inherited) reasons and environmental reasons (how and where individuals live).

Next time »

Unit 4 People have used selective breeding over thousands of years to create more productive plants and animals (page 28).

Unit 4 Cells contain genes made from DNA (page 29).

Previously »

From page 22   Living things are classified according to the characteristics they share.

From page 25   Individual living things of the same species show variation.

Unit 4

Making and using variation

How is variation useful?

We call the differences between individuals of a species 'variation'. Humans have learnt to make use of variation in plants and animals. For thousands of years, people have selectively bred animals and plants to get the varieties they want. In the last 30 years or so, the process has been speeded up by genetic engineering.

Wild wheat, for example, produces quite low quantities of grain suitable to eat. We say it gives a poor 'yield'. Humans have improved wheat by picking out the best variations and concentrating on breeding them. This has led to the modern bread wheat we use today, and many other varieties.

In this Unit, you will learn:

- ○ about genes and DNA;
- ○ how and why people started growing wild plants deliberately;
- ○ why over time the plants became better foods;
- ○ how modern-day crops and farm animals have been derived from wild ancestors by the process of selective breeding;
- ○ why recent discoveries mean we can now engineer crops and animals with the features we want.

Key words

ancestor	genetic modification (GM)
chains	insulin
descendants	mutations
DNA	natural selection
evolution	resistant
farmed	selective breeding
genes	variation
genetic engineering	

What are genes?

The nucleus of every cell in living things contains **genes** – chemical 'codes' that determine how an organism looks, grows and works.

All living things show **variation**, this is due to **mutations** (changes) in the genes passed from the parents on to their offspring. Differences in genes lead to animals or plants growing up differently. We say that in each generation the offspring produced vary.

In nature some variants survive to reproduce more successfully than others. This is called **natural selection** and is the process by which **evolution** works.

 If you put the nucleus of an oak tree into a human egg cell which had had its nucleus removed, would it (in theory) grow into an oak tree or a human?

What is selective breeding?

Around 10 000 years ago, humans began to gather wild animals into herds to produce more milk and meat. One of the first animals humans **farmed** in this way was the auroch, a large four-legged animal with long curved horns that ate plants and produced milk.

Over many hundreds of years, people chose the individuals that produced the best meat or biggest amounts of milk. They bred only the best individuals, so that the genes made each generation of auroch more productive. Today, the auroch no longer exists, but we see its **descendants** in fields all around the world – the domestic cow. We call the auroch the **ancestor** of the cow.

This picking out of the best individuals to reproduce is called **selective breeding**. The same sort of process can be traced for rice, maize, sheep and many, many other animals and plants we take for granted today. Even the domestic dog and cat are the products of selective breeding. Our pet dogs come from wolf-like ancestors, and our pet cats are the descendants of wildcats.

 Find out about some different kinds of horses people ride. Which wild animals did they come from? Where in the world did they or do they live?

It is thought that the last auroch died in 1627. Scientists have started a project to use selective breeding to re-create the auroch, a much bigger animal than a modern cow or bull.

 Investigate what ancestors a modern farm or domestic animal is thought to have had. Do they still exist in the wild?

What is DNA?

In the 1940s it was discovered that genes are made from the chemical **DNA**. A molecule of DNA contains thousands of atoms arranged in patterns called **chains**. These patterns are different depending on the particular species of animal or plant. The DNA is like a code for life.

Each cell in a living thing is like a tiny machine or computer that takes materials in and produces new cells or carries out processes. The DNA works a bit like a computer program that instructs the cell how to function.

 Find out which atoms are present in DNA.

What is 'genetic modification'?

Over the last 60 years humans have been investigating the 'code' of DNA for different plants and animals. Scientists realised that we can change the code to program cells to do exactly what we want them to do. Within the last 30 years it has become possible to put genes from one living thing into another. This is called **genetic engineering** or **genetic modification** (GM).

People with type I diabetes cannot make the hormone **insulin**, meaning their bodies cannot manage sugar levels properly. This can cause very serious illness or even death, so affected people have to inject insulin into themselves. In the past we have had to use insulin from cattle. Human insulin, humulin, is much better suited for us but we could not make it artificially.

One of the earliest achievements of GM was to engineer bacteria to produce the hormone insulin. Scientists found a way to insert the human gene that controls insulin production into bacteria. This causes them to make human insulin, which we can now use to treat diabetes.

 Find out what someone suffering from type I diabetes has to do every day. What happens if they eat too much sugary food? Or not enough?

What are GM foods?

We have also discovered how to change genes in plants and animals, including crop plants like wheat. Food made from plants grown from seeds with altered genes is called GM food. These plants are now grown in some countries around the world, but very little of this food is available in the UK because people are worried about eating it.

Some plants have been genetically modified to create crops that are **resistant** to pests, such as particular kinds of insects. Certain kinds of pest can spoil large quantities of crops, so in the past they would be sprayed with pesticides. Growing pest-resistant plants means no need for chemical pesticides, saving money and reducing damage to the environment.

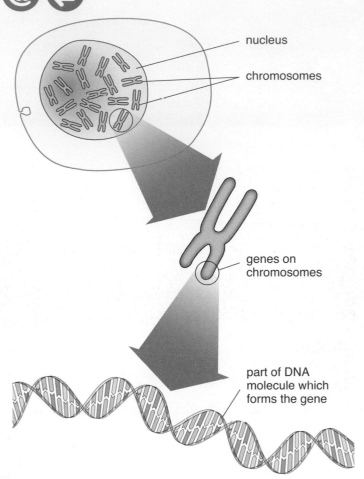

nucleus

chromosomes

genes on chromosomes

part of DNA molecule which forms the gene

? List some countries where GM food can be grown.

This purple tomato has been modified to help protect us against cancers.

What can GM animals do for us?

Genetic modification has also been carried out on animals. For example:

▶ Some people are allergic to chemicals in milk. A variety of cow has been created to produce milk without those chemicals.

▶ More and more of us around the world are becoming overweight, partly because we eat food with too much fat in it (see page 41). A variety of sheep has been developed to produce meat with less saturated fat.

Some people are worried about genetic modification. They feel that this may be a step too far compared with selective breeding, and that we do not understand the long-term effects of growing GM plants and animals.

There is no scientific evidence to suggest GM foods are causing problems; however, there is a lot of research going on to investigate the effects of GM.

? **Choose a particular kind of GM food and investigate how and where it is grown. Produce a summary of arguments people use for and against it being grown.**

You need to remember that:

▶ Cells contain genes, which instruct the cell how to grow and function.

▶ Genes are made from a chemical called DNA.

▶ Different individuals of the same species show variation because of differences in their genes.

▶ Natural selection is the process by which more successful variants dominate and change a species.

▶ People have used selective breeding over thousands of years to create more productive plants and animals.

▶ Modern-day farm animals and pets are the descendants of wild ancestors.

▶ The technology of genetic engineering or genetic modification allows us to put the genes from one organism into the cells of another.

▶ We have used GM to create pest-resistant crops and to grow bacteria that produce insulin.

Next time »

Unit 5 The world is full of amazing living things (page 32).

Unit 14 Living things are adapted to the environment in which they live (page 91).

Previously »

From page 20 — There are millions of species of living things but we don't really know how many.

From page 28 — Variation comes about due to genetic and environmental reasons.

Unit 5

Remarkable nature

How amazing is nature?

This Unit is our 'Guinness Book of Records' for nature. We will learn about a small selection of some of the most remarkable animals and plants on Earth.

In this Unit, you will learn:

- ▷ that blue whales and giant redwood trees are the biggest living things on Earth;
- ▷ how whales live, feed and communicate;
- ▷ why bees are important to us and the Earth;
- ▷ how honeybees communicate information about food to each other;
- ▷ why some animals are threatened by human activity;
- ▷ that parrots are amongst the most intelligent of all birds and can solve problems;
- ▷ that a bristle cone pine tree is one of the oldest things on the planet;
- ▷ that *Welwitschia* is weird!

Key words

baleen	imitate
biomass	intelligence
communicate	krill
conservation status	waggle dance
extinct	*Welwitschia*
girth	

What is special about whales?

There are 86 species of whales, including dolphins and porpoises. Many of them are very rare and one, the Baiji or Chinese River Dolphin, was declared **extinct** (none left alive) in 2005. Here, we will learn about the very large ocean-living whales. We will look in particular at the blue whale, *Balaenoptera musculus*, which at about 30 metres long and weighing in at 200 000 kg is the biggest known animal to ever have existed.

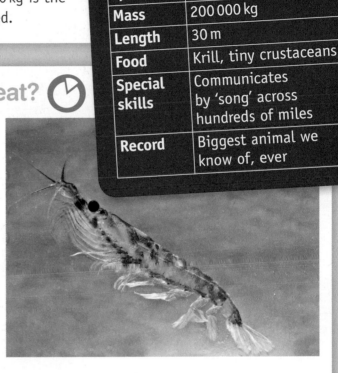

Name	Blue whale
Genus and species	*Balaenoptera musculus*
Mass	200 000 kg
Length	30 m
Food	Krill, tiny crustaceans
Special skills	Communicates by 'song' across hundreds of miles
Record	Biggest animal we know of, ever

What does a blue whale eat?

Possibly the most remarkable thing about this gigantic animal is that its food is tiny! It feeds almost entirely on **krill**, a small crustacean that exists in vast numbers. Let's work out just how much krill food whales could find.

If we add the mass of all the humans on the planet together, we call the total the **biomass** of the human species. In 2012, there were about 7 000 000 000 humans on Earth. On average, a human has a mass of about 50 kg.

So the biomass of humans = 7 000 000 000 × 50 kg = 350 billion kg

One Antarctic krill has a mass of about 0.5 g, so a human has a mass 100 000 times bigger than a krill! We think there are about 800 trillion krill living in the Southern Ocean. So what is the biomass of krill?

Biomass of krill = 800 000 000 000 000 × 0.5 g = 400 billion kg

So the tiny Antarctic krill living in the Southern Ocean has a total biomass more than that of all humans on the planet! That's a lot of food for whales.

However, a blue whale eats around 40 million krill every day. The whale moves forward into a group of krill, and takes them into its massive mouth, together with hundreds of gallons of seawater. The water is squeezed through hard **baleen** plates that hang from the roof of its mouth. Krill cannot pass through the baleen plates and are swallowed.

How much mass of krill does a blue whale eat every day?

How do whales communicate?

Another remarkable feature of some whales is their ability to **communicate** with each other in complex ways. Unfortunately, one thing that cannot be done in a book is to convey sounds.

The most complex song is that of the male humpback whale. Each song can last for up to 20 minutes, and the males will sing all day. We have not yet worked out why they sing these songs or what they mean. They may be challenges to other males. At certain times of the year, the song changes and is used to herd the fish that these whales eat.

 Search online for recordings of whale songs. Try using your descriptive writing ability to convey the songs in words to others. Let them read what you have written, listen to the song and ask them what they think of your description.

Why are whales under threat?

There is much else to learn about whales, but perhaps the most important fact to end with is that humans threaten many of them. So that we can understand which animals are most in danger, the International Union for the Conservation of Nature (IUCN) was formed in 1948. The IUCN is working to give all species of living things a 'conservation status'.

Because of hunting and other human activities, many species of whale are threatened.

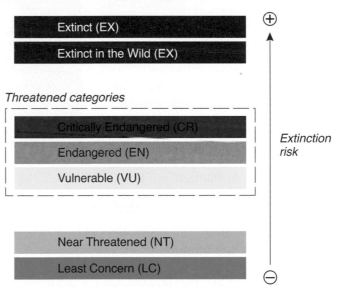

The categories the IUCN uses to describe how much at risk a species can be.

Species	World population	Conservation status
Blue whale	under 25 000	EN Endangered
Fin whale	under 100 000	EN Endangered
North Atlantic right whale	under 300	EN Endangered
Sperm whale	under 2 million	VU Vulnerable
Common minke whale	not known	NT Near Threatened

What is special about bees?

Bees are a huge group of insects (about 20 000 species) closely related to ants and wasps. Here we are going to look at the Western honeybee, *Apis mellifera*, and in particular its ability to communicate.

Name	Western Honeybee
Genus and species	*Apis mellifera*
Mass	0.25 g (a colony of 50 000 bees would weigh about 12 kg)
Length	Just over 1 cm
Food	Nectar and pollen
Special skills	Lives in big colonies Communicates by 'dances'
Record	Helps flowering plants and many crops reproduce through pollination

How do honeybees live?

Honeybees live in colonies of up to 80 000 individuals. They feed on nectar and pollen collected from local flowers. When a foraging worker finds a new patch of flowers it can communicate information about it to others. The returning bee performs a 'round dance', telling others that food is within 50 m. It then does a '**waggle dance**', which provides more detailed information about the distance and direction of the food.

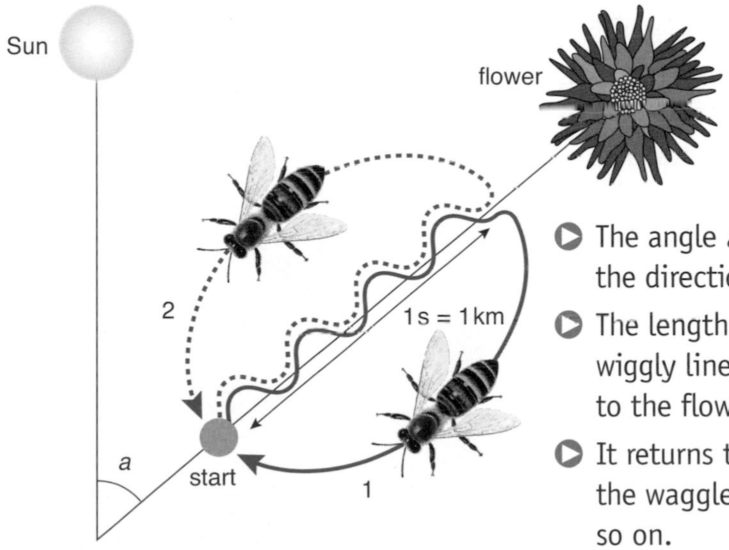

- The angle *a* of its dance to the vertical shows the direction of the flower relative to the Sun.
- The length of time it takes to dance the wiggly line, in seconds, measures the distance to the flower in kilometres.
- It returns to the start from the right, repeats the waggle, then returns from the left, and so on.

THINKING BEYOND...

Bees are not the only animals that use unusual methods of communicating with each other.

Find out more about bee dances and, in a table, compare this method of communication with that of three other animals and humans. Can you find out any information about communication in plants?

Why are bees under threat?

Honeybees are very important to us and the environment.

▶ They provide us with honey when we keep them in beehives.

▶ They make sure most flowering plants and crops reproduce, because they pollinate the flowers.

Unfortunately, a combination of natural and human causes means bee numbers have reduced dramatically.

▶ Over the last hundred years the number of beehives in the UK has declined from over 1 million to only 280 000.

▶ There are several diseases that threaten bees – in 2008, 30% of all bees in the UK were lost to such diseases.

▶ Human activity means that large areas where bees live and forage have disappeared. These areas include traditional meadows and heather moors.

 Explain why bees are important to the environment around us. What do you think can be done to help bees?

What is special about parrots?

It is well known that parrots can **imitate** human speech, but being able to imitate is not the same as having **intelligence**. Better evidence comes from experiments showing that parrots can solve puzzles. In addition, some parrots have been shown to use language in a creative way. One, an African grey parrot called N'kisi, is said to have a vocabulary of 950 words. Once, when the chimpanzee expert Jane Goodall visited N'kisi, the bird said 'got a chimp' because it had seen a photograph of her with chimpanzees.

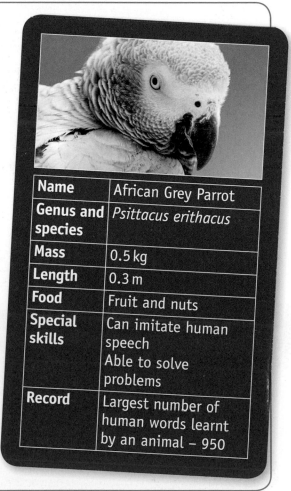

Name	African Grey Parrot
Genus and species	*Psittacus erithacus*
Mass	0.5 kg
Length	0.3 m
Food	Fruit and nuts
Special skills	Can imitate human speech Able to solve problems
Record	Largest number of human words learnt by an animal – 950

 1 Find out how many words a human child will learn by the age of three. What does that suggest about N'kisi's intelligence?

2 Keep a vocabulary log by noting every new word you learn in a week. You may be surprised!

What is special about 'General Sherman' @ and the bristle cone pine?

If the blue whale is the biggest animal ever to have lived, the giant redwood is probably the biggest plant. For example, the tree called 'General Sherman' is the biggest alive today. It is 83.8 m (275 feet) high and has a **girth** (distance around it) of over 30 m (100 feet). It is thought to weigh over 2 000 000 kg. It accumulates new wood at a rate equivalent to the wood in a 30-year-old oak tree every year. The General Sherman grows, along with other giant redwood trees, in the Sierra Nevada Mountains of California.

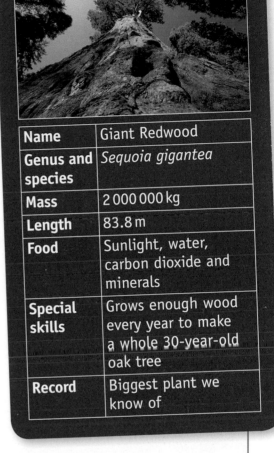

Name	Giant Redwood
Genus and species	*Sequoia gigantea*
Mass	2 000 000 kg
Length	83.8 m
Food	Sunlight, water, carbon dioxide and minerals
Special skills	Grows enough wood every year to make a whole 30-year-old oak tree
Record	Biggest plant we know of

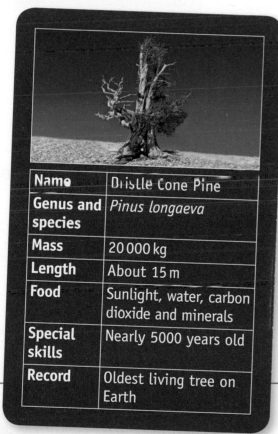

Name	Bristle Cone Pine
Genus and species	*Pinus longaeva*
Mass	20 000 kg
Length	About 15 m
Food	Sunlight, water, carbon dioxide and minerals
Special skills	Nearly 5000 years old
Record	Oldest living tree on Earth

Not very far away in the White Mountains of California grows a bristle cone pine tree called Methuselah, which is nearly 5000 years old!

  THINKING BEYOND...

The 'General Sherman' is not in fact the largest living thing on Earth, nor is 'Methuselah' the oldest. 'General Sherman' is the largest single-stemmed tree and 'Methuselah' is thought to be the oldest non-clonal living thing.

? Using the clues above, see if you can find out which are truly the largest and oldest living things. Write a paragraph about each of them.

Why is *Welwitschia* truly special?

Welwitschia has been given a number of different descriptions; the world's ugliest, weirdest, strangest, most wonderful and most bizarre plant.

Welwitschia is the only species in its genus, the only genus in its family and the only family in its order. There is no other species of living thing even remotely like it!

It lives on the coast of Namibia and Angola in South West Africa. This region is a dry desert but water is available in early morning mists. *Welwitschia* consists of a long taproot, a short trunk and just two leaves. The leaves grow throughout the life of the plant, which can be as long as 2000 years. The leaves curve downwards, so that they collect the mist into water droplets. These droplets run into the soil and to the roots.

Growing plants have leaves about 2 m long, but the wind blowing them against the sand wears away the growth. If they weren't constantly worn away like this it is thought each leaf would be well over 100 m long!

Name	Welwitschia
Genus and species	*Welwitschia mirabilis*
Mass	100 kg
Length	About 2 m
Food	Sunlight, water, carbon dioxide and minerals
Special skills	Lives in very harsh conditions
Record	Very, very unique

You need to remember that:

- ▶ The world is full of amazing living things.
- ▶ Blue whales are the biggest animals that have ever lived.
- ▶ Whales feed off some of the smallest animals on the Earth.
- ▶ Whales communicate with each other by 'singing' under water.
- ▶ Honey bees communicate information about food to each other through 'waggle dances'.
- ▶ Whales and bees are threatened by human activity.
- ▶ Parrots are amongst the most intelligent of all birds and can solve problems.
- ▶ The biggest giant redwood trees are some of the largest living things on the planet.
- ▶ Bristle cone pine trees can live to be some of the oldest things on the planet.
- ▶ *Welwitschia* is weird!

Next time »

Unit 15 Each living thing is adapted to the place it lives, its habitat (page 95).

Unit 16 There are over 7 billion people on Earth, which puts a big strain on the environment (page 104).

Unit 6

Nutrition and diet

Why do living things need food?

All living things need food. Plants can make their own food in a process called photosynthesis, but all animals need to eat plants or other animals. The basic needs of animals and plants are materials for growth, energy and water.

Living things make use of a wide range of materials taken from carbohydrate, proteins, vitamins and minerals. The main source of energy for both animals and plants is carbohydrate. Fat is also used to store energy. Water is all around us in rain, rivers, lakes and oceans, but a lot of the water that an animal needs is found in the food it eats.

In this Unit, you will learn:

- ▶ how the process of photosynthesis makes carbohydrate;
- ▶ that plants need minerals to make use of carbohydrates;
- ▶ about the seven components of a balanced diet for humans;
- ▶ where we can get the seven components of a balanced diet;
- ▶ how we digest and absorb food;
- ▶ how diets of other animals compare with ours.

Key words

absorbed	chloroplasts	gut
absorption	digestion	malnutrition
assimilated	egestion	minerals
balanced diet	enzymes	photosynthesis
breaking down	excreted	proteins
carbohydrates	faeces	stomata
chlorophyll	glucose	villi

What is photosynthesis?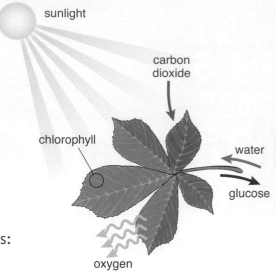

Plants make all the food on the Earth, in a process called **photosynthesis**. Carbon dioxide in the atmosphere and water from the soil are joined together. These react to make **glucose** (a carbohydrate) and oxygen (a gas that is given off as a waste product).

Photosynthesis goes on in the green leaves of plants. Leaves are green because they contain a substance called chlorophyll. **Chlorophyll** absorbs the sunlight energy and converts it into chemical energy.

We can write a word equation for photosynthesis:

$$\text{carbon dioxide + water} \xrightarrow[\text{light energy}]{\text{chlorophyll}} \text{glucose + oxygen}$$

Carbohydrates like glucose provide the energy for most of the processes of life.

What do leaves do?

The leaves of a plant are adapted to their job. Here is a picture of a whole leaf and a cross-section of a leaf.

Here are some features of leaves:

- for most plants, they have a large surface area;
- they have pores (holes) on the lower surface called **stomata**, which can be opened and closed;
- they have air spaces inside;
- they are packed with cells containing chloroplasts;
- the **chloroplasts** contain the chlorophyll.

The leaves' large surface area allows for the **absorption** (taking in) of lots of light energy.

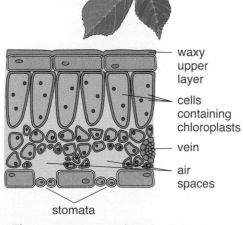

Carbon dioxide enters the plant through the stomata. The stomata can be closed at night, so that the plant does not lose water. The air spaces inside the leaf allow carbon dioxide to circulate easily and enter the chloroplasts in the cells.

 Explain why the features of leaves listed above are important for plants.

The leaves of different plants show a large amount of variety. For example, the leaves of a pine tree are long, thin and waxy, but the leaves of samphire are succulent (moist and fleshy). The plants have adapted to their different environments.

? Pick three examples of plants with different leaves and describe the different features of their leaves. Explain how each plant has adapted its features to suit its environment.

Why do plants need minerals?

In photosynthesis, plants are only able to make carbohydrate and oxygen. Like all living things, to grow they also need protein, fats and many other substances, including chlorophyll for photosynthesis.

To make these other substances they need **minerals**, which they get from the soil. For example, to make **proteins** they need nitrogen and sulfur. A plant with plenty of light, carbon dioxide and water still won't grow well if it doesn't get the right minerals. This is why farmers and gardeners add fertilisers to their soil.

 ? What chemicals does 'NPK' fertiliser contain?

What is a balanced human diet?

Just like all living things, humans need nutrition. The energy and materials we take in are used for a range of different processes.

A good diet is a **balanced diet**, that is one with all the necessary components in the right amounts. The seven components of a balanced diet are:

- ● carbohydrates
- ● proteins
- ● fats
- ● vitamins
- ● minerals
- ● fibre (sometimes called roughage)
- ● water

Too little or too much of any of these can lead to **malnutrition** (illness due to eating badly). Obesity (being overweight) is a form of malnutrition. Being too thin because of not eating enough is also a form of malnutrition.

Why do we need all these things in our diet?

Here are some of the uses of all these different substances and the foods they come from:

Substance		From which foods?	Use
carbohydrates		wheat products, sugars	for energy
proteins		meat, fish, dairy products	for growth
fats		meat, dairy products	for storing energy and keeping us warm
vitamins		different vitamins from different vegetables and fruit	to help with chemical reactions in the body
minerals		different minerals from different vegetables and fruit	for healthy bones, teeth and blood, and other purposes
fibre		dark parts of rice or wheat (like bran)	to help food move through the digestive system
water		most vegetables and fruit, and water drinks	for all the chemical reactions in the cells

In order to make sure that you eat a balanced diet, you should make sure your food is varied. Meat, dairy products and fruit and vegetables should all be included. If you are vegetarian, you need to make sure you eat enough foods containing protein instead of meat.

How does digestion work?

Big chunks of food cannot be taken into the body across the wall of the gut. Even large molecules cannot be taken in. The process of **digestion** works by **breaking down** big things into smaller things:

1. The big chunks of food are broken down into smaller chunks.

2. These chunks are broken down into molecules.

3. These large molecules are broken down into smaller molecules.

There are two kinds of digestion:

1. Mechanical digestion – works on the chunks. The teeth do some slicing and grinding, and the digestive system muscles do some churning.

2. Chemical digestion – works on the molecules. The body makes chemicals called enzymes that break large food molecules into small ones.

gut blood body
wall stream cells

protein → enzyme (protease)

fat → enzyme (lipase)

starch (a carbohydrate) → enzyme (carbohydrase)

What are enzymes?

Enzymes are specialised chemicals that speed up reactions. Enzymes are proteins.

Once the molecules are small enough they are **absorbed** across the wall of the **gut**. The gut lining has millions of folds called **villi**. These villi have properties that mean they are very good at absorbing all the molecules of broken-down food:

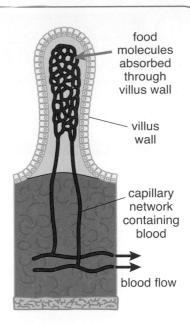

food molecules absorbed through villus wall

villus wall

capillary network containing blood

blood flow

- They are folded up tightly, so the gut wall has a very large surface area.
- They have thin walls, so there is not much to stop the molecules of food.
- They have a very good supply of blood, which carries the molecules away quickly.

Some parts of food cannot be broken down by the digestive system. This is collected together as solid **faeces**. Your body gets rid of faeces in a process called **egestion**.

Most absorbed food molecules are **assimilated**; molecules that cannot be assimilated are **excreted** in the urine.

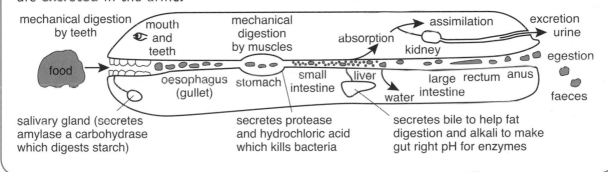

mechanical digestion by teeth

food

mouth and teeth

salivary gland (secretes amylase a carbohydrase which digests starch)

oesophagus (gullet)

mechanical digestion by muscles

stomach

secretes protease and hydrochloric acid which kills bacteria

small intestine

liver

water

absorption

kidney

large intestine

secretes bile to help fat digestion and alkali to make gut right pH for enzymes

assimilation

rectum anus

excretion urine

egestion

faeces

How are the diets of other animals different?

The diets of animals are very varied. Humans eat a massive range of foods. Other animals are very specialised. For example, aphids (greenfly) only drink plant sap, so their digestive systems are very simple. However, from the sap they get all the carbohydrates, fats and proteins they need.

Many other animals need most of the same minerals as we do.

Different animals need different vitamins. For example, humans are unusual in not being able to make Vitamin C, so we need to eat plenty of fruit containing Vitamin C.

How much Vitamin C should we consume each day?

The macaws of South America get the minerals they need from licking clay.

 ? Research and explain the other way in which macaws use clay in their digestion.

You need to remember that:

- All living things need food.
- Plants make their own food in photosynthesis.
- The chemical reaction for photosynthesis is:

$$\text{carbon dioxide + water} \xrightarrow[\text{light energy}]{\text{chlorophyll}} \text{glucose + oxygen}$$

- Plants need minerals to make other substances and to grow.
- Humans need a balanced diet to stay healthy.
- A balanced diet should include carbohydrates, proteins, fats, vitamins, minerals, fibre and water.
- Food comes in large chunks.
- Large chunks of food are broken down into smaller chunks by mechanical digestion.
- Molecules in food are broken down into smaller molecules by chemical digestion.
- Chemical digestion uses enzymes.
- Once the molecules in food are small enough, they are absorbed across the gut wall.
- Any food that cannot be broken down forms faeces and is egested.
- All absorbed food is assimilated.
- Food that cannot be assimilated is excreted.
- Animal diets differ but they all need the same basic things.

Next time »

Unit 7   Energy is released from food in respiration (page 46).

Unit 12   Our health depends on many things, and we are protected from many infections by our immune system (page 76).

Previously »

| From page 13 | Cells can specialise and then work together to form tissues and organs. |
| From page 13 | To work, cells need to get food and oxygen in, and give waste products out. |

Unit 7

Respiration and breathing

What are respiration and breathing?

Plants trap light energy and convert it into chemical energy in food (see page 40). To use this energy, plants and animals carry out a process called respiration.

Sometimes oxygen is used and this is called aerobic respiration. If oxygen is not used the process is called anaerobic respiration. Much more energy is released in aerobic respiration.

Some animals get their oxygen through their lungs. The process of bringing fresh air into the lungs and getting rid of the used air is called breathing. Breathing and respiration are not the same thing!

In this Unit, you will learn:

- ▶ how aerobic respiration releases lots of energy from glucose;
- ▶ how anaerobic respiration releases much less energy from glucose;
- ▶ that anaerobic respiration is used in the drinks industry to make alcohol;
- ▶ how breathing and respiration are different things;
- ▶ how breathing involves the ribs and the diaphragm;
- ▶ that the lungs are very spongy and contain alveoli;
- ▶ why the alveoli have thin walls and a good blood supply;
- ▶ how smoking can damage your lungs.

Key words

aerobic respiration	breathing	gas exchange	ribs
alcohol	cancer	lactic acid	smoking
alveoli	diaphragm	pressure	thorax
anaerobic respiration	emphysema	pressure gradient	volume

How does aerobic respiration work?

In our machines and power stations, we burn fuels such as hydrocarbons – coal, oil, gas or petrol (see page 292). When they are burnt, the fuels give out energy that we can use. 'Burning' means 'reacting with oxygen'.

In our bodies, we use the carbohydrate glucose as a fuel. When it reacts with oxygen, it gives us energy. Our bodies do not 'burn' glucose, but they do something very similar. And just like with a burning fuel, if we take oxygen away the reaction stops.

As with photosynthesis, we can represent **aerobic respiration** with a word equation.

glucose + oxygen → carbon dioxide + water + energy

Notice how this equation is the reverse of the one for photosynthesis on page 40.

If we don't have enough oxygen though, we can still get some energy from glucose. We then use a reaction called anaerobic respiration.

How does anaerobic respiration work?

In some living things, including parts of humans, energy can be released from glucose without oxygen. This is called **anaerobic respiration**. It only gives living things about 5% of the energy that is released in aerobic respiration.

Organisms that live in places where there is no oxygen use anaerobic respiration to get energy. For example, many bacteria depend on anaerobic respiration. An example is *Clostridium botulinum*, a species that causes food poisoning in humans.

Anaerobic respiration is also used when there is some oxygen around, but not enough for full aerobic respiration. For example, when an athlete runs a race:

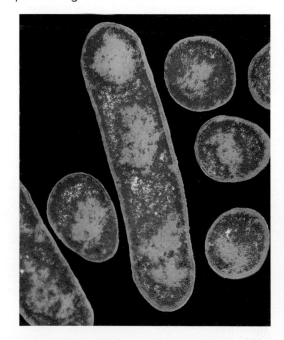

- Most of the time they use aerobic respiration.
- As they run longer distances and need to breathe harder, they are not getting enough oxygen into the blood through their lungs.
- Anaerobic respiration can give them that extra last boost of energy they need to finish the race.

If anaerobic respiration is used, the body produces **lactic acid**. It is the build-up of lactic acid in the muscles that causes cramp.

We also make use of anaerobic respiration to produce alcoholic drinks. We use an organism called yeast to turn the glucose in fruit or barley into **alcohol** (see page 181).

How do we breathe in?

It is important to remember that breathing and respiration are NOT the same thing. Just as eating and digestion get us the food we need, **breathing** gets us the oxygen. About 21% of the air is oxygen, so we are not usually short of oxygen!

To understand how we breathe, we need to look at the structure of the **thorax** (also known as the chest).

To breathe in, air is drawn into the lungs through the nose and back of the throat (pharynx) when:

- the muscles between the ribs contract;
- the **ribs** rise up;
- at the same time, the **diaphragm** muscles pull the diaphragm flat;
- this increases the **volume** of the thorax.

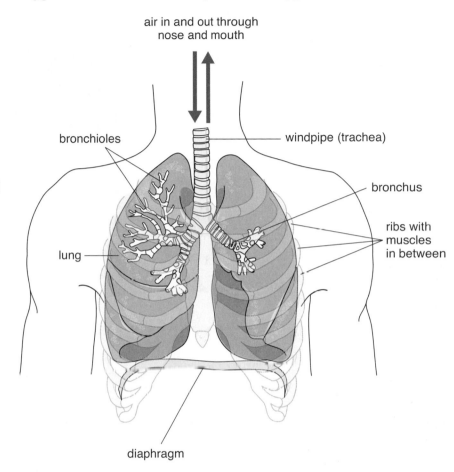

air in and out through nose and mouth

bronchioles

windpipe (trachea)

bronchus

ribs with muscles in between

lung

diaphragm

When the volume of something goes up, the **pressure** of the air inside it goes down. So, now the pressure inside the thorax is less than that in the atmosphere. We say there is a **pressure gradient** between the air outside the body and the air inside the lungs.

Air flows from places with high pressure to places with low pressure, so air rushes into the lungs down the pressure gradient.

All these steps happen automatically, so we never need to think about it.

We can show the process in a flowchart:

rib muscles contract	→	ribs rise up	→	thorax volume increases	→	thorax pressure decreases (below atmospheric)	→	air rushes into lungs down pressure gradient

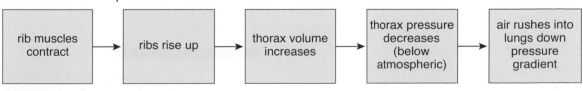

Explain how breathing is different from aerobic respiration.

What do alveoli do?

Once the air is inside the lungs it enters air sacs called **alveoli**. All the alveoli inside each of the lungs covers an area as big as a tennis court! Every one of them is covered with a network of blood vessels to take in the oxygen. These have a very thin wall so the oxygen in the air can pass into the blood. At the same time, waste carbon dioxide passes out of the blood into the alveoli. This is called **gas exchange**.

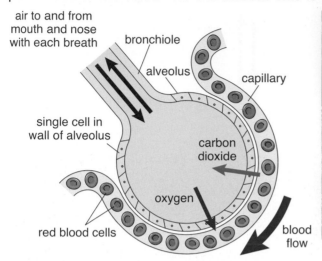

air to and from mouth and nose with each breath
bronchiole
alveolus
capillary
single cell in wall of alveolus
carbon dioxide
oxygen
red blood cells
blood flow

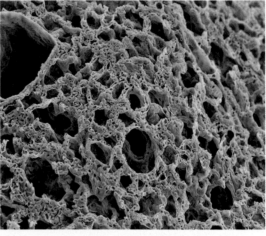

The alveoli inside a lung make it seem spongy.

Explain how the alveoli have a large surface area. (Hint: Compare the alveoli with the villi in the gut – see page 43.)

How do we breathe out?

To breathe out:

- the muscles between the ribs relax;
- the ribs fall;
- the diaphragm pushes upwards;
- the volume of the thorax goes down.

This causes the pressure in the lungs to go up and the air is pushed out.

The 'bell jar' model can help us to understand this process. Pull on the rubber sheet and the balloon expands, showing how breathing works. Push on the rubber sheet to 'breathe out'.

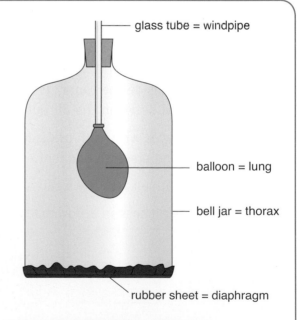

glass tube = windpipe
balloon = lung
bell jar = thorax
rubber sheet = diaphragm

Draw a 'breathing out' flowchart in the same style as the 'breathing in' flowchart on page 47. Start with the oxygen exchange box.

Why take care of your lungs?

As you can see from the picture below, the lungs are very delicate organs. The thin walls of the alveoli are very easily damaged. When this happens, less oxygen is taken into the blood when you breathe.

One of the worst things you can do is to take damaging substances into your lungs. Sometimes, you may have little choice about this because you live in an environment where there is air pollution. But something over which you do have a choice is **smoking**.

What damage can smoking cause?

Tobacco smoke has a number of harmful effects.

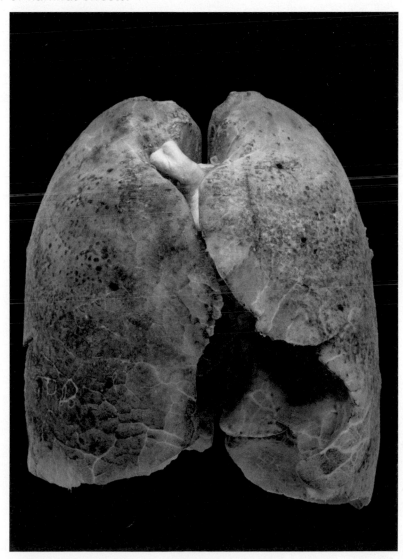

- ▶ It will damage the walls of the alveoli. This will make a person short of breath, and over time it can cause a condition called emphysema.

- ▶ **Emphysema** is where the alveoli are so badly damaged, the thin walls have broken down. This condition greatly reduces the surface area of the lungs, making it hard to breathe or even move about.

- ▶ Some chemicals in smoke can cause **cancer**, where cells are damaged and grow out of control to make lumps called tumours. Smoking often causes cancer in the throat or lungs. Cancers can kill you.

- ▶ Stale tobacco smoke coming out of the lungs really does not smell good!

Add all these effects to the huge cost of cigarettes and smoking begins to look like a really bad idea!

For a long time, people did not think smoking was at all harmful, even though it might seem almost obvious to us now. Many cigarettes were advertised with all sorts of questionable benefits to health that we now know were false. Richard Doll and Austin Bradford Hill conducted one of the first studies to link lung damage with smoking. All cigarettes now have to be advertised with a health warning!

? Find out about the work of Richard Doll and Austin Bradford Hill. Explain why there was a lot of resistance to their work at the time.

You need to remember that:

- Energy is released from food in respiration.
- Aerobic respiration uses oxygen.
- Anaerobic respiration is where no oxygen is used.
- More energy is released in aerobic respiration than in anaerobic respiration.
- The chemical reaction for respiration is the reverse of photosynthesis:

    glucose + oxygen → carbon dioxide + water + energy

- Anaerobic respiration by yeast is used in the drinks industry to make alcohol.
- Muscles in the thorax (chest) move the ribs and diaphragm when you breathe.
- The rib and diaphragm movements cause the thorax volume to change.
- The change in volume means the pressure inside the lungs changes.
- Pressure changes cause air to rush in or out of the lungs.
- The lungs are spongy because they are full of air sacs called alveoli.
- The alveoli have thin walls to allow oxygen into the blood and carbon dioxide out of it.
- Smoking damages the lungs and can cause cancer.

Next time »

Unit 8   **Your circulatory system brings food and oxygen together to your cells (page 52).**

Unit 8   **Blood carries food molecules and waste dissolved in the watery plasma (page 54).**

Previously >>

From page 43 | Your body digests food into small molecules that are carried by the blood.

From page 46 | Oxygen is brought into the blood through breathing and aerobic respiration.

Unit 8

Circulation

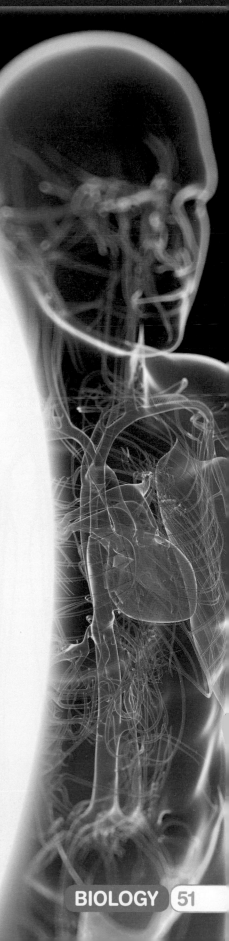

What is circulation for?

When oxygen and food have been brought into the body, humans need some way of getting them to every cell all over the body.

Blood is not just a liquid; it contains specialised cells designed to collect food from the gut and oxygen from the lungs. The blood is then carried all round the body through a huge network of tubes called vessels. This network is powered by a machine that works every second of our lives: the heart. The blood, vessels and heart together are called the circulatory system.

In this Unit, you will learn:

- ▶ how the circulatory system brings food and oxygen to the cells;
- ▶ how the circulatory system also takes away waste from the cells;
- ▶ about the vessels that carry the blood around the body;
- ▶ what blood contains;
- ▶ why oxygen is carried by specialised red blood cells;
- ▶ what red blood cells are made of;
- ▶ how white blood cells protect us from diseases;
- ▶ how the blood protects us when we are injured;
- ▶ how the heart works.

Key words

arteries	haemoglobin	red blood cells
blood vessels	heart	scab
capillaries	heartbeat	valves
clot	plasma	veins
dissolve	platelets	white blood cells

What is the circulatory system?

Your circulatory system is a huge network of pipes, containing blood, and a pump. We call the pipes '**blood vessels**', and the pump is the heart. If you could take all the blood vessels out of your body and lay them end to end, they would form a line over 60 000 miles long!

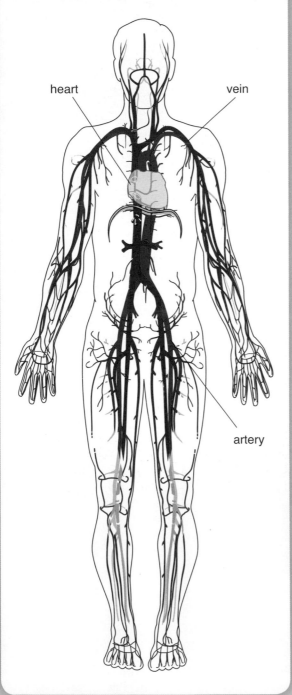

heart

vein

artery

How does the circulatory system work?

In Unit 6, we saw how the body digests food into small molecules. In Unit 7, we saw how oxygen is breathed in, and how cells use the oxygen to get energy through respiration. The body also gets rid of waste products from the cells and breathes out carbon dioxide.

Once oxygen and food molecules have been brought into the body, a way is needed to transport them to all of the cells. The circulatory system takes the blood around every part of the body to 'fuel' every cell. It also carries the waste products away.

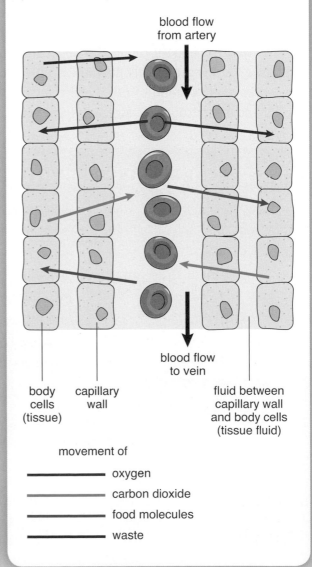

blood flow from artery

blood flow to vein

body cells (tissue)

capillary wall

fluid between capillary wall and body cells (tissue fluid)

movement of

———————— oxygen

———————— carbon dioxide

———————— food molecules

———————— waste

What do blood vessels do?

There are three different types of blood vessels in the body.

○ Large, thick-walled blood vessels called **arteries** take blood from the heart to all the organs of the body.

○ Large, thin-walled blood vessels called **veins** take blood from the organs back to the heart.

○ Small blood vessels called **capillaries** link the two.

Large blood vessels are like 'major roads'. They have muscles to help push the blood in the arteries, and **valves** to stop blood flowing backwards in the veins.

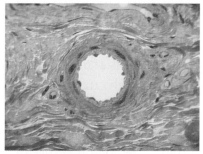

Cross-section of artery.

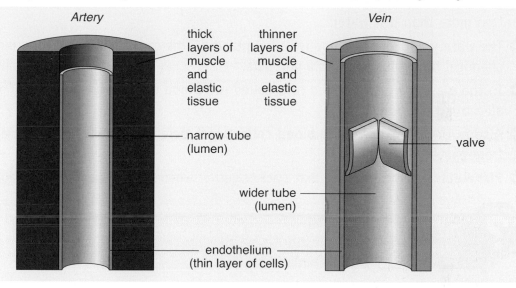

The capillaries allow oxygen and food to move across the walls into cells. They also allow waste materials to move from cells into them. To do these things they have very thin walls.

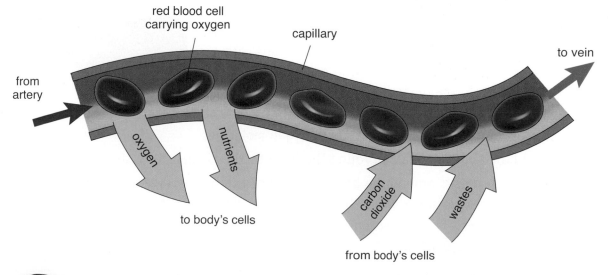

Draw a table to compare an artery, a vein and a capillary.

What is blood made from?

Animals with very basic circulatory systems use just water to transport things. This works because many things needed for life will **dissolve** in water. Unfortunately, oxygen only dissolves a little in water.

Large, active, warm-blooded animals like us need lots of oxygen. So our blood needs to contain more than just water.

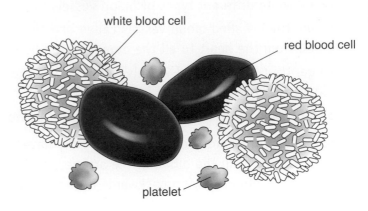

white blood cell

red blood cell

platelet

▶ The watery part of the blood is called **plasma**. This carries dissolved food molecules, chemical hormones and waste products.

▶ In the plasma are specialised cells called **red blood cells**. These cells carry oxygen all around the body.

▶ Also in the blood are **white blood cells**, which defend the body against infection from bacteria.

▶ **Platelets** are tiny granules that stick together when a blood vessel is damaged.

 Draw a spider diagram showing the components of blood and what each component does.

How do red blood cells work?

Red blood cells are red because they contain the chemical haemoglobin. **Haemoglobin** is a protein that binds with and releases oxygen. A single red blood cell contains about 280 million haemoglobin molecules!

▶ In the alveoli in the lungs, there are lots of oxygen molecules (see page 48). Here, each haemoglobin 'collects' four oxygen molecules.

▶ The red blood cells are carried round the body by the circulatory system.

▶ The rest of the cells around the body need oxygen to respire (see page 46). Here, the haemoglobin releases the oxygen molecules for the cell to use.

▶ The red blood cell is then carried back to the lungs by the circulatory system, and the cycle starts again.

 Why is blood thicker than water?

How does your blood protect you? @

White blood cells help protect your body from diseases. Some white blood cells wrap themselves around bacteria to kill them. Other types of white blood cell help the body 'remember' what bacteria have entered the blood. They help create antibodies – chemicals that protect against infections.

If a blood vessel is damaged, platelets **clot** the blood to form a protective barrier to stop infections. If you cut yourself, platelets form a **scab** over the wound.

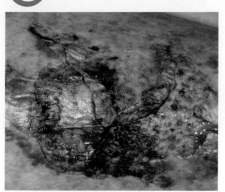

? Research how much blood a human usually contains. Explain why someone who loses a lot of blood in an accident needs to be given more blood.

How does the heart work? @

The **heart** is a pump made of muscle. The muscles in the heart contract in a particular order that pulls blood into the heart and pushes it back out again. Each complete set of contractions is a **heartbeat**. Each time the heart beats, it pushes some blood to the lungs and some round the rest of the body.

○ The blood that goes to the lungs picks up oxygen and throws away carbon dioxide (see page 48).

○ The blood that goes to the body delivers oxygen and picks up waste carbon dioxide.

The best way to understand what the heart is like is to look at one. Here is a photograph of a heart that has been cut open.

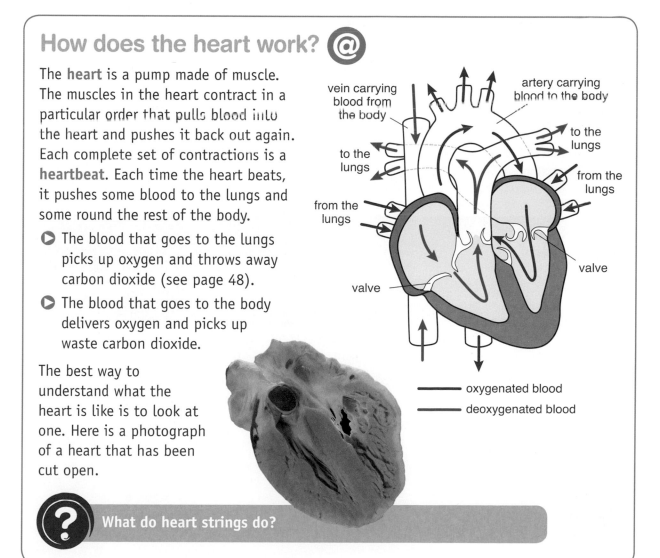

vein carrying blood from the body

artery carrying blood to the body

to the lungs

to the lungs

from the lungs

from the lungs

valve

valve

——— oxygenated blood
——— deoxygenated blood

? What do heart strings do?

Look again at the photograph and diagram of the heart on page 55.

Investigate and explain how the heart makes the blood go round in the way shown by the arrows. You will need to find out about *heart muscles* and *valves*.

You need to remember that:

- ▷ The circulatory system brings both food and oxygen to all the cells in the body.
- ▷ It also takes wastes away from the cells.
- ▷ The circulatory system contains vessels, blood and the heart.
- ▷ Arteries have thick walls and take blood from the heart and lungs.
- ▷ Veins have thin walls and take blood back to the heart and lungs.
- ▷ Capillaries have very thin walls and allow substances to move across them to and from cells.
- ▷ Blood carries food molecules and waste dissolved in the watery plasma.
- ▷ Oxygen is carried in red blood cells by a chemical called haemoglobin.
- ▷ White blood cells protect the body against diseases.
- ▷ The heart pumps blood to the lungs, where it collects oxygen.
- ▷ The heart also pumps blood around the body, where it can release this oxygen to cells that need it.

Next time ≫

Unit 9   The bone marrow inside bones makes red blood cells and white blood cells (page 58).

Unit 12   The immune system protects against many infections (page 78).

Previously »

| Remember | Humans and many other animals have skeletons and muscles to help them to move. |
| From page 43 | The thorax (chest) contains muscles that move the ribs and thorax when you breathe. |

Unit 9

Movement

Which living things move?

One of the seven characteristics of life is movement. We can see movement most clearly in larger animals. For example, a horse running a race or a monkey jumping from branch to branch in a tree. But movement is not obvious in all animals, even though it does happen. Plants move too!

The easiest kind of movement to see is what we do as humans. To move we need something to create the movement – muscles – and something to move – the skeleton.

In this Unit, you will learn:

- ◗ how all living things, including plants, move;
- ◗ that humans have a supportive skeleton;
- ◗ how your skeleton is made of bone;
- ◗ how each bone is connected to others by joints;
- ◗ how muscles work by contraction and pulling;
- ◗ why muscles cannot push, so they have to work in pairs.

Key words

antagonistic pair	muscles
biceps	pathogens
bone	skeleton
bone marrow	synovial fluid
cartilage	synovial joints
joint	triceps

How do plants and corals move?

Movement in plants can be seen inside their cells. However, there are some plants, such as the sensitive plant (*Mimosa pudica*) that can move whole leaves. Another group of plants, the fly traps, move their leaves in order to catch flies which they then digest.

Animals such as corals, barnacles and sea anemones do not move from place to place but do have parts that make movements. Barnacles, for example, move their legs backwards and forwards to filter food from the water.

 Research and explain how a sensitive plant moves.

What is bone made from?

The human skeleton, like that of all mammals, is made of **bone**. Bone combines strength with flexibility. It does this by being made of non-living and living components.

- The non-living component of bone is made of the minerals calcium and phosphate. This makes bones strong and difficult to bend. If the non-living component is removed, bones are easily bent. We say they are decalcified.

- Living cells are mixed in amongst the minerals. These cells build and repair bones, and make them difficult to break. If the living component is removed, bones become brittle and easily broken.

Decalcified bone.

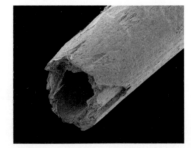

Brittle bone.

spongy bone

compact bone

marrow

An individual bone has a strong, dense outer layer with a flexible, spongy layer inside. In the very middle is the **bone marrow** through which blood vessels pass. The bone marrow contains specialised cells that make our blood cells.

 Suggest why bones have blood vessels.

How do joints work?

Anywhere where two bones meet is a **joint**.

- Some joints are immovable (they cannot move), like those in the skull.
- Some joints can be moved in one direction, like the knee.
- Some joints can be moved in a number of directions, like the shoulder.

In order for the joint to move smoothly and painlessly it is lined with a soft substance called **cartilage**. To reduce friction further, our bodies make a liquid called **synovial fluid**. This works like oil in a car engine (see page 222). This gives the movable human joints their name, **synovial joints**.

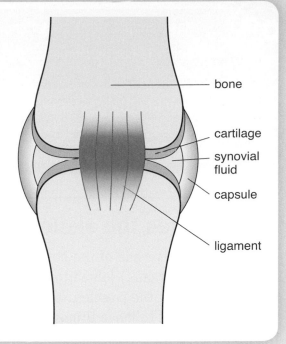

bone

cartilage

synovial fluid

capsule

ligament

How do muscles work?

Muscles contain elastic (stretchy) tissue made from specialised cells. Muscles work by contraction, where they use up energy to get shorter and fatter. This means they can only 'pull' – they cannot 'push'.

What are antagonistic muscles?

Let's think about a simple joint like the elbow.

- One muscle, the **biceps**, *pulls* the forearm upwards.
- Another muscle, the **triceps**, *pulls* the forearm down.

It is easy to see how the pulling up works on a diagram, but the pulling down is not so clear.

1. Try touching your biceps muscle whilst pulling your forearm upwards. You should feel it get shorter, thicker and 'harder' as it contracts.
2. Now touch your triceps muscle as you lower your forearm. You should now feel that get shorter, thicker and 'harder' as it contracts.

biceps

triceps

The biceps muscle and the triceps muscle work together as an **antagonistic pair**.

 Explain how the knee joint works in a similar way.

Many people think that flamingos have 'backwards' knees.
But it is not as simple as this.

 Compare the skeleton and bones of the flamingo leg with that of the human. Explain why they do not, in fact, have 'backwards' knees.

What does the skeleton do?

The **skeleton** is made of the bones (about 200 of them!) joined to each other and, with the muscles, it allows us to move and to move things.

The skeleton does other things too:

- ▶ It protects vital organs. For example, the skull protects the brain, and the rib cage protects the heart and lungs.
- ▶ It makes red and white blood cells in the bone marrow.
- ▶ It holds vital organs such as the heart and kidneys in place.
- ▶ It gives the body a shape.

The skin also helps to protect the organs inside the body. It is tough and helps stop **pathogens** (viruses or bacteria) that might cause disease.

1 Explain why it is important to protect your bones if you are playing sports. If you break a bone, what would happen if it did not repair itself?

2 Vitamins and minerals are needed for healthy bones. Which foods should we eat to keep our bones healthy?

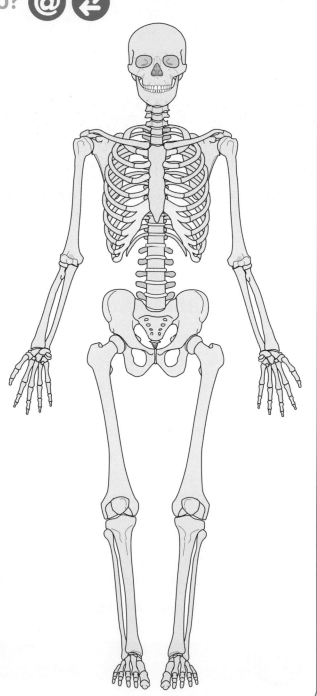

You need to remember that:

- ▷ All animals and plants move, but sometimes the movement is not obvious.
- ▷ Humans and other mammals have an internal skeleton made of bone.
- ▷ Bones meet each other in joints.
- ▷ Some joints cannot move, like those in the skull.
- ▷ Some joints can be moved, like those in the elbow and shoulder.
- ▷ Muscles pull on bones to create movement.
- ▷ Muscles pull by contracting (getting shorter).
- ▷ Muscles cannot push, so they work together in antagonistic pairs.
- ▷ The skeleton protects vital organs and gives your body its shape.
- ▷ The bone marrow inside the bones makes red and white blood cells.

Next time »

Unit 10   Flowering plants disperse their pollen grains in the environment (page 64).

Unit 12   Exercise reduces diseases of all kinds and helps you feel healthier (page 81).

Previously »

| Remember | All living things reproduce. |
| Remember | You should know about the main stages in the human life cycle. |

Unit 10

Reproduction

What is reproduction?

All living things reproduce. For a species to survive, it needs to create copies of itself through reproduction. There are two ways in which living things reproduce: sexual and asexual.

In this Unit, you will learn:

- ▶ that all living things reproduce;
- ▶ about the two kinds of reproduction – sexual and asexual;
- ▶ how asexual reproduction only needs one individual;
- ▶ how sexual reproduction needs a male and a female;
- ▶ how sex cells are produced and join together through fertilisation;
- ▶ about the production of human eggs in the menstrual cycle;
- ▶ about the production of human sperm;
- ▶ that humans go through a process called puberty in which the production of sex cells is 'switched on'.

Key words

asexual reproduction	follicle	ovaries	sperm
binary fission	fruit	ovulation	stamens
carpels	gametes	ovules	stigma
contraception	germinates	penis	testes
eggs	hormones	pollination	uterus
embryo	implants	puberty	vagina
females	males	seed	zygote
fertilisation	menstrual cycle	sexual intercourse	
foetus	menstruation	sexual reproduction	

What is asexual reproduction?

From simple single-celled organisms such as *Amoeba*, to a few vertebrates like lizards, reproduction without sex is the rule. We call this **asexual reproduction**. *Amoeba* undergoes a process called **binary fission** in which a cell simply splits in half.

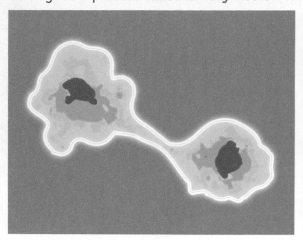
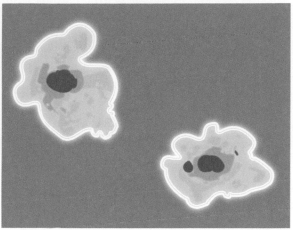

Every New Mexico whiptail lizard is a female. There are no males! Each lizard lays four eggs in the summer, from which a new lizard grows. The eggs do not need to be fertilised. The lizards appear to take part in mock (pretend) mating, which we think causes them to produce their eggs.

 Explain how aphids (greenfly) reproduce asexually.

What is sexual reproduction?

In **sexual reproduction**, two different types of specialised sex cells called **gametes** are brought together. The different sex cells are produced either by different individuals (**males** and **females**), or by different parts of the same individual. These sex cells fuse together to make one new cell, a **zygote**. The zygote splits many times to form an **embryo**. This embryo grows up to form a new individual.

The process of sexual reproduction takes many forms. We will look at it in detail for flowering plants and humans.

Some animals reproduce asexually, others reproduce sexually. Some do both under different circumstances and at different times of year. Here are some examples:

▶ many greenfly are sexual in the autumn, asexual in the summer;

▶ many desert animals and animals at the poles are asexual;

▶ animals in rainforests are nearly all sexual.

? What pattern can you see in the list above of animals that reproduce sexually, asexually or both? What explanation can you provide for it?

How do flowering plants reproduce?

In most, although not all, flowering plants the flower contains both male and female sex organs. The male sex organs are called **stamens** and the female sex organs are called **carpels**.

The male gamete in flowering plants cannot move on its own, so it has to be carried from flower to flower. It is inside a structure called a pollen grain. Different plants use all sorts of different ways to get these pollen grains moved about.

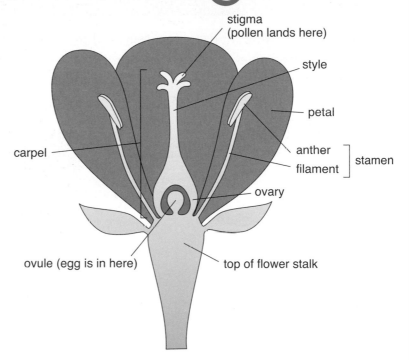

stigma (pollen lands here)

style

petal

anther
filament
} stamen

carpel

ovary

ovule (egg is in here)

top of flower stalk

▶ Some pollen grains are light and specially shaped so they are blown about by the wind.

▶ Some are sticky or have hooks on their surface, so they are carried on the bodies of animals such as insects (like bees) or even bats.

Flowers have structures and shapes designed to catch the pollen grains on the carpel.

? Search online to find a number of electron microscope pictures of different pollen grains. See if you can explain how each type of pollen is adapted to be dispersed in the environment.

What happens when the male gamete arrives at the carpel?

Inside a flower, the top part of the carpel is called the **stigma**. Inside the carpel are **ovules** that contain the female gametes, called **eggs**.

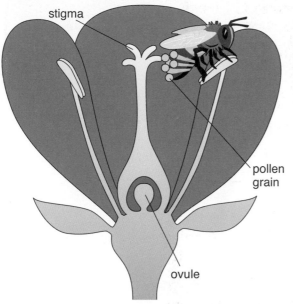

stigma

pollen grain

ovule

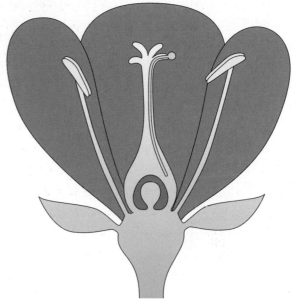

1. Some pollen grains are transferred from the backs of insects or the wind onto the stigma. This is called **pollination**.

2. The pollen grain **germinates** and a tube passes down through the stigma into the ovule.

3. The tube bursts and releases the male gamete into the ovule.

4. The male gamete joins with the female gamete to form an embryo. This is called **fertilisation**.

Remember that pollination and fertilisation are different parts of the process.

How does a new plant grow from the embryo?

The embryo now grows, together with other parts of the ovule, to form a **seed**. Many seeds may form inside a structure called the **fruit**.

seeds

▶ A fruit is often fleshy and nutritious, to tempt animals to eat it. The seeds are not digested, so they are carried to a different place where they are egested in the animals' faeces (see page 43).

▶ A fruit protects the seeds and falls to the ground, where the fruit rots and the seed is left on the ground.

In these ways, seeds are dispersed (moved around) the environment. If a seed lands in a suitable place it will germinate, sending a root into the ground and a shoot upwards. Eventually, this young plant will flower and the life cycle starts again.

THINKING BEYOND...

Sexual reproduction between two different individuals produces great variation in offspring. It is thought that this helps a species to evolve. The 'best' variations create the plants most likely to live longer, reproduce more successfully, resist diseases and so on. Natural selection 'chooses' the best variations for the next generation.

In many plants, the male and female parts are on the same flower (we say they are *hermaphrodite*). This means one individual plant could pollinate and fertilise itself. However, this would mean that the purpose of sexual reproduction to create variation would not be achieved.

? Research and explain how hermaphrodite flowers ensure they do not self-pollinate. How else do flowering plants avoid self-pollination? (Hawthorn and holly are examples of plants you might choose.)

How do humans reproduce?

In all mammals, including humans, the male gamete is called the **sperm** and can swim. Sperm are produced in the **testes**.

The female gamete is an **egg**, is very much bigger than the sperm, and cannot swim. Eggs are produced in the **ovaries**, in a process called **ovulation**.

A man and a woman bring their sex organs together in **sexual intercourse**. The man's **penis** becomes erect so that it can be inserted into the woman's **vagina**. Millions of sperm are pushed from the man's testes, through his penis, into the vagina. If the woman has an egg in the Fallopian tube leading to her **uterus**, it produces chemicals that attract the swimming sperm. Only one of the many millions of sperm that were introduced can eventually join with the egg and fertilise it.

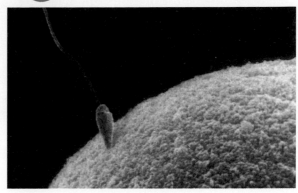

Only one sperm joins with the egg to fertilise it.

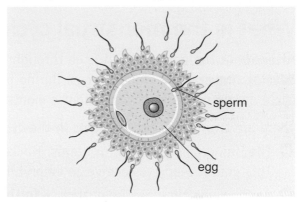

sperm

egg

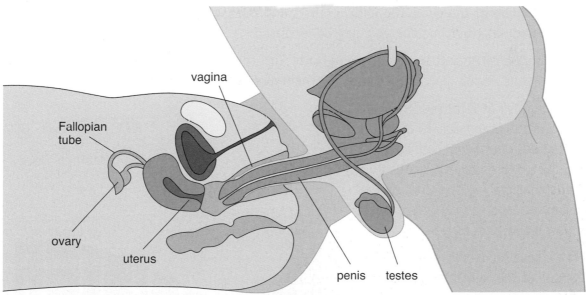

vagina

Fallopian tube

ovary

uterus

penis   testes

Sexual intercourse.

It is not certain that fertilisation will occur. As with most mammals, human eggs are only present for a few days each month because of the menstrual cycle.

How are the sperm and egg suited to their functions as sex cells?

Contraception is where a man and woman choose to prevent the sperm from fertilising the egg. One method of contraception is called the rhythm method.

This relies on the fact that an egg is only present in the woman for part of each month. If sexual intercourse occurs outside this time, pregnancy will not result. Unfortunately, it is not very reliable – sometimes an egg will be fertilised even though the rhythm method was used.

 Research the rhythm method and suggest why its failure rate is quite high.

What is the menstrual cycle? @

After about the age of 12, girls go through **puberty**. This is where the sex organs develop and start to produce eggs. During puberty, the **menstrual cycle** starts. Each full cycle of egg production lasts about a month.

There are two main sets of events in the cycle.

▶ The lining of the womb, or uterus, thickens and becomes well supplied with blood. This gets it ready to receive an embryo if fertilisation happens.

▶ At the same time, in the ovaries, a **follicle** develops with an egg inside it. At about the middle of the cycle the follicle bursts and releases the egg. If there are sperm in the body at this time the egg may be fertilised.

If the egg is fertilised, the embryo **implants** into the thick lining of the uterus. The embryo cells divide many times until the embryo develops into a **foetus**.

If the egg is not fertilised, the lining of the uterus breaks down and passes out of the vagina. This part of the process is called **menstruation**. Menstruation can be painful, and can cause tiredness or low mood.

All of these processes need to happen at the right time and in the right sequence. The body controls this by changing the amounts of different chemical **hormones** in the body over the month.

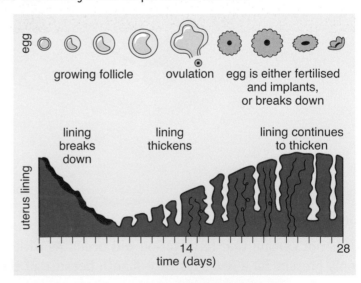

 Make a table of the stages involved in the menstrual cycle and explain what happens at each stage.

You need to remember that:

- There are two kinds of reproduction – sexual and asexual.
- Many plants and some animals use asexual reproduction.
- Flowering plants and mammals use sexual reproduction.
- A flower contains the sex organs: the stamens (male) and carpels (female).
- The male gamete is in a pollen grain; the female gamete is called the ovule.
- In pollination, the pollen grain is carried to the female part of another flower by wind or animals.
- The pollen grain then grows down into the carpel, where the male gamete is released and joins the ovule in fertilisation.
- A fruit with seeds in it then develops and the seeds are dispersed into the environment.
- In mammals, the male gametes are sperm that can swim.
- Sperm are produced in the male's testes, and eggs are produced in the female's ovaries.
- Millions of sperm are introduced into the female's vagina during sexual intercourse.
- If an egg is present, fertilisation may occur.
- After fertilisation, an embryo forms and implants into the lining of the uterus.
- Eggs are produced every month during the menstrual cycle.

Next time »

Unit 11 In humans, the fertilised embryo grows by cell division to form a blastula and then a foetus (page 73).

Unit 11 In humans, the baby is born around nine months after fertilisation (page 74).

Previously »
| Remember | All living things reproduce and grow. |
| From page 13 | Cells can specialise and then work together to form tissues. |

Unit 11

Growth

How do living things grow?

All living things grow, and all living things are made of cells. These two facts are linked because growth involves an increase in cell number or in cell size, or both.

In this Unit, you will learn:

- ▶ that plants grow by increasing cell size and numbers;
- ▶ how plant cells get bigger by absorbing water;
- ▶ how cell numbers increase through mitosis;
- ▶ that animals grow mostly by increasing cell numbers;
- ▶ how a human embryo divides to form a blastula and then a foetus;
- ▶ how the foetus is fed and protected as it grows;
- ▶ how a baby is born;
- ▶ how children grow quickly and then at the age of 12, start to go through puberty;
- ▶ what changes take place during puberty and adolescence.

Key words

acne	embryo	puberty
adolescence	foetus	roots
amnion	labour	shoots
auxin	meristems	testosterone
blastula	mitosis	umbilical cord
cervix	oestrogen	uterus
dendrochronology	placenta	

How do plants grow?

Plants grow in two ways:

● by increasing the size of their cells;
● by increasing the number of their cells.

A plant cell gets bigger by absorbing water into its cell vacuoles (see page 14). When the cell is young or under the influence of growth chemicals, the cell wall can stretch. Unlike animals, which grow in all parts of their bodies, only certain parts of plants grow. These **meristems** are at the tips and round the edges of **shoots** and **roots**. This allows growth in length and in thickness.

Plant cells increase in number by dividing in a process called **mitosis**. Growing regions of plants, particularly the roots, are good places to see cell division.

Trees outside the tropics grow in spring and summer and not in winter. This leads to the formation of rings of spring and summer wood which can be counted to find out how old the tree is. The study of tree rings is called **dendrochronology**.

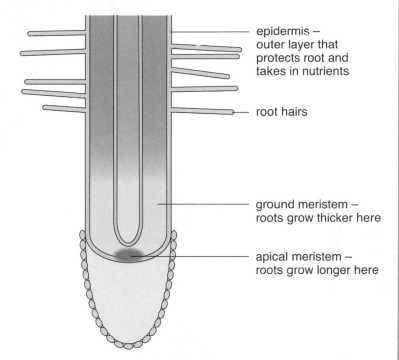

epidermis – outer layer that protects root and takes in nutrients

root hairs

ground meristem – roots grow thicker here

apical meristem – roots grow longer here

 How could you find out how old a tree is without cutting it down?

 THINKING BEYOND

Not only can we find out how old a tree is but also how suitable for growth the weather was by the thickness of the rings.

How has studying tree rings helped to tell us about climates in the distant past? What are the conclusions of this research?

How do the cells change as a plant grows?

After division, the cells take up water and swell. This is important in causing plant movement as well as growth. If a plant is placed on a windowsill with light coming from one side, it will bend towards that light.

A plant hormone called **auxin** is made at the tip of the shoot and moves down inside the shoot to cause the swelling of cells. When light is shone from one side, more auxin collects on the *unlit* side. This causes the cells on the unlit side to get bigger than the cells on the lit side, pushing the shoot over towards the light.

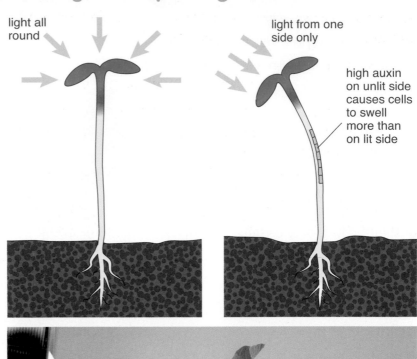

light all round

light from one side only

high auxin on unlit side causes cells to swell more than on lit side

 Plan an experiment to show that young plant shoots respond to the direction of light. Remember to include a control – a pot of seedlings where you don't change the experimental conditions.

 THINKING BEYOND...

Charles Darwin is well known for his 'Theory of Evolution by Natural Selection'. It is not so well known that he also did experiments on a wide variety of other biological topics. He was one of the first people to research how plants move as they grow.

 Find out about Darwin's work on growth movements in grass seedlings. How were his conclusions refined by Boysen-Jensen and F. W. Went?

How does a human foetus grow?

In animals, most growth occurs through increasing the numbers of cells. The cells divide in the process called mitosis (see page 69).

We saw in Unit 10 how humans reproduce. The fertilised **embryo** implants into the wall of the **uterus** (womb), and the cells start to divide.

▶ The dividing cells form into a ball called a **blastula**.

▶ The cells in the blastula continue to divide and change into different types of specialised cells.

▶ The blastula turns into a **foetus**, and we can start to recognise some human features.

For the foetus to grow, energy and materials from food are needed, and wastes need to be carried away. This is done through the **placenta**, an organ connecting the foetus to its mother. The placenta is filled with blood vessels that allow food and oxygen molecules to cross from the mother's blood to the foetus's. It also takes away waste molecules, and helps to protect the growing foetus from infections that might be in the mother's blood. The placenta is connected to the foetus by the **umbilical cord**.

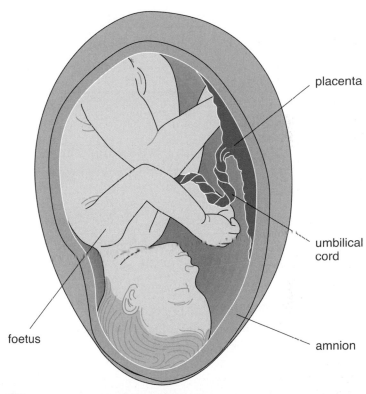

placenta

umbilical cord

foetus

amnion

Substances passed to the foetus by the mother	Substances passed to the mother from the foetus
sugars (food)	urea (waste)
amino acids (food)	carbon dioxide
oxygen	

The foetus is protected from being bumped or damaged by a bag, the **amnion**, filled with a watery liquid called amniotic fluid.

 By what process do substances pass from mother to foetus and from foetus to mother? Explain, in detail, how this can continue to happen throughout the life of the foetus.

How do humans give birth?

About 9 months after fertilisation, the foetus has grown into a baby that can breathe, move and digest food for itself. It usually turns in the uterus so its head is pointing downwards. The opening of the uterus, called the **cervix**, relaxes and the protective bag of amniotic fluid bursts.

This happens near the start of the process called **labour**. Strong muscles around the uterus contract to push the baby out, head first. The baby emerges from its mother's vagina, with the umbilical cord still attached. The cord then needs to be cut and sealed. Labour finishes when the placenta or 'afterbirth' is pushed out.

 Find out about what causes the process of labour to begin.

What is puberty?

After being born, babies grow rapidly into children. In our first few years, we learn how to eat, move about, see, hear and communicate. We also grow taller and stronger as our bones and muscles develop.

After growing for about 12 years, further changes occur that lead to **puberty**.

▶ In girls, levels of a chemical hormone called **oestrogen** start to go up. This leads to the development of the female sex organs, together with breasts, increased body fat and pubic hair.

▶ In boys, a chemical hormone called **testosterone** leads to the development of the male sex organs. At the same time, body hair and muscular strength increase, and the voice 'breaks' (sounds deeper).

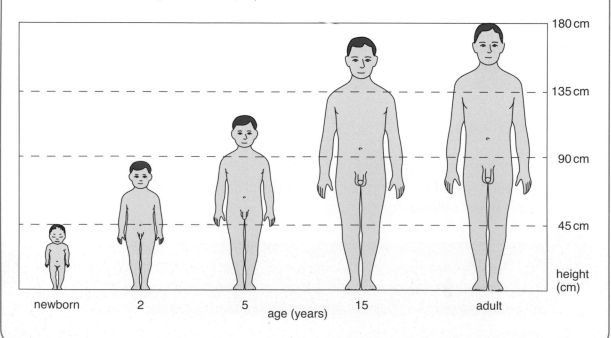

What is adolescence?

The full development of all the changes started at puberty takes up to 8 years, a period known as **adolescence**. The huge changes, together with sudden increases in hormone levels, can lead to physical and emotional difficulties. **Acne**, a sore spotty skin condition, is one such problem.

We also change emotionally in many ways as we grow up.

- We develop a wish to be independent and 'do our own things'.
- We may become rebellious as we test out our limits.
- Our increased hormones cause us to explore sexual activities.
- We develop emotions such as love.
- We also learn to care about other people and act to help them.

Adolescence usually draws to a close around the age of 18, at which point we become adults.

? Find out about the changes in hormones that lead to the changes during adolescence. Make a table to compare the situation in boys and girls.

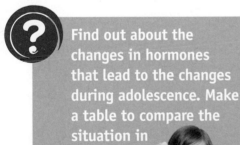

You need to remember that:

- All living things grow.
- Plants grow through increasing the size and numbers of their cells.
- Only certain parts of a plant grow – the meristems.
- Plants are sensitive to light and weather, and grow towards sunlight.
- Animals grow mainly by increasing the numbers of their cells.
- In humans, the fertilised embryo grows by cell division to form a blastula and then a foetus.
- Food and oxygen cross the placenta to the foetus from the mother.
- Waste materials and carbon dioxide cross the placenta from the foetus to the mother.
- The placenta is an organ full of blood vessels, connected to the foetus by the umbilical cord.
- After 9 months of growth and development, the mother goes into labour and the baby is born.
- Children grow taller and stronger quickly, and learn how to eat, see, hear and communicate.
- At about 12 years of age, hormones are produced in the process called puberty.
- Girls produce the hormone oestrogen, which causes their sex organs to develop and their menstrual cycle to start.
- Boys produce the hormone testosterone, which causes their sex organs to develop and their voice to change.
- Puberty is the start of the 8-year growth spell called adolescence.
- During adolescence, major physical and emotional changes take place.

Next time »

Unit 12   Diseases caused by organisms such as bacteria and viruses make many people unhealthy (page 77).

Unit 13   Plants can sense gravity and grow shoots away from its pull, and roots towards it (page 85).

Previously »

| From page 41 | Humans need a balanced diet to stay healthy. |
| From page 49 | Smoking damages your lungs and can cause cancer. |

Unit 12

Health

How healthy are we?

Health is partly 'not feeling ill', but it is also about how happy we feel and how fit we are. Our health depends on many things, not all of which we can control by ourselves. For example, our health can be affected by our income, our environment, our level of education and where we work. In this Unit we will look at some of the biological things that affect our health.

In this Unit, you will learn:

- ▷ how some diseases are caused by bacteria and viruses;
- ▷ how your body can stop those organisms from getting into you;
- ▷ how your immune system tries to destroy them if they do get in;
- ▷ about the weaknesses of your immune system;

- ▷ how vaccination helps your immune system to respond more quickly;
- ▷ how antibiotics work;
- ▷ how some medicines can reduce the symptoms of disease;
- ▷ how and why exercise makes you healthier;
- ▷ how drugs such as alcohol and cannabis can affect your health.

Key words

addictive	diseases	memory cells	relieve
alcohol	evolve	MRSA	skin
antibiotic	illegal drugs	mucus	symptoms
antibodies	immune	over-the-counter drugs	vaccinated
antigens	immune response	phagocytosis	viruses
bacteria	immunisation	prescription drugs	white blood cells
cannabis	infection	recreational drugs	

How do bacteria and viruses cause diseases?

We have only known for about one hundred years that **bacteria** and **viruses** cause **diseases.** But during that time we have been able to prevent many of these diseases in the modern world. In fact, in 1979 the World Health Organization declared that smallpox had been eradicated (completely killed off in the wild). However, some other diseases are still important and life-threatening in less developed countries.

Some common bacterial and viral diseases are shown in the table.

Disease	Organism	Symptoms
common cold	rhinovirus	headaches, sore throat, muscle stiffness, sneezing
influenza	flu virus	headaches, joint pain
measles	*Morbillivirus*	rash of red spots, cough, runny nose, red eyes, fever
food poisoning	*Salmonella* bacteria	stomach cramps, vomiting, dehydration
tetanus (lockjaw)	*Clostridium tetani* bacterium	joint stiffness, muscle spasms, fever
Legionnaires disease	*Legionella* bacterium	headaches, joint pain

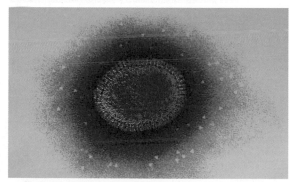

Influenza virus.

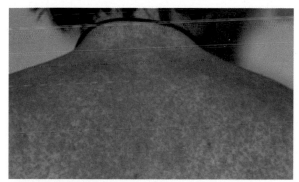

Effect of measles.

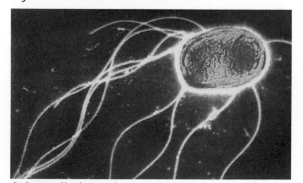

Salmonella bacterium.

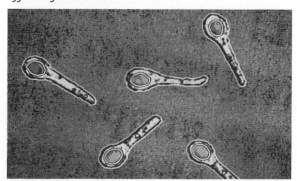

Tetanus bacteria.

Make a table to show the differences between bacteria and viruses.

What barriers to disease do we have? @

Your **skin** provides a tough barrier around the body through which bacteria cannot pass. The barrier has some holes in it: your mouth, anus, urinary tube, ears and nostrils. But all these openings are lined with sticky **mucus** that can trap bacteria.

You have another line of defence too. If bacteria do get into your body through your mouth, acid in your stomach can kill them.

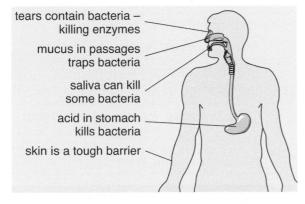

tears contain bacteria – killing enzymes

mucus in passages traps bacteria

saliva can kill some bacteria

acid in stomach kills bacteria

skin is a tough barrier

If your skin is cut or grazed, bacteria can enter. Your body protects you here too.

1. Blood flows outwards and can help wash the bacteria away.

2. Platelets in the blood stick together to form a clot over the cut (see page 55).

3. The clot dries and turns into a scab.

4. Cells work to heal the skin, under the protection of the scab.

If all these methods fail and bacteria or viruses do get into your blood, we say you have caught an **infection**. It is the turn of your immune system to deal with them.

Write down some ways in which you can help your body protect itself against bacteria. (For example, by blowing your nose into a tissue, or by not picking scabs.)

How does the immune system fight diseases?

Your immune system is made up of a number of different specialised cells and chemicals that work together to kill off infections.

In your blood, there are many different kinds of **white blood cells**. Some of these can simply wrap themselves around a bacterium or virus and kill it. This is called **phagocytosis**.

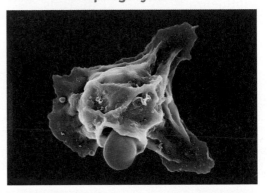

Such cells are not usually able to kill all the infecting organisms by themselves. They have a way of telling other cells in the blood about the infection.

▶ Parts of the killed bacterium are displayed on the surface of the white blood cell that killed it. These parts are called **antigens**; the cells displaying them are called antigen-presenting cells.

▶ Other cells detect the antigens and start a process leading to the production of antibodies. **Antibodies** are chemicals that contain specially shaped 'holes', which fit perfectly over the antigens.

▶ These antibodies can now destroy huge numbers of the particular infecting organism.

This chain of events is called the **immune response**.

Why don't we catch many diseases twice?

Whenever your immune system comes across an organism for the first time, it takes time to 'recognise' the antigens and make enough antibodies. So you are likely to develop an illness with **symptoms** like a fever or cough. Luckily, most infections (like colds) will not kill you!

Once your body has killed off the infection, some cells called **memory cells** 'remember' the antigens for the rest of your life. If you are infected again with the same organism, antibodies are made very quickly and you don't become ill. You are now **immune** to that disease.

? Explain why children who catch mumps or chicken pox don't usually catch it again.

Why do you think we suffer from colds quite often?

How does vaccination help us?

Unfortunately some diseases, such as typhoid, hepatitis, polio and smallpox, can cause such severe symptoms they may kill you. In 1796, Edward Jenner showed that it was possible to protect someone against smallpox.

▶ The person is injected with a sample of a related, but less dangerous, disease: cowpox.

▶ The person's immune system develops antibodies to cowpox, which also protect against smallpox.

▶ The person is now immune to smallpox. We say they have been **vaccinated**; the cowpox is a vaccine.

Before 1796, we think about 60% of the world's population got smallpox, and 20% died from it. In 1979, after many decades of vaccinating as many people as possible, the World Health Organization declared that smallpox had been eradicated.

People are now vaccinated against a wide range of diseases. We may well see more diseases eradicated.

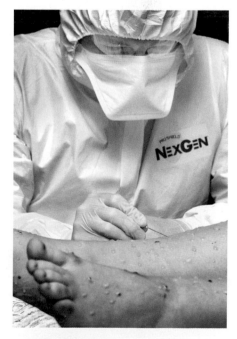

Thanks to vaccination, no-one will ever catch smallpox again.

? Find out which diseases you have been vaccinated against.

Immunisation and vaccination are not the same thing, but they are related.

 Find out precisely what immunisation and vaccination are.
Explain how they are different.

How did we discover antibiotics?

Although our immune systems are very powerful, we can still suffer from illnesses caused by bacteria. In 1928, Alexander Fleming accidentally discovered that a particular fungus makes a chemical that can kill bacteria. This is the chemical penicillin, which we now synthesise (make) in large quantities (see page 192). Penicillin was the first **antibiotic**. Many other antibiotics have now been discovered, each of which can kill particular kinds of bacteria.

Antibiotics are used all over the world to treat many different infections. But over time, bacteria are able to **evolve** (change) so that they are no longer killed by a particular antibiotic. Also, antibiotics don't work against viruses.

There are now some bacteria that cannot be killed by *any* known antibiotics. The most famous of these is **MRSA** (methicillin-resistant *Staphylococcus aureus*). This is why your doctor won't usually give you antibiotics for simple illnesses like sore throats.

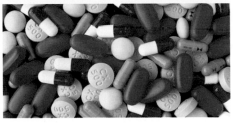

 Research how hospitals are trying to prevent the spread of MRSA.

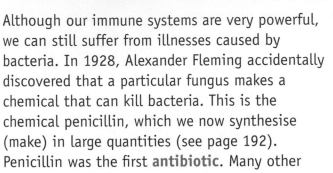

antibiotic
non-resistant bacteria
resistant bacteria

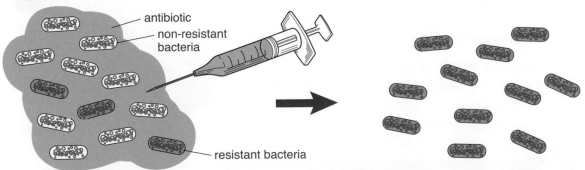

An antibiotic is used to kill off bacteria in an infection, but some are resistant.

The resistant bacteria reproduce, so only they are left. The antibiotic cannot kill them.

What other medicines are there?

A major group of other medicines are those that **relieve** symptoms. They make us feel better but they don't cure the illness. These include painkillers, throat tablets, anti-nausea tablets, anti-itching creams, and many more.

 Find out from your family which common medicines you keep at home.

Why is exercise important?

For us to stay healthy, it is not enough to eat well (see page 41) or to take medicines when we are ill. Exercise is one of the best ways for us to stay healthy. There are some things to remember when we exercise:

◗ Exercise helps all our cells and systems work at their best.

◗ We don't have to exercise for long. Even 30 to 45 minutes is enough, so long as we work up a sweat.

◗ It's more important to make sure we exercise regularly – at least four or five times a week.

◗ Sports are good, but other things like walking, running, cycling, skateboarding, trampolining and even cutting the lawn count!

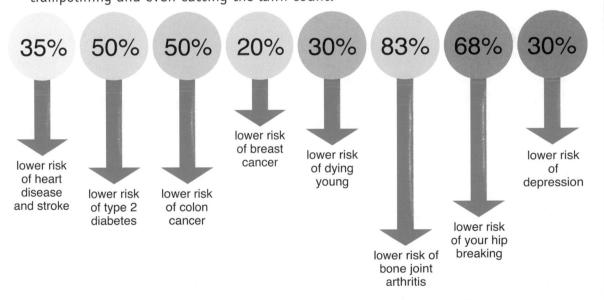

35% — lower risk of heart disease and stroke

50% — lower risk of type 2 diabetes

50% — lower risk of colon cancer

20% — lower risk of breast cancer

30% — lower risk of dying young

83% — lower risk of bone joint arthritis

68% — lower risk of your hip breaking

30% — lower risk of depression

The National Health Service has worked out how much less likely we are to suffer illnesses if we exercise regularly.

 Write a table of the days of the week showing what types of exercise you do and for how long.

What are 'drugs'?

The word 'drugs' covers a wide range of chemical substances. All of them affect our bodies or our minds by changing how the chemicals and cells inside us work. Most drugs also have 'side effects' – our bodies may react in ways we cannot control. Some drugs that have dangerous effects or side effects are banned to protect us – these are **illegal drugs**.

- ▶ **Prescription drugs** are medicines like antibiotics, which your doctor may give you to treat illnesses. They can be dangerous if not used properly, so they are carefully controlled.

- ▶ **Over-the-counter drugs** are medicines like painkillers or cough syrup, which can be bought from a pharmacy to treat illnesses. They are less dangerous, but taking too much of one can still cause harm. For that reason, the sales of some of them are restricted. For example, you are restricted in the number of packs of paracetamol you can buy at a time.

- ▶ **Recreational drugs** are not medicines. Some people use them to relax or to change their mood, but all of them can be dangerous. Some are so dangerous they are illegal.

What problems can drugs cause?

Alcohol is a legal recreational drug for people over the age of 18 in the UK. The table shows some effects of different amounts of alcohol. One unit is about half a pint of beer or a small glass of wine.

Units of alcohol	Effect on an adult man's body
1–3	relaxed, more talkative, skin flushed
4–6	slower to react, high risk of having an accident
7–9	blurred vision, speech affected, can be aggressive
10–15	loss of balance and memory, can be violent
16–25	cold skin, pupils of eyes dilated
Over 26	unconscious, possible death

Alcohol affects people's health too. If someone drinks too much on a regular basis, it can:

- ▶ make them obese;
- ▶ cause cancer and diabetes;
- ▶ permanently affect their mood;
- ▶ damage their liver.

Cannabis (also called marijuana, weed or hemp) is an illegal drug in the UK. It affects the brain and nerves, and is habit-forming. It can:

- ▶ make someone forgetful;
- ▶ affect breathing;
- ▶ cause mental health problems to grow worse.

Other illegal recreational drugs, such as heroin and cocaine, or 'crack', are more damaging to health and can kill. They are also highly **addictive**, meaning someone who takes them even once can find it almost impossible to stop taking them.

 Find out what the NHS recommends as a maximum number of units of alcohol for adults to consume in a week. Why is it different for men and for women?

You need to remember that:

- ▶ Health depends on many things, not just the things we can control ourselves.
- ▶ Diseases caused by organisms such as bacteria and viruses make many people unhealthy.
- ▶ We have learnt how to prevent or treat many diseases.
- ▶ Your body protects you from infection by diseases, using your skin, mucus and acid in your stomach.
- ▶ Your body protects you when your skin is cut, by forming a scab.
- ▶ Some bacteria and viruses do still enter your body, but these can be destroyed by your immune system.
- ▶ Your immune system produces antibodies to kill harmful organisms.
- ▶ Producing the right antibodies takes time when you are infected by an organism your immune system has not met before.
- ▶ Your immune system stores memory cells to stop you being infected by the same disease twice.
- ▶ Different diseases produce different symptoms when you are unwell.
- ▶ Vaccination and immunisation can prevent diseases.
- ▶ Antibiotics help your immune system destroy bacteria, but some bacteria are resistant to antibiotics.
- ▶ Antibiotics don't work against viruses.
- ▶ Other medicines are available to reduce the symptoms of diseases.
- ▶ Evidence shows that exercise reduces diseases of all kinds and helps you feel healthier.
- ▶ Prescription drugs are given by doctors to treat serious illnesses.
- ▶ Over-the-counter drugs are sold by pharmacy shops to treat mild illnesses.
- ▶ Some recreational drugs like alcohol are legal for adults.
- ▶ Other recreational drugs like cannabis are illegal.
- ▶ All drugs can be harmful.

Next time »

Unit 13   We have five senses that involve a sense organ converting a stimulus into a nerve impulse (page 85).

Previously »

| From page 59 | In animals with a skeleton, muscles pull on bones to create movement. |
| From page 72 | Plants are sensitive to light and weather, and grow towards sunlight. |

Unit 13

Sensitivity

What is sensitivity?

Sensitivity allows living things to detect events going on around them and do something about them. Even plants are sensitive. They can detect which way light is coming from and move toward it by growing (page 72). They also sense gravity, putting roots down and sending shoots up.

Humans have five senses: sight, hearing, taste, smell and touch.

In this Unit, you will learn:

▷ how plants grow roots towards gravity and shoots away from gravity;

▷ how animals convert light, sound, taste, smell and touch into nerve impulses.

Key words

auxin	'heavy' touch	sense organ
balance	iris	sight
cones	'light' touch	smell
ear canal	lens	stimulus
eardrum	nerve impulses	taste
exposed	olfaction	taste buds
five senses	olfactory cells	temperature
focused	Pacinian corpuscle	touch
gravity	retina	transducers
hearing	rods	vibration

How are plants affected by gravity?

We saw on page 72 how plants bend towards light, but what about gravity?

The cress seedlings in the picture have been grown in a Petri dish held in a vertical position. The roots have bent downwards and the shoots have bent upwards.

The dish was kept in the dark. At the tips of the root and the shoot are cells that can detect **gravity**.

We don't quite know how this works, but it leads to the movement of a chemical called **auxin** down to the bottom of cells.

▶ In shoots, the chemical causes the cells nearest the bottom to take in *more* water and swell. This pushes the shoot upwards.

▶ In roots it is different. Here, auxin causes the cells nearest the bottom to take in *less* water. The cells at the top swell more, pushing the root downwards.

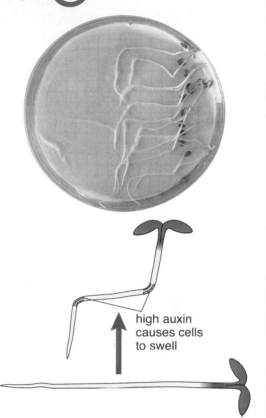

high auxin causes cells to swell

 Explain why the dish was kept in the dark. What could have happened if it had been left out in the light?

What are our five senses?

Most animals, including humans, can see, hear, taste, smell and detect touch. These are the **five senses**.

Each sense involves the use of a **sense organ**.

The information picked up by the sense organs is sent to the brain as **nerve impulses** – electric currents. All that sense organs do is to convert what they sense, the **stimulus**, into nerve impulses. They are **transducers**.

Sense	Sense organ
sight	the eye
hearing	the ear
smell	the nose
taste	the tongue
touch	the skin

For example, a sound wave causes air molecules to push against our eardrums (see page 87). The eardrums and bones in our ears vibrate. This moves hairs and is converted into electric currents that are sent by our nerves to our brain. The sound wave is the stimulus.

 Write a table listing the different senses and what stimuli cause our sense organs to send signals to our brain.

How do we see?

Even very simple organisms can detect light. The human eye allows us to do much more than this. It contains specialised structures:

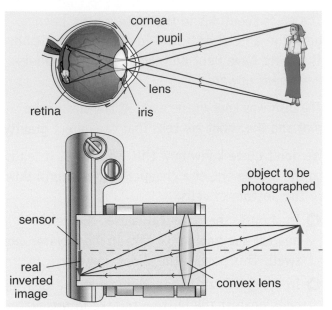

▶ The **iris** controls the amount of light entering our eye, so we can adjust to very bright or very dark environments. When the amount of light entering our eye is just right for us to see the details of an object, we say it is correctly **exposed**.

▶ The **lens** adjusts to change the direction of the light rays entering our eye. When the light rays from an object are all directed to the same point on the back of our eye, we say it is correctly **focused**. We see a sharp image.

The eye is rather like a camera. You can see that in the two drawings.

The part at the back of our eye that converts light into nerve impulses is the **retina**. This is made of special cells called rods and cones.

▶ **Rods** detect the amount of light only. They allow us to see in black-and-white, particularly when it is very dark.

▶ **Cones** also detect the frequency of the light (see page 272). This means they allow us to see different colours. They work best in brighter light.

The cones are concentrated near the centre of the retina, and the rods are arranged around them.

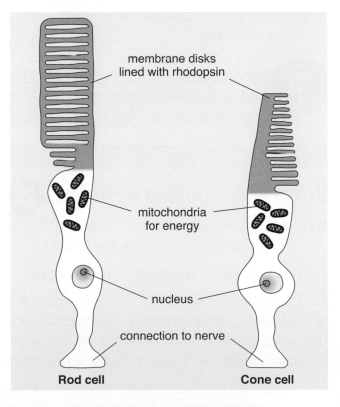

 In daylight, we look straight at something to get the best image. At night, it often helps to point the centre of our eyes slightly to one side of an object to get the best image. Explain why this is.

How do we hear?

The ear converts sounds into nerve impulses using bending hairs.

- When a sound wave passes into your ear, it pushes air molecules backwards and forwards down your **ear canal**.

- These movements cause the **eardrum** to vibrate.
- These vibrations make a liquid inside your ear move.

- The moving liquid makes very fine hairs bend.
- The moving hairs cause a nerve impulse to be sent to your brain.

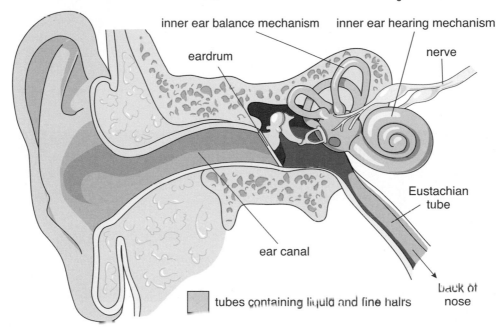

inner ear balance mechanism   inner ear hearing mechanism

eardrum

nerve

Eustachian tube

ear canal

back of nose

tubes containing liquid and fine hairs

The liquid and hairs inside our ear can also sense our position and body movements. This helps with our sense of **balance**.

 When you catch a cold or have an ear infection, you may feel dizzy and lose your sense of balance. Explain why this may happen.

How do we taste and smell?

On the surface of your skin inside your nose, there are thousands of sensing cells. You have thousands of similar cells on the top and sides of your tongue. Each time these cells detect a different chemical, they send different nerve impulses to your brain.

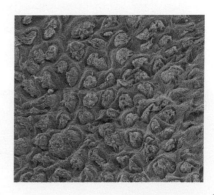

- The sense cells on your tongue are called **taste buds**.
- The sense cells in your nose are called **olfactory cells**.

The process of smelling something is called **olfaction**.

How do we sense things through touch?

The skin contains millions of touch-sensitive cells. There are four main types of cells, each sensing different things:

- ▶ **'heavy' touch** – such as pushing something;
- ▶ **'light' touch** – such as stroking fur;
- ▶ **temperature**;
- ▶ **vibration**.

One of the most common touch-sensitive cells is the **Pacinian corpuscle**. The diagram shows how it works.

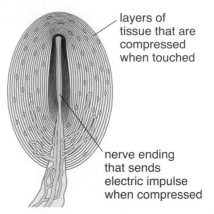

layers of tissue that are compressed when touched

nerve ending that sends electric impulse when compressed

THINKING BEYOND...

Some people claim humans have a 'sixth sense' that might help us to predict the future.

?

1 How could you investigate whether this 'sixth sense' exists?

2 Some animals can detect things that we cannot. Find out about two animals which have 'sixth senses'.

You need to remember that:

- ▶ Plants can sense light and grow shoots towards it.
- ▶ Plants can sense gravity and grow shoots away from its pull, and roots towards it.
- ▶ Humans have five senses.
- ▶ We see using our eyes – light is focused on to the retina, which contains two kinds of cells: rods and cones.
- ▶ We hear using our ears – the eardrum vibrates, which makes a liquid move small hairs inside the ear.

- ▶ We taste using our tonque – cells called taste buds detect different chemicals.
- ▶ We smell using our nose – olfactory cells detect different chemicals.
- ▶ We touch using our skin – the skin contains four different sense cells that detect heavy touch, light touch, temperature and vibration.
- ▶ All our senses involve a sense organ converting a stimulus into a nerve impulse.

Next time »

Unit 15   Each living thing is adapted to its habitat (page 96).

Unit 15   Living things interact by feeding off each other (page 96).

Previously »

| Remember | Different plants and animals are found in different habitats. |
| From page 35 | Many animals, such as honeybees, are very important to us and the environment. |

Unit 14

Ecology and the environment

What do ecologists do?

Many scientists study living things in the laboratory. Ecologists are scientists who study living things in nature. They learn about the features of the natural environment and how living things are adapted to their environment and behave in it. They also learn about how living things interact with each other, for example through feeding. From this they can understand how populations grow and are controlled.

Another important thing that ecologists do is help humans look after the environment, by understanding how it works. In this and the next two Units we will look at the work of ecologists.

In this Unit, you will learn:

- ○ that the environment consists of living and non-living things;
- ○ how ecologists measure non-living things;
- ○ how organisms are adapted to the environment in which they live;
- ○ how and why some organisms hibernate or migrate.

Key words

abiotic factors	diurnal	nocturnal
adapted	environment	probes
biotic factors	hibernate	sensors
data logger	migrating	

How do we study the environment?

The **environment** is everything around us. That means all living and non-living things. They affect us and we affect them.

If we go out to study a piece of the environment like a woodland, we can see all the living things such as humans, trees, birds, flowering plants, insects and so on. We call these **biotic factors**. We can observe and record all the different life processes for each of these living things.

In any environment, there are a number of other non-living things we can measure. These are called **abiotic factors**. Some examples include:

- ▶ the pH of the soil;
- ▶ the temperature of the air and the soil;
- ▶ the light intensity;
- ▶ how much water is in the soil;
- ▶ the mineral content of the soil;
- ▶ the quantities of gases in the atmosphere such as oxygen and carbon dioxide.

These abiotic factors, and many more, can be measured using **sensors** or **probes**. We can set most of these measuring devices up to work automatically using a **data logger**. This means we can take regular measurements over a long period of time, and analyse the results using our computers.

 Choose another type of environment (for example, a seashore). List at least six biotic factors and six abiotic factors. How would you measure each of these factors?

What is 'adaptation'?

To get what it needs to survive – food, water, oxygen and so on – a living thing has to be **adapted** to the environment in which it lives. Camels would not survive in the Arctic and polar bears would not do too well in the Sahara! The things they need are available in different forms. The particular biotic and abiotic factors are different.

The camel is very well adapted to life in the desert. A camel:

- ▶ has large feet to stop it sinking in sand;
- ▶ has nostrils that close to stop sand getting in;
- ▶ has a fat store in its hump, for food and energy;
- ▶ has long legs to keep its body and head away from hot sand;
- ▶ has bony ridges over its eyes for shade;
- ▶ has long eyelashes and extra eyelids to keep out sand;
- ▶ has flat-edged teeth to chew vegetation;
- ▶ can go without water for up to six months;
- ▶ can drink over 130 litres of water in five minutes.

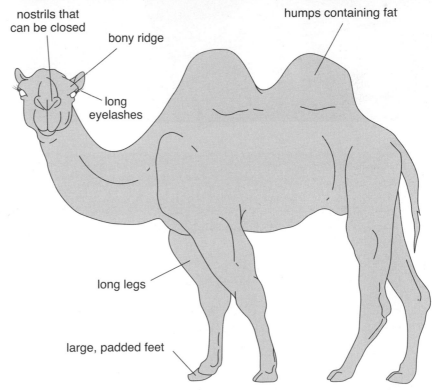

nostrils that can be closed

bony ridge

humps containing fat

long eyelashes

long legs

large, padded feet

 Describe the features of a polar bear and how they help it adapt to its environment.

There are nearly as many ways of living on Earth as there are places to live.

? Choose two or three animals and/or plants and find out where they live and how they are adapted to live there.

Which animals live in daily cycles?

Nocturnal living things are active only at night.

Diurnal living things are active during the day.

Copy and complete the following table of animals, explaining which are diurnal and which are nocturnal.

Animal	Diurnal or nocturnal?	Why?
badger		
tawny owl		
giraffe		
butterfly		
peppered moth		
cat		
great grey slug		

In the third column of your table, add a reason why each animal might be more active during the day or night.

Which animals live in yearly cycles?

Some living things are only active for part of the year. Polar bears, for example, are not active in the coldest part of the winter. This is because food is too hard to find and temperatures are too low to survive outside. They find a warmer place to shelter in, and slow down their body processes. We say that they **hibernate**.

Another way of avoiding harsh conditions is to move away. Many birds do this by **migrating**. For example, swifts spend the northern winter in warm parts of Africa. In about May they come back to the north, where it has warmed up and there is now plenty of food. This is where they reproduce and bring up their young. When they have done this they, and their young, migrate back to Africa.

Many insects also migrate. In America, the Monarch butterfly spends the summer months in the northern USA and Canada. It migrates to spend the winter in Mexico and Cuba.

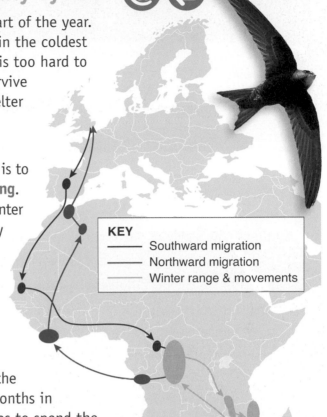

KEY
— Southward migration
— Northward migration
— Winter range & movements

On an outline map of North and Central America, draw where the Monarch butterfly spends its summers and winters, and map its migration routes.

Many animals avoid harsh conditions such as cold or drought by hibernating or migrating.

? Find out about two examples of animals that hibernate and two that migrate. See if you can discover which animal hibernates for the longest amount of time, which migrates the greatest distance and which sleeps the most.

You need to remember that:

▶ Ecology is the study of the environment and the organisms in it.

▶ The environment of an organism is everything around it, living and non-living.

▶ Living things are biotic; non-living things are abiotic.

▶ Sensors, probes and data loggers can be used to measure abiotic factors.

▶ Living things are adapted to the environment in which they live.

▶ Some living things are active during the day (diurnal), others are active during the night (nocturnal).

▶ Living things avoid harsh conditions by sleeping, hibernating and migrating.

Next time »

Unit 15 The natural world is divided into a number of ecosystems (page 96).

Unit 16 There are over 7 billion people on Earth, which puts a big strain on the environment (page 104).

Previously »

From page 39 — Plants make their own food in photosynthesis; animals need to eat plants or other animals.

From page 90 — The environment of an organism is everything around it, living and non-living.

Unit 15

Ecosystems

What are ecosystems?

You are probably used to the idea of a habitat – the area in which a particular organism lives. When we think about many organisms and their habitats in one area, they all overlap and depend upon each other. This connected set of living things and their habitats is an ecosystem.

In this Unit, you will learn:

- ● what an ecosystem is and what its main parts are;
- ● how living things and non-living things affect each other;
- ● how energy flows through an ecosystem;
- ● about food chains and food webs;
- ● about pyramids of numbers and biomass;
- ● how nutrients cycle and the importance of decay;
- ● how populations grow and are controlled.

Key words

average	diversity	populations
biomass	ecosystem	predator–prey cycle
biome	energy flow	predators
birth rate	food chain	preserved
carbon cycle	food web	prey
carnivore	habitats	pyramid of numbers
communities	herbivore	random sampling
competition	Lincoln Index	sampling
death rate	macro-decomposers	
decomposition	micro-decomposers	

How are ecosystems described?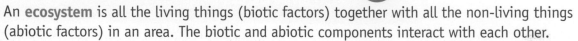

An **ecosystem** is all the living things (biotic factors) together with all the non-living things (abiotic factors) in an area. The biotic and abiotic components interact with each other.

The living things in an ecosystem are organised into:

- **populations** – the total of all individuals of the same species in the area;
- **communities** – all the different species found in a particular ecosystem;
- **habitats** – the place where the population of a species lives, finds food and reproduces.

So an ecosystem consists of *communities* of different living things, in single species *populations* living in their *habitats*.

We call a set of similar ecosystems a **biome**. A biome can cover a very large area of the Earth. We classify biomes depending on the type of climate and vegetation found there. For example, the biome of tropical forests has:

- an average temperature of 20–25 °C;
- only two seasons – rainy and dry;
- large amounts of rainfall throughout the year;
- many layers of vegetation, with not much light reaching the ground;
- the biggest number of species of plants and animals of any biome – we say it has the greatest **diversity**.

How do food chains work?

Living things interact with each other in ecosystems. The most obvious way they do this is through feeding. On page 40 we learnt that plants make food. Animals cannot make their own food, so they have to feed on plants or other animals.

- An animal that feeds on plants is called a **herbivore**.
- An animal that feeds on other animals is a **carnivore**.

Big carnivores such as lions or ground beetles are called **predators**. The animals they eat are called **prey**. We can draw a chain of food leading from plants, through animals that eat those plants, all the way up to the top predator. This is called a **food chain**.

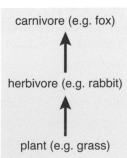

 Draw out three food chains. One should include a grass snake, one a green woodpecker and the final one a lion.

What are food webs?

When we study these feeding relationships in more detail, we find that it is more complicated than this. For example, foxes do not just eat rabbits. They will also eat birds, earthworms and many insects. Food chain ❶ on the right shows this.

But then, what do the earthworms, birds and insects feed on? Food chain ❷ shows this.

When we then think about the rabbit, you can probably guess that other animals may feed on that as well! The whole diagram gets more and more complicated, to form a **food web** ❸.

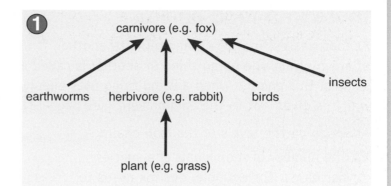

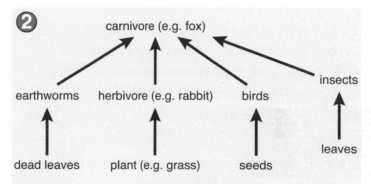

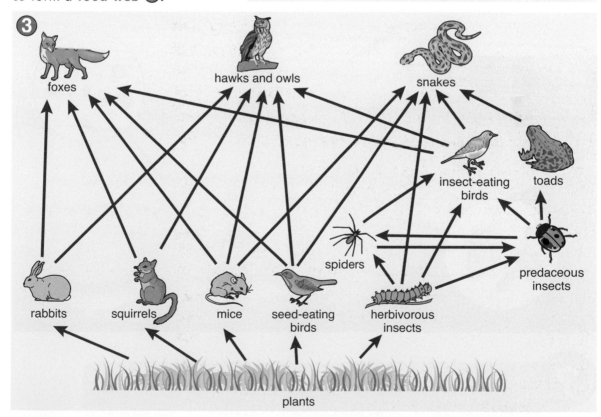

 From the food web, draw out three food chains with different numbers of links.

How many individual living things are there in a food chain?

As food passes from one living thing to another, it takes energy with it. The movement of energy from one living thing to another is called **energy flow**. Each living thing uses some of this energy. When a living thing uses energy, it is mostly converted into heat, which is given out to the environment (see page 18).

As we go up the levels of the food chain:

▶ The number of individuals of a species decreases. For example, one fox needs to feed on many different smaller animals.

▶ The total mass of all the individuals of one species (the **biomass**) goes down. For example, one fox has much less mass than all the mass of its prey added together.

▶ The amount of energy available from food goes down.

A simple diagram to show this is called a **pyramid of numbers**. Look at the pictures.

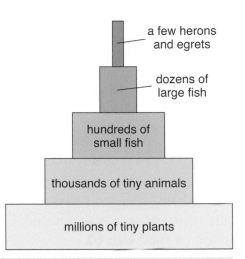

a few herons and egrets

dozens of large fish

hundreds of small fish

thousands of tiny animals

millions of tiny plants

Draw a pyramid of numbers for each of the following food chains:

1. grass → rabbit → fox
2. oak tree → winter moth caterpillars → robin
3. phytoplankton → zooplankton → herring → sea lion

What is the 'carbon cycle'?

Food contains materials, such as minerals. As one animal eats a plant, or another animal, these minerals also flow from one living thing to another. Unlike energy, minerals are not converted into heat. They stay within the living thing, and are either eaten by another animal or fall onto the ground when the living thing dies. So minerals travel in a cycle called a mineral or nutrient cycle.

One mineral that cycles in this way is carbon. Carbon travels around whole ecosystems in the **carbon cycle**.

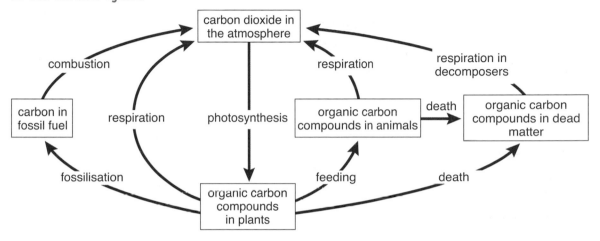

One very important part of all mineral cycles is what happens to those minerals when a living thing dies. The tissues of the living thing are broken down into atoms and molecules of minerals by **decomposition** or decay. Decomposition is actually carried out by yet more living things!

▶ **Macro-decomposers** are bigger animals like earthworms and woodlice. Earthworms are vitally important because as they digest dead organisms, they egest fertile soil.

▶ **Micro-decomposers** are much smaller organisms, like bacteria and fungi. For example, when food goes mouldy, that is a micro-decomposer hard at work!

1 Find out about the nitrogen cycle and draw a diagram of it, similar to the one for the carbon cycle.

2 Make a comparison of the carbon and nitrogen cycles.

Humans have a number of ways of stopping food from decomposing. We say that food can be **preserved**.

 Find out about ways of preserving food and explain what this tells you about the conditions needed for efficient decay. How could you apply this knowledge to looking after a compost heap?

How big is a population?

The total number of individuals of one species in a habitat or ecosystem is called a population. The most obvious question about a population is, how big is it? This can be answered in all sorts of ways. If it was antelope on the African plains, we might be able to count them from a hot air balloon.

What about buttercups in a field? There would just be too many to count individually. So we count them using **sampling**.

1. We make a map of the field and divide it up into equally sized numbered squares. (We often use squares 1 m × 1 m, called quadrats.)

2. We then count the buttercups in a sample of the squares – just some of them.

3. We then multiply the **average** number of buttercups in a square by the number of squares, to get an estimate of the total population.

Not all the squares will be identical – for example, some may have a slope or be wetter or drier than the others. To make the sampling fair, we use a computer program to decide randomly which squares to look at. This is **random sampling**.

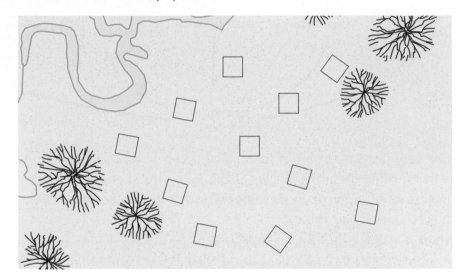

 Some students sampled a meadow with buttercups. It measured 300 m by 400 m. What is its total area in square metres?

In the ten 1-metre-square quadrats they sampled they got the following results:

Quadrat number	1	2	3	4	5	6	7	8	9	10
Number of buttercup flowers	14	17	21	9	12	5	23	16	18	21

What is the average number of buttercup flowers per square metre?

Using this figure and the total area of the field, calculate the total number of buttercups in the field.

The plant sampling method will not work with living organisms that move about, like most animals. To find out how big an animal population is:

1. We catch and mark some of them. For example, we can put coloured rings on the legs of birds.
2. We release the marked ones unharmed back into the wild.
3. Later, we repeat the process with another sample.

In the second sample, we will catch some that were marked the first time, and some that were not.

We will get three numbers:
- ▶ Number in first sample.
- ▶ Number of marked animals in second sample.
- ▶ Number of unmarked animals in second sample.

Using these numbers, we can estimate the size of the whole population. This method is called the **Lincoln Index**.

? Using either a real animal, for example grasshoppers, or some beads or pieces of card, research and try out the Lincoln Index method.

How and why do populations change in size?

Populations in an ecosystem get bigger if more individuals arrive than leave.
- ▶ Individuals arrive by being born or by immigrating into the ecosystem.
- ▶ Individuals leave by dying or by emigrating from the ecosystem.

The rate at which individuals are born is called the **birth rate**. The rate at which individuals die is called the **death rate**.

If no individuals immigrate or emigrate, and if the birth rate and the death rate are equal, the population size doesn't change.

Actually, most populations grow, as shown in the graph.

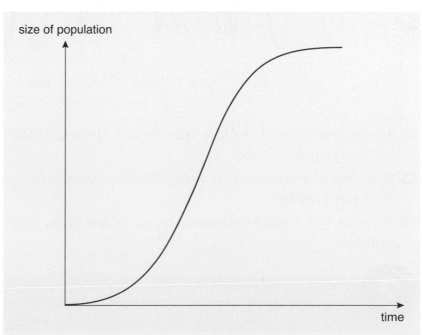

Why do populations level off at the top?

When a population is small, there is plenty of food, space, nest sites and everything else the animals need. As the population grows, all of these things start to run out. We say there is **competition** for food, space and other things. This means there is a limit to how big a population can grow.

Disease and predators also affect the size of a population. For example, a species of cat called the lynx is a predator of hares. The populations of lynx and hares were followed for over 80 years in northern Canada. The graph shows the changes.

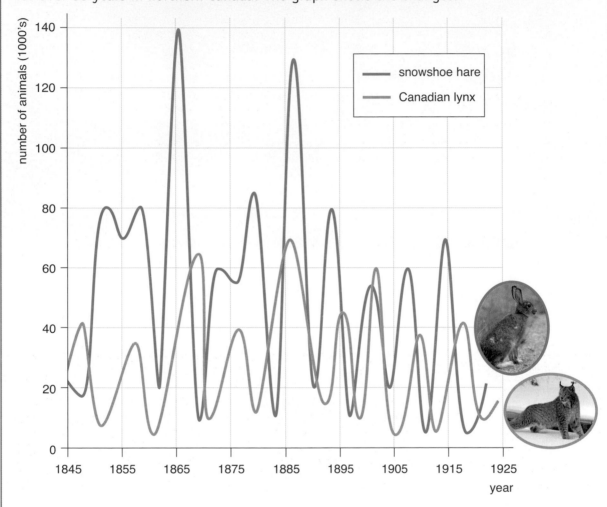

- ▶ As the population of the hare falls, so does the population of lynx. This is because the lynx run out of food.
- ▶ When the lynx population is small, the hare population rises again, because there are fewer predators.
- ▶ Then the lynx population goes back up and the cycle, called a **predator–prey cycle**, continues.

? Look at the graph. Why do the lynx population increases tend to lag a little behind the hare population increases?

You need to remember that:

- The natural world is divided into a number of ecosystems.
- Ecosystems consist of non-living things (abiotic factors) and living things (biotic factors).
- The living things in an ecosystem form a community.
- Each living thing is adapted to the place where it lives, its habitat.
- Living things interact by feeding off each other.
- Plants are eaten by herbivores, which in turn are eaten by carnivores in a food chain.
- Food chains can be linked together to show more complicated feeding relationships in a food web.
- The total mass of all the individuals of one species is called the biomass.
- One carnivore needs to eat many other animals, so the number of individuals at each level of a food chain forms a pyramid.
- Energy flows in the food from one level of the food chain to the next, but some is given out as heat on the way.
- Nutrients such as minerals also pass along the food chain.
- Minerals return to the ground when an animal dies, through the process of decomposition.
- Nutrients move from ground, to plants, to animals and back to the ground in a cycle.
- The populations of living things change due to changes in birth rate and death rate.
- Disease, competition and predators all affect the size of a population.

Next time »

Unit 16 There are over 7 billion people on Earth, which puts a big strain on the environment everywhere (page 104).

Unit 16 Poisonous chemicals can become concentrated along the food chain. This may harm top predators (page 106).

Previously »

From page 91 — Living things are adapted to the environment in which they live.

From page 99 — Carbon travels around whole ecosystems in the carbon cycle.

Unit 16

Humans and the environment

How are we changing our world?

Like all animals on the planet, as human beings we depend on our environment for everything we need. Between the years 1900 and 2000, the number of people on Earth quadrupled.

There are now so many of us – over 7 billion – that we have started to damage our environment. In this Unit, we will look at some of the ways in which we are damaging our environment. We will also look at some of the ways in which we can protect it.

In this Unit, you will learn:

- ▶ how humans are damaging environments on Earth;
- ▶ how some poisonous chemicals we use harm other living things;
- ▶ how burning fossil fuels can cause climate change;
- ▶ how every one of us can change our lifestyle in order to protect the Earth's environments.

Key words

bio-magnification	habitat destruction
carbon dioxide	herbicides
climate	nature reserves
climate change	pesticides
global warming	resources
fossil fuels	thought experiment
greenhouse effect	

How does an increasing population affect our environment?

As the population of any species gets bigger it uses more **resources**. This changes the environment. The main resources that we humans need from our environment include:

- ▶ food;
- ▶ fuel (including oil, coal, gas and wood);
- ▶ metals and minerals;
- ▶ space to live in.

In order to obtain most of these resources, we are changing or destroying the habitats of other living things. **Habitat destruction** is the main way in which we are affecting the Earth's environments.

 Farming is the activity from which we get food. How might farming destroy habitats for:

- ▶ woodland birds like the great spotted woodpecker?
- ▶ freshwater birds like a mallard duck?
- ▶ the wild saltmarsh grass *Spartina*?

In a country like the United Kingdom, there is very little natural habitat left. Nearly all the land around us has been farmed, built on or neglected. The few places that look natural are usually managed by people as **nature reserves**. Many nature reserves themselves have not always contained the same habitats. They may be 'second growth' areas – areas used for farming, industry or building in the past but which have now been allowed to go back to nature.

 Find out as much as you can about a local nature reserve. In your report, describe:

- ▶ how it is managed now;
- ▶ what animals and plants live in it, especially the rarer ones;
- ▶ what it may have been used for in the past;
- ▶ whether it is under threat of being developed again.

What effects do toxic chemicals have?

Farmers use **pesticides** to kill crop pests and **herbicides** to kill weeds. Pesticides and herbicides have to be poisonous but they are normally diluted, meaning small amounts of the poisonous chemical are dissolved in large quantities of water. These very low concentrations do not directly harm larger animals or people.

Even diluted poisonous chemicals can still cause a problem called **bio-magnification**. As larger animals eat smaller animals or plants containing the chemical, the amounts of chemical add up. Small amounts of pesticides can become larger along the food chain.

To understand this better, we will go through a **thought experiment**. This is where we imagine what will happen, instead of carrying out a real experiment.

Imagine a pesticide called XYZ is normally diluted and sprayed on crops. Some of it is washed into lakes by rain.

1. 10 grams of XYZ is enough to harm a fish eagle.

2. XYZ is diluted to a concentration that means tiny plants in the water get 0.01 grams each.

3. A tiny water animal eats 10 of these plants, so the water animal ends up with 0.1 grams of XYZ.

4. Now a small fish eats 10 of the tiny water animals, so the fish ends up with 1 gram of XYZ.

5. A bigger fish eats 10 small fish, so the big fish ends up with 10 grams of XYZ.

6. A fish eagle eats 10 of the bigger fish and ends up with 100 grams of XYZ, ten times the dose that can harm it!

 We could dilute the chemical more to reduce the amount the fish eagle eats. How much would each tiny plant need to get before it was safe for the fish eagle?

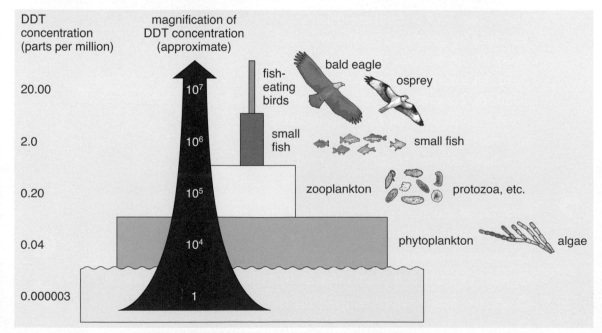

Bio-magnification happened around the world with the pesticide DDT.

Bio-magnification along food chains was one of the first environmental concerns to be written about. In 1962 Rachel Carson published a book called 'Silent Spring'. This is often said to be when the environmental movement was born.

 Find out all you can about Rachel Carson and her famous book. Write a short biography of her.

What is the 'greenhouse effect'?

When we burn **fossil fuels** (oil, coal and gas), **carbon dioxide** is produced (see page 283). This gas reflects heat radiation back down to the surface of the Earth. We call carbon dioxide a 'greenhouse gas' because it keeps heat in the atmosphere. Glass in a greenhouse works in the same way.

In fact, this **greenhouse effect** is a good thing for life. A little carbon dioxide in the atmosphere helps keep the world warm enough to live on. Unfortunately, the more carbon dioxide there is in the atmosphere, the warmer the Earth gets. Now that we are adding more carbon dioxide by burning fossil fuels, most scientists believe that it is causing **global warming**. This is where the greenhouse effect is made stronger, and the temperature is continually rising.

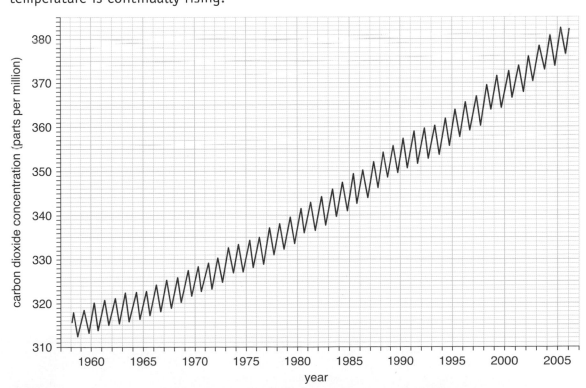

 List as many sources of carbon dioxide as you can. What other greenhouse gases do humans produce?

How is our climate changing?

Climate is the word we use to describe the patterns of temperature, air pressure, humidity, rainfall and so on over long periods of time. The rising temperature is changing our climate. As the average temperature across the whole world rises, it changes many things including:

- ▶ ice at the poles melts, raising sea levels;
- ▶ the natural flow of warm water to colder areas of the ocean changes, changing currents in the oceans;
- ▶ patterns of rainfall change, so some places get drier and other places get wetter;
- ▶ the flow of weather patterns can change, meaning some areas experience more storms or more extreme weather.

For example, you might think it would be nice if the UK were drier and warmer. Unfortunately, **climate change** isn't that simple. Many scientists think that the UK may become colder and wetter, because the ocean current called the 'Gulf Stream' may stop flowing. Warm water that flows to the UK from the Caribbean may stop, making our winters colder and our summers wetter.

How will climate change affect living things? @

Even small changes to climate can affect plants, animals and other living things.

The cycle of reproduction in animals depends upon the availability of particular kinds of food. Here is an example.

- ▶ Leaves emerge on trees when the daily temperature rises above a particular level.
- ▶ Certain kinds of butterflies lay their eggs so that the caterpillars emerge when fresh green leaves are growing.
- ▶ Blue tits nest at a particular time so their chicks hatch at the same time as the caterpillars appear in large numbers.

If the average temperature rises steadily over many years, whole food chains will be changed. Whole populations and habitats can be affected.

Off the north-west coast of the United Kingdom, puffins have been breeding poorly. Puffins eat sand eels, which they catch at sea. But puffins nest on land.

? **Find out about how climate change may have changed where sand eels live. How could this have led to poor reproduction in puffins?**

What can we do to protect our environment?

Because people cause these problems, people can help to solve them.

- We can reduce the amount of energy we need by turning off lights and appliances.

- We can insulate our homes to keep heat in.

- We can use public transport, car share, walk or cycle to reduce the amount of fuel we burn to move ourselves around.

- We can also find other, renewable energy sources like wind or wave power.

All of these changes can help reduce the amount of fossil fuels we burn. This in turn will reduce the amount of carbon dioxide we produce.

It is more difficult to solve habitat loss. Everyone needs to think about the demands they make on the environment. For example, every piece of paper that is used has to come from a tree. We get most of our paper from pine trees. Sometimes, older forests and woodlands of deciduous trees are destroyed to grow pine trees to make paper. Pine woodland is not so rich a habitat as the natural deciduous forest it replaces. So reusing and recycling paper can help save natural habitats.

Deciduous woodland.

Pine woodland.

Write a short account of how people could change their lifestyle, so that they might help to save habitats. Say what type of habitats could be saved and explain how.

You need to remember that:

- There are over 7 billion people on Earth, which puts a big strain on the environment.
- Poisonous chemicals used on crops at low concentrations can become very concentrated along the food chain. This may harm top predators.
- Burning fossil fuels produces carbon dioxide.
- Carbon dioxide is a greenhouse gas, meaning it helps trap heat in the Earth's atmosphere.
- Increased carbon dioxide can cause global warming, which leads to climate change.
- Climate change may cause many problems including increased drought, severe weather and rising sea levels.
- Climate change affects habitats, so all the animals in food chains are also affected.
- People can help by using less energy in transport and in the home.

Introducing Chemistry

The science of chemistry is the investigation of what substances are made of and what they do. Finding out how chemicals react together, and how to make new chemicals, has changed our daily lives in all sorts of ways. For example, the coloured inks on this page have all been developed by chemists. Mobile phones depend on elements such as lithium in the battery and indium in the screen.

Isabella Karle developed new ways of showing the crystal structure of molecules, including the use of X-rays.

What are chemicals?

All the objects around us are made from chemicals. When we look really closely at all substances, we can see they are made up from billions of tiny particles called atoms and molecules.

◗ Each atom contains a nucleus surrounded by even tinier particles called electrons.

◗ Molecules are made from atoms that are joined together.

What we study in chemistry is how these particles move around and join together. For example, we have found 118 different types of atoms that we call elements. Learning the properties of these elements helps us explain how living things work, from tiny bacteria to complicated human beings. It also helps us make things, like fuels to create energy, fabrics and foods, and all sorts of electronic devices.

An important part of all science is to make predictions and test them in experiments. Reacting chemicals together is a great way to find out how science works.

What do chemists do?

Chemistry is a vital part of many careers.

- Medicinal chemists and biochemists are developing new medicines all the time, including trying to find cures for cancers.
- Atmospheric chemists all over the world are investigating how the climate works and changes, so we can reduce the effects of global warming.
- Chemists are creating new materials with special properties, such as lighter, airier fabrics to wear and substances that store energy for use in our mobile devices.

What will you see?

In this book, we will explore and investigate many substances, and how they interact. We will look at:

- What substances are made from, including atoms and molecules, and how they join together.
- How substances change when we heat them up or cool them down.
- How we can catalogue all the substances by understanding what elements are and what properties they have.
- How we can react substances together to generate energy or make new substances.
- Why there are only limited amounts of many substances and how we can use them more wisely so that we don't run out of them.

We extract raw materials from the Earth to use in chemical reactions. We need to manage our use of these resources carefully.

Previously »

Remember | Solids, liquids and gases are different in how they move and keep their shape.

Unit 1

Particles

What are particles?

Everything is made up from tiny pieces of matter called particles. The model scientists use to describe the way these particles behave is called Particle Theory. Matter can take the form of solids, liquids or gases. Particles packed closely together so they cannot move around each other form solids. Liquids are also made up of particles packed closely together, but they can move over and around each other. Gases contain particles that are far apart, and which can move around freely in all directions.

In this Unit, you will learn:

- ▶ what matter is made from;
- ▶ what atoms contain;
- ▶ how we tell the difference between types of atoms;
- ▶ what an element is;
- ▶ what molecules contain;
- ▶ how particles are packed together;
- ▶ how particles can move around;
- ▶ the differences between solids, liquids and gases.

Key words

atoms	gases	Particle Theory
attraction	liquids	particles
compressed	matter	protons
density	molecules	solids
electrons	neutrons	volume
elements	nucleus	

Solid

Liquid

Gas

What are atoms?

All the 'stuff' around us and inside us is called **matter**. Matter is made up of tiny **particles** called **atoms**. Atoms are so tiny, that you would have to line up about 10 million hydrogen atoms to go across the dot in the exclamation mark at the end of this sentence! The way we describe how atoms are arranged inside matter to form gases, liquids and solids is called **Particle Theory**.

Atoms are made up made from even smaller particles called electrons, protons and neutrons. **Protons** and **neutrons** are packed tightly together in the centre of an atom, in the atom's **nucleus**. Protons are positively charged and neutrons are neutral. **Electrons** are negatively charged and fly around the nucleus at high speed.

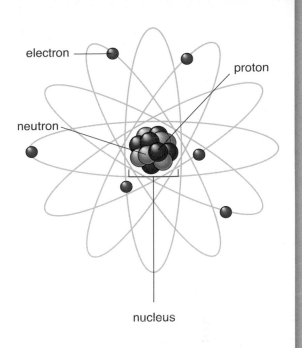

electron

proton

neutron

nucleus

What are elements?

There are many different types of atoms, which we tell apart by the numbers of protons they contain. Some materials are made up from only one type of atom and these are called **elements**. For example, diamonds are made from atoms of the single element carbon. The carbon atoms are arranged in a particular way to produce the hard, shiny diamond crystal.

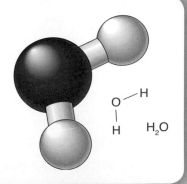

 ? **How many elements can you list?**

What are molecules?

Different types of atoms can join together to form **molecules** like water. A water molecule contains two atoms of hydrogen and one atom of oxygen. Most materials are made up from molecules.

The types of atoms and molecules that make up matter give materials their different properties.

O—H

H H_2O

What are the features of solids?

Examples of **solids** are all around us, like the bricks in walls or the metal in cars.

○ Solids take up a fixed amount of space – we say they have a fixed **volume**. The shape of a solid does not easily change even when compressed (squashed).

○ Solids also have a high density because the particles in solids are closely packed together.

○ The particles in solids do not move because they are held tightly together by strong forces of attraction.

 Look around you. What other examples of solids can you list?

What are the features of liquids?

Water and petrol are examples of **liquids**.

○ Liquids have a fixed volume and cannot easily be compressed.

○ Liquids do not have a fixed shape; they take on the shape of the container they are held in. For instance, if you pour out a bottle of drink into a glass, it will change shape to fill your glass. But the volume stays the same as it was in the bottle.

○ Liquids are dense because their particles are closely packed together, but they are less dense than solids.

○ Unlike solids, liquids move easily. This is because the forces between the particles are weaker than those in solids.

What are the features of gases?

The oxygen and nitrogen in the air around us are examples of **gases**.

○ Gases do not have a fixed volume because the particles are not held together by strong forces of **attraction**.

○ Gases have a low **density** because there are very large spaces between particles. This means that gases can be **compressed** quite easily.

○ The particles in a gas move very quickly in all directions.

Particle theory explains the way in which solids, liquids and gases behave. The particles are held together by forces of different strengths. We can create a 'model' to explain this.

▶ Think of a crowd of people standing very close together, unable to move about much. If they link arms, this is like the forces of attraction between the particles in a solid.

▶ If the people unlink arms but hold hands, they can move around at arms' length – just like the forces of attraction in a liquid.

▶ If the people stop touching completely, they can easily move around and the crowd starts to break up – just like in a gas.

 Use this model to explain the main characteristics of solids, liquids and gases to your friends or family.

You need to remember that:

▶ Matter is made up from particles that are atoms or molecules.

▶ Atoms contain protons, neutrons and electrons.

▶ We tell atoms apart by the number of protons they contain.

▶ Matter made up of just one type of atom is called an element.

▶ Atoms of different elements combine to make molecules.

▶ The model that describes the way these particles behave is called Particle Theory.

▶ Particles are held together by forces of attraction.

▶ The behaviour of these particles gives materials their different properties as solids, liquids or gases.

Property	Solid	Liquid	Gas
shape	fixed	can change	changes
volume	fixed	fixed	changes
density	very high	high	low

Next time »

Unit 2   The behaviour of particles changes the properties of matter (page 116).

Unit 2   Density is a measure of how heavy a material is for its size (page 118).

Previously 》

From page 113 — Matter is made up from particles that are atoms or molecules.

From page 113 — The behaviour of these particles gives materials their different properties.

Unit 2

Particle behaviour

Why is particle behaviour important?

The behaviour of particles changes the properties of matter. For instance, as particles are heated they move more rapidly and as they are cooled they move more slowly. These changes alter the distance between the particles and also the strength of the forces of attraction that hold them together as solids, liquids or gases. So, the properties of materials change with temperature. For example, solids can turn into liquids, and liquids can turn into gases as the temperature increases. The opposite can also happen as the temperature decreases.

In this Unit, you will learn:

- ▶ how particle behaviour affects properties of materials;
- ▶ about expansion and contraction;
- ▶ how we measure expansion and contraction;
- ▶ what diffusion is and how it works;
- ▶ about density and how we measure it;
- ▶ about the pressure of gases and what it affects;
- ▶ about changes of state including melting and boiling.

Key words

boiling point	diffusion	melts
changing state	expands	pressure
contracts	gauge	sublimes
density	melting point	vaporises

What are expansion and contraction?

Although solids have a fixed shape and volume at room temperature, the particles in a solid are vibrating ever so slightly all the time. We can't feel the vibrations but we can see them if we use an electron microscope to zoom in on the individual atoms.

The volume of a solid **expands** when it is heated and **contracts** when it is cooled down. This is because the particles that make up a solid vibrate faster as the temperature rises. This makes the spaces between the particles increase, causing the material to expand. As a solid is cooled, the opposite happens. The particles vibrate more slowly as the temperature falls and the distance between the particles decreases, causing the material to contract.

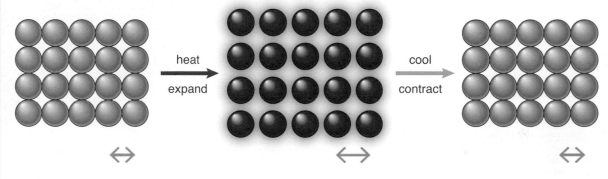

 What materials do you know that change when they are heated or cooled?

How do we measure expansion and contraction? @

Expansion and contraction can be measured by controlling the temperature and measuring small changes in the length of a solid such as a metal rod. As you increase the temperature of the metal rod you can measure how much it expands. Similarly, as you decrease the temperature, you can measure how much it contracts. These changes are often very small, so we use a very sensitive device called a **gauge**.

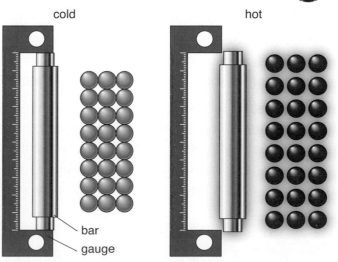

cold   hot

bar
gauge

When many thousands of very large pieces of metal are used to build a bridge, even small changes can make the bridge bend out of shape or collapse. Engineers need to understand precisely how much the metals will expand in the summer and contract in the winter in order to design and build safe bridges.

What is diffusion?

The particles in liquids move more freely than those in solids and less freely than those in gases. The particles in liquids and gases move by a process called **diffusion**.

You can see this happening in liquids by dissolving a few crystals of a purple substance called potassium permanganate in a beaker of water. The crystals dissolve and you can see spots of purple that slowly move to make swirling patterns in the water. Eventually the whole beaker of water becomes pale purple.

This is because the purple particles have spread (diffused) evenly throughout the water to make a pale purple liquid.

The same thing happens if you add orange squash to a large glass of water without mixing it. The orange becomes paler as it diffuses into the water.

What is density?

Density measures how much mass of a material there is in a particular volume (see page 234). The density of a material is higher if the particles are packed more tightly together. Different solids, liquids and gases have different densities. For example, solid metals are denser than wood. Wood floats on water but metals do not.

Usually, the solid form of a material is denser than the liquid form. However, water is different! Water is most dense as a liquid at 4 °C and not in the solid state of ice at 0 °C or below. This is important for fish living in ponds. Ice forms on the *top* of a pond in freezing weather. The water below stays slightly warmer, and denser, so the ice floats on top. The fish do not freeze and are able to survive the winter!

?

1 In some regions of the world temperatures can reach as low as −30 °C. What do you think would happen to the water in a pond at this temperature?

2 What effect do you think density has on whether an object floats or sinks?

What is pressure?

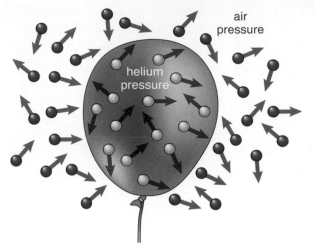

Gas particles are constantly moving freely in all directions. If a gas such as helium is sealed inside a balloon, the movement of the particles keeps the balloon inflated. If you increase the temperature, the gas particles move faster. This means more particles push with greater force against the inside of the balloon. We say the **pressure** inside the balloon increases as the balloon heats up.

The air around us is a gas that behaves in exactly the same way. The air pushes against everything, including us, all the time. When you inflate a balloon by blowing into it, you are pushing warm air particles into the balloon at a higher pressure than the air around you. This is why the balloon expands. If you untie the opening of a balloon full of air, the pressure of the air outside the balloon pushes all the air out of the balloon. The balloon deflates.

How does a material change state?

To get from a solid to a liquid, or from a liquid to a gas, a material has to be heated to a particular temperature. These changes are called **changing state**. For example, when solid ice cubes are placed in a drink, the ice warms up and **melts** to become liquid water. The temperature at which this occurs is known as the **melting point**. For water, this is 0 °C. This happens because, as the temperature increases, the molecules in the ice vibrate so much they start to loosen the connections between them and move around.

When water is heated in a kettle, it changes from a liquid to a gas: steam. As the liquid is heated, the particles move faster and faster. Eventually they move so much they break apart from each other so they start to move freely. The liquid **vaporises** and becomes a gas. The temperature at which this occurs is known as the **boiling point**. For water, this is 100 °C.

For most materials, the melting point and boiling point are at different temperatures. However, carbon dioxide changes directly from a solid (known as 'dry ice') into a gas. We say the dry ice **sublimes**. As this happens, a white smoky effect is created. This is often used to make artificial smoke or fog in films, gigs and stage shows.

 Explain how a thermometer shows changes in temperature.

The behaviour of particles changes as they get hotter or colder. We have talked about why engineers need to understand how metals (solids) expand and contract as the weather gets hotter and colder. It's harder to imagine how gases expand and contract because we can't easily see the changes.

If you turn a beaker of air upside down and lower it carefully into a bowl of water, the air stays in the beaker. If you heat the bowl up, bubbles start appearing in the water from the bottom of the beaker.

?

Why does air start to escape from the beaker as the air is heating up?

Explain what is happening to the particles in the gas to make this happen.

You need to remember that:

- ◯ The behaviour of particles changes the properties of matter.
- ◯ As temperature increases, particles vibrate more in solids, and move about more in liquids and gases.
- ◯ Solids expand as the temperature increases and contract as the temperature decreases.
- ◯ We measure expansion and contraction using a gauge.
- ◯ The particles in liquids and gases move by diffusion.
- ◯ Density is a measure of how heavy a material is for its size.
- ◯ Density increases the more tightly packed the particles are.
- ◯ Pressure is a measure of how hard a gas pushes against its surroundings.
- ◯ Pressure increases with temperature.
- ◯ Melting is when a solid changes state to a liquid.
- ◯ Boiling is when a liquid changes state to a gas.
- ◯ Sublimation is when a solid changes state straight to a gas.
- ◯ Changes of state occur at particular temperatures, depending on the material.

Next time »

Unit 3   Mixtures consist of two or more different substances that are not chemically joined (page 122).

Unit 5   Physical changes are reversible (page 136).

Previously »

Remember   Some solids dissolve in water to give solutions, but some do not.

Remember   We can separate some mixtures by sieving, filtering or evaporation.

Unit 3

Mixtures and solutions

What kinds of mixtures are there?

When you make a mixture of substances, they don't chemically react. You can mix different amounts of substances to make a mixture and you can separate the substances back out again later. The way you do this will depend on the properties of the substances you have mixed. Air is a mixture, mainly of oxygen and nitrogen, but with smaller amounts of other gases too.

Solutions are mixtures of substances that dissolve. As the substance dissolves, the particles spread out into the liquid. This is what happens when you dissolve sugar in tea. Solutions are transparent. Substances that don't dissolve are insoluble, but we can still make mixtures with them. Milk is a mixture of insoluble substances in water. These mixtures are called suspensions and you can't see through them.

In this Unit, you will learn:

- ▶ about mixtures and how to make them;
- ▶ about types of mixtures (soluble, saturated and insoluble mixtures);
- ▶ about factors that affect solubility;
- ▶ how mixtures can be separated;
- ▶ how mixtures can be investigated;
- ▶ what mixtures are used in everyday life.

Key words

chromatography	fractional distillation	soluble
condenses	insoluble	solute
constituent part	mixture	solution
crystallisation	opaque	solvent
dissolve	saturated solution	suspension
evaporation	separate	transparent
filtration	solubility	

What is a mixture?

A **mixture** contains different substances put together that are not chemically joined. Mixtures are common in everyday life. An example is seawater, which is a mixture of salt and water and several dissolved gases. Mixtures can be separated using physical methods, meaning we don't need to react chemicals together to get the different substances out.

 Name some other mixtures and list the substances they contain.

What are solutions?

When copper sulfate crystals are added to water they **dissolve** and the water turns blue. This is an example of a **soluble** mixture or **solution**. The substance that dissolves is called the **solute**. The liquid the substance dissolves in is called the **solvent**. In this case the copper sulfate crystals are the solute and water is the solvent. We can see through solutions – they are **transparent**.

If you keep adding copper sulfate to a beaker of water, eventually the crystals stop dissolving. This is called a **saturated solution** because the water cannot dissolve any more of the crystals.

 List some examples of soluble mixtures that you come across every day.

What mixtures can we make with substances that don't dissolve in water?

Water is not the only solvent that can be used to dissolve substances to form mixtures. For example, fatty substances, such as candle wax, dissolve in oil but not in water. We add washing up liquid to water so that the grease and fat on dirty plates will dissolve.

Some substances, like sand, do not dissolve in a solvent and so form **insoluble** mixtures. When insoluble substances are mixed with water they are called a **suspension**. Suspensions are **opaque** (you can't see through them). Milk is a suspension.

THINKING BEYOND...

Knowing whether a solution is soluble or insoluble can be very useful. For example, nail varnish can be made from lacquers, enamels, paints and pigments. It is often brightly coloured and very sticky. If someone spills nail varnish onto their bathroom floor, they have to use special nail varnish remover to clear it up. Nail varnish remover is a substance called acetone that easily dissolves the nail varnish.

 Explain why even hot water does not help remove nail varnish.

What affects solubility?

Solubility is a measure of the amount of solute that dissolves in a solvent before the solution becomes saturated. Solubility depends on:

- ▶ the type of solute – for example, more salt than sugar will dissolve in water;
- ▶ the type of solvent – more salt will dissolve in water than in oil;
- ▶ the temperature – more salt will dissolve in hot water than in cold water.

 Describe how you could investigate the effect of temperature on the amount of salt you can dissolve in water.

How can we separate mixtures?

Each substance in a mixture is called a **constituent part.** We choose from four different methods to **separate** mixtures into their constituent parts:

- ▶ filtration
- ▶ evaporation
- ▶ chromatography
- ▶ fractional distillation

We choose the best method according to the properties of the constituent parts.

How do filtration and evaporation work?

Rock salt is a mixture of salt and sand that is scattered on roads to stop cars skidding in icy weather. We can separate the salt from the sand by **filtration**, where we pass the mixture through a fine grid or paper.

1. First we put the mixture of salt and sand in water. Salt dissolves in water but sand does not, so we get a mixture of salt solution and insoluble sand particles.

2. Filter paper has tiny holes that stop the large sand particles. Sand collects on top of the filter paper.

3. The water and dissolved salt particles are small enough to go through the tiny holes and can be collected in a boiling tube underneath. This liquid is called the filtrate.

4. We then take the salt solution, heat it and leave it to dry out. The water is carried away in the warm air by **evaporation.**

5. The salt particles are left behind and form crystals. This last step is known as **crystallisation.**

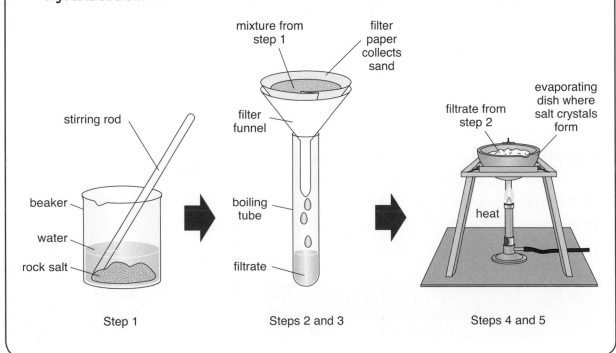

What is chromatography?

Mixtures of dissolved, coloured substances can be separated so we can see the different colours. This process of separating colours is called **chromatography**. For example, ink is a mixture of different coloured substances. We can see its constituent parts as follows:

1. We place a spot of black ink near the bottom of a strip of filter paper.

2. We then dip the bottom of the strip nearest the ink spot into some water and fix the dry top end of the paper so the water can soak up through the paper.

3. As the water soaks into the filter paper strip, the black ink dissolves and moves up the filter paper with the water.

4. The components of the black ink are carried different distances by the water, so we see separate spots of different coloured substances.

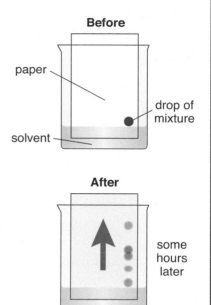

Chromatography can be used to investigate natural substances like chlorophyll (the green colour in plants) and haemoglobin (the red colour in blood).

How can we separate colourless liquid mixtures?

Liquids have different boiling points – they turn into gases at different temperatures. For instance, alcohol boils at a lower temperature than water. Liquids that are mixed can be separated by **fractional distillation**, where the mixture is heated carefully so one liquid turns into a gas but the other substances in the mixture stay as liquids. For example:

1. To separate a mixture of alcohol and water, we heat it carefully.

2. We keep the temperature lower than 100 °C so that the water does not boil, but higher than 78.3 °C, which is the boiling point of alcohol.

3. Alcohol boils and escapes as a gas into a collection tube.

4. As the alcohol moves down the tube, it cools and forms a liquid again. We say the alcohol **condenses** and drips into a beaker.

5. Once all the alcohol has separated from the mixture, only water is left behind and we can stop heating it.

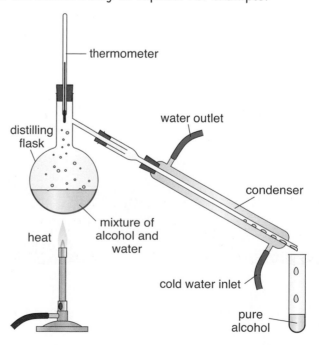

What mixtures do we use in everyday life?

Mixtures of all kinds are very important to us. Seawater is a mixture of sodium chloride (salt), water, oxygen and carbon dioxide. The air we breathe is actually a mixture of gases like oxygen and nitrogen and a small amount of carbon dioxide. The black ink in your pen and the paint on your bedroom wall are mixtures of different coloured substances.

1 You want to paint your bedroom green but you only have blue, yellow and red paint. Which colours would you mix to make the colour that you really want?

2 Distilled water is water free from all impurities (other chemicals). Explain how you would collect distilled water and salt crystals from a jar of salty water. (Hint: You will need to combine two methods described in this Unit.)

You need to remember that:

- Mixtures consist of two or more different substances that are not chemically joined.
- When salt is mixed with water it dissolves to make a soluble salt solution.
- If you keep adding salt to water, eventually it will not dissolve any more. This is a saturated salt solution.
- Solubility depends on the type of solute and solvent as well as the temperature.
- Sand mixes with water to make an insoluble mixture.
- Mixtures can be separated into their constituent parts.
- Insoluble mixtures can be separated by filtration.
- A soluble substance (solute) can be separated from the solvent by evaporation.
- Mixtures of coloured liquids can be separated by chromatography.
- Mixtures of liquids can be separated by fractional distillation.
- Mixtures like seawater, the air we breathe and ink are common in everyday life.

Next time »

Unit 11   Acids are solutions with a pH less than 7 that will neutralise alkalis (page 172).

Unit 11   Alkalis are solutions with a pH greater than 7 that will neutralise acids (page 172).

Previously »

From page 113 The behaviour of particles gives materials their different properties.

From page 119 Changes of state occur at particular temperatures, depending on the material.

Unit 4

Making things happen

How can we change and measure things?

Making things happen is the fun part of science! Scientists make things happen to help them understand how things change. To do this, they do experiments and measure what changes. There are lots of properties that can be measured to help understand chemicals and reactions. The results of experiments provide the clues that help reveal the secrets of science!

In this Unit, you will learn:

▶ how to use a Bunsen burner safely;
▶ about evidence of reactions;
▶ how to measure different types of change;
▶ about identifying gases;
▶ about measuring temperature;
▶ about detecting acids and alkalis;
▶ how to work out and explain what results mean.

Key words

adjustable air hole	experiment	physical changes
Bunsen burner	gas pipe	pop test
burner tube	gas tap	results
chemical reactions	heatproof mat	safety goggles
collar	indicator	temperature changes
endothermic	lighted splint	thermometer
evidence	limewater	weigh
exothermic	litmus paper	

How should we use a Bunsen burner?

Chemical reactions often need to be heated to make them happen. Scientists use a piece of equipment called a **Bunsen burner** to do this.

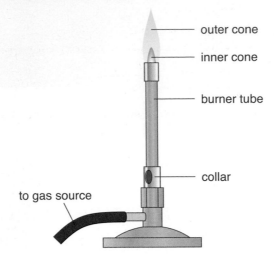

outer cone

inner cone

burner tube

collar

to gas source

It is very important to use a Bunsen burner safely. You will need to wear **safety goggles** and tie back long hair. You should then follow these steps to prepare your equipment.

1. Place the Bunsen burner on a **heatproof mat** and connect the **gas pipe** to the **gas tap**.
2. Make sure the gas tap stays turned off until you are ready to light the Bunsen burner.
3. Turn the **collar** on the **adjustable air hole** on the Bunsen burner so that it is in the closed position.
4. Collect a lighted splint and be ready to light the Bunsen burner.
5. Turn on the gas tap as you hold the **lighted splint** at the top of the **burner tube**.
6. When the Bunsen burner is alight, put out the splint carefully.

The colour of the flame depends on whether the adjustable air hole is open or closed. When the air hole is completely closed, you see a yellow flame. When the air hole is completely open you see a pale blue flame and should also hear a 'roaring' sound. The blue flame is hotter than the yellow flame. If you look carefully at the blue flame, you will see an outer cone and an inner cone. The inner cone is the hottest part of the flame. You can adjust the temperature of the flame by changing the size of the air hole.

Most experiments are done using a blue flame (air hole open). When you are not using the Bunsen burner, you should close the air hole (yellow flame). The yellow flame is easier to see so you will be less likely to touch the flame accidentally.

When you have finished your experiment you should extinguish the flame by turning off the gas. Remember, the Bunsen burner will be hot! Let it cool down before you touch it and put your equipment away.

 List and explain all the safety precautions you should take before, during and after using a Bunsen burner.

What kinds of changes can we measure?

The changes that happen in a chemical reaction can be measured in many different ways. This helps scientists understand what is happening when things change.

Physical changes happen without altering the mass of the substance or any chemical bonds (see page 136). Physical changes can be reversed.

For example:

● if you **weigh** 20 g of ice and melt it, you will have 20 g of water;

● if you heat the water so that it turns to water vapour and collect the vapour carefully, you will have 20 g of water vapour;

● if you cool the water vapour down again, you will get 20 g of water back.

This is because the substance (water) is the same, we say it is just in different physical states (solid, liquid or gas).

Chemical reactions make new substances. There are a few tell-tale signs or pieces of **evidence** to look out for that show you a reaction is happening.

This evidence can include:

● changes in temperature because heat is produced or taken in;

● changes in colour;

● other changes in appearance, like a solid appearing in a liquid (a precipitate);

● fizzing of gas bubbles.

 When water is heated in a saucepan or by a Bunsen burner, we see bubbles appearing. Explain what is happening. Is this a physical or chemical change?

How can we measure changes in heat?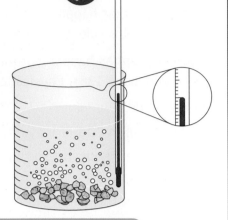

All chemical reactions involve heat energy being given out or taken in. We can tell when this happens by measuring the temperature of the substances that react at regular times to see changes. These **temperature changes** are measured in degrees Celsius (°C) using a **thermometer**.

Exothermic reactions give out energy and **endothermic** reactions take in energy from the surroundings (see page 164).

? You have a thermometer containing coloured alcohol, but the temperature scale has fallen off. Describe how you can use the properties of water to calibrate it (add a new temperature scale).

How can we see changes in reactions? @

Reactions often involve a colour change. If you put an iron nail in a solution of copper sulfate, the solution becomes pale blue/green and the nail becomes copper coloured. This is because the iron in the nail reacts with the copper in the blue solution to make a coating of copper on the nail and the solution is now iron sulfate, which is a pale blue/green.

? Describe what happens when iron rusts. Is this a physical or a chemical change?

How can we check if reactions make gases?

Chemical reactions often produce gases and this is evidence of a reaction happening. You can see bubbles but it is also useful to know how much gas is being produced. You can measure the amount of gas being produced simply by counting the number of bubbles produced if the reaction is slow. You can also collect the gas by sealing the neck of the flask with a balloon. The balloon inflates as the pressure increases.

It can also be useful to know what type of gas is being made. Hydrogen and carbon dioxide are often produced in chemical reactions.

What is the 'pop test' for hydrogen?

To test for hydrogen, add some zinc granules to some dilute hydrochloric acid in a test tube. Cover the top of the test tube with a piece of card and watch as bubbles of hydrogen appear. Take the card away and quickly put a lighted splint near the top of the tube. You'll hear a squeaky popping sound as the hydrogen makes a tiny explosion. This is the '**pop test**'.

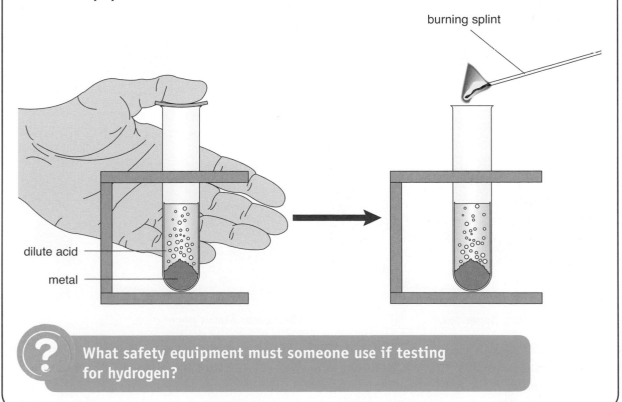

burning splint

dilute acid

metal

? **What safety equipment must someone use if testing for hydrogen?**

What is the test for carbon dioxide?

To test for carbon dioxide, the gas needs to bubble through a solution of calcium hydroxide. This is usually called **limewater**. The carbon dioxide reacts with the calcium hydroxide to make calcium carbonate. This is insoluble so the solution becomes cloudy, showing you that the gas is carbon dioxide.

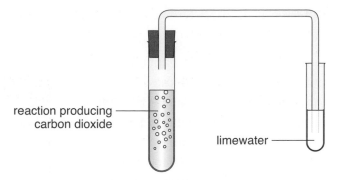

reaction producing carbon dioxide

limewater

 ? Why do we need to make sure the gas tube is sealed in the top of the test tube with a bung?

How can we tell acids and alkalis apart?

Acids and alkalis (see page 172) can be distinguished using **litmus paper**. This is a strip of paper that is coated in a substance that changes colour when it comes into contact with an acid or alkali. This called an **indicator**.

Acid turns litmus paper red.

Alkali turns litmus paper blue.

Acids and alkalis also come in different strengths. Lemon juice is a weak acid but sulfuric acid in a car battery is a strong acid. We can measure the strength of an acid or an alkali using different indicators to show the pH (see page 173).

How can we show our measurements?

You can see that there are lots of properties you can measure to show you that changes or reactions are happening. You need to be able to put these measurements together to see what is happening in an **experiment**.

For instance, you might do an experiment to find out how quickly water heats up. You would measure the temperature of the water before you start heating (at 0 minutes) and then every 5 minutes. You use a table like this to record your measurements (**results**):

Time (minutes)	Temperature (°C)
0	18
5	25
10	57
15	76
20	96

These results can then be plotted on a graph so that you can clearly see the changes in temperature as time goes on. Graphs also help when you are trying to explain what you saw to other people.

Your graph might look something like this:

Communicating results is very important because the best ideas often happen when you are swapping information. Scientists also need records of every experiment to ensure we can spot patterns or repeat the same experiment later to prove new discoveries. There is more about data handling in the special Unit on pages 320 to 323.

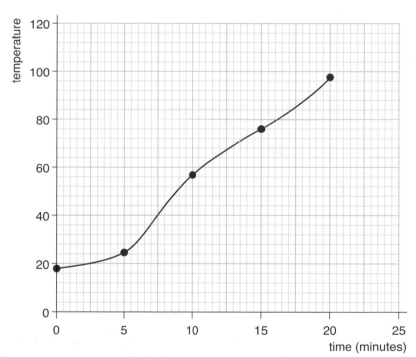

The experiment results carried on to look like this:

Time (minutes)	Temperature (°C)
25	100
30	100

Using a new sheet of graph paper, plot the full set of results from 0 to 30 minutes. What is happening at the end of the experiment?

Have you ever wondered why something happens but you have not been sure how to find out? Science is all about questions and answers. Scientists learn about the world we live in by asking questions and carrying out investigations to try to answer the questions. The results provide the clues that help the scientists work out the answers.

To follow the scientific approach, you should write up and report all your investigations using the same headings:

- ▶ Aim – What do you want to find out by doing your experiment?
- ▶ Methods – What will you do or test to answer your question?
- ▶ Results – Record the things that happen or you measured in a table. Do this very carefully with lots of detail – you never know what will be important!
- ▶ Conclusion – Once you've thought about what your results mean, you can try to answer your 'Aim' question. You might not be able to do this straight away. Your results might make you think of another question to investigate.

Many of your science lessons will be all about planning, carrying out and writing up investigations in this way.

? **You've been given a solution and you don't know if it's an acid or an alkali. Write the aim, methods, results and conclusions of an experiment you would carry out to find the answer.**

You need to remember that:

- ▶ It is important to use a Bunsen burner safely.
- ▶ Changes in temperature or colour, formation of a solid (precipitate) from two solutions or fizzing of gas bubbles are all signs that a chemical reaction is happening.
- ▶ Temperature changes are measured in degrees Celsius (°C) using a thermometer.
- ▶ You can measure the volume of a gas being produced by collecting the gas.
- ▶ You can identify hydrogen using the pop test.
- ▶ You can identify carbon dioxide by its reaction with limewater.
- ▶ Acids and alkalis can be identified using an indicator like litmus paper.
- ▶ You can record the changes you measure in a table.
- ▶ You can show the changes you measure in a graph.
- ▶ It is important to understand what your results mean and explain them to other people.

Next time ≫

Unit 5   Physical changes do not make new substances; chemical bonds are not made or broken (page 136).

Unit 11   Universal indicator is a mixture of different dyes that we use to measure the pH of a solution (page 17:

Previously ≫

From page 119 — Changes of state occur at particular temperatures, depending on the material.

From page 129 — We can measure and record many properties to show that changes are happening.

Unit 5

Changing materials

How do we change materials?

Water changing state from liquid to gas or solid, and back again, is probably one of the most common examples of reversible changes. It's happening all around but most of the time we don't even think about it.

There are a lot of materials that can change from one form to another and back again. Jelly comes as a sticky solid block. Melt it in hot water and then cool it in the fridge and it sets and becomes solid again – it's just another reversible change.

In this Unit, you will learn:

- about changes that are reversible;
- what happens to particles when a substance changes state;
- about melting and boiling points;
- what happens to particles when they are dissolved or crystallised.

Key words

boiling point	fractional distillation
boils	freezes
condenses	melting point
crystallisation	melts
dissolves	physical state
energy	reversible changes
evaporates	solution
forces of attraction	

What is a reversible change?

Physical changes are examples of **reversible changes**. These types of changes do not make new substances. The substance changes state but the amount of substance stays the same. The particles are rearranged without changing any chemical bonds.

For instance, if we cool liquid water to 0 °C it **freezes** to make solid ice. We can reverse this process by warming it up so the ice **melts** to make water again.

When water **boils** at 100 °C it makes water vapour (a gas), but it is still water. The water changes its **physical state** (see page 119), but it still contains the same molecules.

How can we get water vapour without boiling water?

We don't have to heat a whole beaker of water to 100 °C to get some water vapour. Even at the temperatures in school rooms, a little water **evaporates** from a beaker full to make water vapour. If you put a saucer of water on a windowsill in the sunshine, the water will eventually disappear – it isn't magic, it's evaporation! The liquid turns to water vapour a little at a time, very slowly, until eventually it has all turned to gas.

How can we get liquid water back from water vapour again? @

There is water vapour mixed in with the air all around us. In cold air, the water can change back into a liquid. Water vapour **condenses** on a cold surface to make liquid water again. This is why water droplets (condensation) appear on your window early on a cold morning. The moisture in the warm air inside your house cools very quickly when it touches the cold glass and condenses to make water patterns on your windows.

? If you go camping, the tent can get wet on the inside even if the weather is dry. Explain why.

How can we measure all these changes in experiments?

We can measure all these changes as we heat up or cool down a substance by using a thermometer and a stopwatch. If we plot a graph of temperature against time, we can see what is happening to the substance.

The graph shows the change in temperature of some ice as heat is added at a constant rate. The different parts of the graph show how the water changes.

1. This part of the graph is where the ice is still solid, but it is warming up.

2. Here, the heat is being used to change the solid ice into liquid water. The temperature doesn't change until all the ice has melted.

3. In this part, the beaker contains only liquid water, and the temperature rises again. This is where a little bit of the water will evaporate very slowly.

4. Now we have reached 100 °C, and the water boils. The temperature stops changing until all the water has turned to gas.

5. Finally, all the water has changed to gas and the temperature starts to rise again.

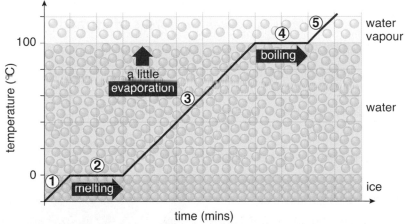

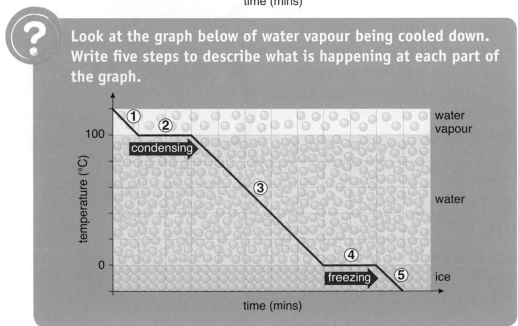

? Look at the graph below of water vapour being cooled down. Write five steps to describe what is happening at each part of the graph.

Water is a key part of how our climate and weather work. For example, we measure the amount of water vapour in the air to help us predict what weather is coming. This is a quantity called humidity. The higher the humidity, the greater the chance clouds will form and rain will fall.

? List the different states of water involved in different types of weather and build a 'flow chart' showing the changes between states.

@

What happens in changes of state?

A substance must be heated to make it melt. In the solid state, the particles are very tightly packed and do not move about. When the solid is heated, the **energy** of the particles increases and the particles start to move faster. When the particles are moving fast enough and have enough energy to weaken the **forces of attraction** between them, the solid melts to make a liquid.

For example, when ice is warmed to 0 °C, the water molecules have enough energy to weaken the forces of attraction between them and the ice melts to make water.

When water is heated to 100 °C, it boils to make water vapour. The forces of attraction between the water molecules are broken. Then the molecules are able to move freely in all directions and the liquid water changes to a gas.

These changes of state are reversible. When water vapour cools to 100 °C, it condenses to become liquid again. The energy of the particles decreases and the forces of attraction between the particles are able to hold them together again.

When water is cooled to 0 °C, it freezes and becomes ice. The energy of the particles is so low that the forces of attraction between them are able to stop the particles moving about at all.

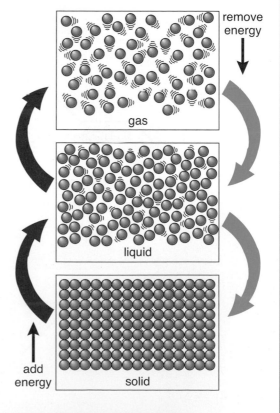

remove energy

gas

liquid

add energy

solid

? When particles are cooled and lose energy, where do you think the energy goes?

How are melting and boiling points useful?

Ice melts to make water at 0 °C. This is called the **melting point** of water.

Water boils to make steam at 100 °C. This is called the **boiling point** of water.

All substances have their own melting and boiling points. If you can measure or are told the melting and boiling points of an unknown substance, it can help you work out what the substance is.

For instance, metals tend to have very high melting points and non-metals tend to have low melting points (see page 145).

We can separate a mixture of two substances if we know their boiling points. If you heat the mixture to the lower of the two boiling points, one substance evaporates while the other stays as a liquid. This process is called **fractional distillation** (see page 125).

The melting and boiling points of some common substances.

Substance	Melting point (°C)	Boiling point (°C)
water	0	100
ethanol (alcohol)	−114	78
carbon dioxide	−55	−78

 Copy and extend the table above to include the elements oxygen, nitrogen, mercury, iron and lead. You will need to find the melting points and boiling points from a reliable online source.

What other physical changes are there?

When a solid substance **dissolves** it doesn't disappear. It changes state to form a **solution** (see page 122).

For example, when you add 10 g of salt crystals to 100 g of water in a beaker, you get 110 g of salt solution. The salt particles in the crystals separate and mingle with the water particles. It weighs 110 g because no particles are lost, they are just rearranged.

If you then evaporate the water, the salt particles rearrange themselves again and you get 10 g of salt crystals back. This is called **crystallisation**.

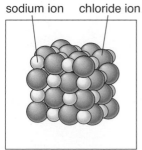

sodium ion   chloride ion   water molecules

sodium chloride crystal ⟶ sodium chloride solution

 If you collected all the water vapour evaporated from the salt solution, how much do you think it would weigh?

You need to remember that:

- ▶ Physical changes are reversible.
- ▶ Physical changes do not make new substances; chemical bonds are not made or broken.
- ▶ Changes of state are examples of physical changes.
- ▶ Solids melt to make liquids.
- ▶ Liquids freeze to make solids.
- ▶ Liquids boil or evaporate to make gases.
- ▶ Gases condense to make liquids.
- ▶ Substances must be heated to make them melt or boil, and cooled to make them condense or freeze.
- ▶ Heating makes particles move faster and weakens the forces of attraction between the particles.
- ▶ Cooling slows the particles down and strengthens the forces of attraction between the particles.
- ▶ Substances melt and boil at particular temperatures called the melting and boiling points. These are different for each substance.
- ▶ Some solids dissolve to make solutions.
- ▶ Solids can be made from solutions by crystallisation, where the solvent is evaporated.
- ▶ When a substance dissolves or is crystallised, the amount of substance does not change.

Next time ⟫

Unit 6   Elements are made up of a single type of atom (page 142).

Unit 7   The elements in the Periodic Table are arranged in groups that have similar properties (page 150).

Previously »

Remember — We can sort materials into groups based on their properties.

From page 113 — Atoms contain protons, neutrons and electrons.

Unit 6

Elements

Why are elements important?

There are over 100 different elements and each is made up of only one type of atom. Pure gold contains only gold atoms and pure lead contains only lead atoms. The structure of each type of atom gives the element its properties. Gold is very heavy but quite soft and doesn't react easily. Lead is also heavy and soft but reacts much more easily than gold. Long ago, alchemists tried very hard to change lead into gold but never managed it. This is because elements can't be changed chemically; chemical reactions don't affect the contents of an atom's nucleus.

In this Unit, you will learn:

- about elements and what makes each one different;
- which elements were discovered first;
- the symbols used to represent the elements;
- what is meant by 'relative atomic mass' and the 'atomic number';
- about the Periodic Table of the elements;
- about metals and non-metals (and some exceptions);
- about compounds and what they are made from.

Key words

atom	Group	Periodic Table
atomic number	insulators	relative atomic mass
compound	metals	symbol
conductors	non-metals	
elements	Period	

What are elements?

Elements are substances made up of a single type of **atom**. Different types of atoms are identified by the number of protons that they contain. This is called the **atomic number**. This number also gives us a clue as to how heavy the atom is.

When we find elements in their natural state, some contain individual atoms (like helium or neon, which we find as gases). Others contain molecules made of two or three of the element's atoms joined to each other (like oxygen or nitrogen in air). These molecules still contain only one type of atom.

Sulfur forms molecules of eight atoms.

Bromine gas Br$_2$ *Iodine gas I$_2$*

How do we measure the mass of elements?

Atoms with more protons in the nucleus tend also to contain neutrons, which help to keep the nucleus together. The mass of protons + neutrons + electrons gives us the mass of each atom. Because it would be a waste of time to measure the mass of EVERY atom one by one, we take an average over a very large number of atoms. We call this the element's **relative atomic mass**.

What symbols do we use for elements?

We use symbols to represent the elements. The **symbol** is usually the first one or two letters of the name of the element.

Element	Symbol
carbon	C
nitrogen	N
oxygen	O
sulphur	S
aluminium	Al
silicon	Si
helium	He

The symbols used for some elements are taken from the Latin name of the element.

Element	Latin name	Symbol
sodium	natrium	Na
lead	plumbum	Pb
iron	ferrum	Fe

1 Work out the symbol for elements like chlorine, magnesium, argon, and calcium. Check your answers against the Periodic Table on page 144.

2 For a challenge, see if you can work out what elements are represented by the symbols Cu, W and Ag. Why do they have these symbols?

How do we show these symbols and properties?

We can put all the main information about an element into a simple 'card'. You will see many forms of this card in tables and charts, but most of them will show at least this information:

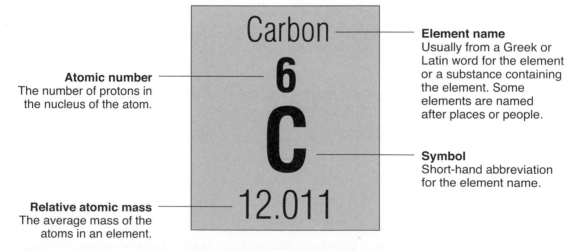

Carbon
6
C
12.011

Atomic number
The number of protons in the nucleus of the atom.

Relative atomic mass
The average mass of the atoms in an element.

Element name
Usually from a Greek or Latin word for the element or a substance containing the element. Some elements are named after places or people.

Symbol
Short-hand abbreviation for the element name.

Pick one of the elements from the tables of symbols above. Create an element information card for it.

The Periodic Table

In the 17th century, scientists noticed that some elements have things in common. Dmitri Mendeleev from Russia realised he could organise the elements in groups according to their properties. He listed these elements in the **Periodic Table**, which was published for the first time in 1869. Today, we have discovered many more elements and Mendeleev's table has grown to contain 118!

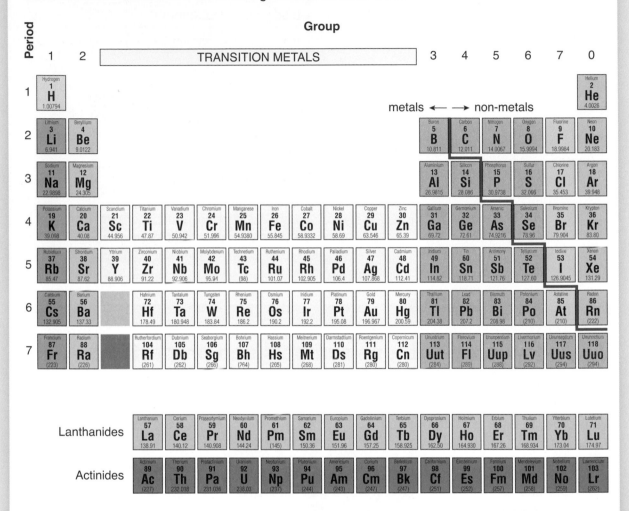

- ▶ The elements are listed in order of increasing atomic number. This tells us the number of protons in the nucleus of an atom of each element.

- ▶ Elements with similar properties are arranged in columns. Each column is called a **Group**.

- ▶ Each horizontal row is called a **Period**. There is a gradual change or 'trend' in the properties of the elements across a Period.

The first 92 elements have all been discovered in nature. We have had to manufacture elements 93 to 118 using nuclear reactions. We may yet create more elements!

The elements above and to the right of the stepped diagonal line are **non-metals**. All the rest are **metals**.

There is a bigger version of the Periodic Table on page 336.

What is the difference between metals and non-metals?

As you can see, the elements in the Periodic Table are divided into metals and non-metals.

Metals are:	Non-metals are:
able to transfer electricity and heat well (good **conductors**)	poor conductors of electricity and heat (**insulators**)
shiny, especially when you polish or cut them	dull, not shiny (many are gases or liquids at room temperature)
hard and strong	not strong or hard-wearing
malleable (bendy)	brittle (not bendy and break easily)
sonorous (they make a ringing sound when you hit them)	do not make a ringing sound when you hit them
have high melting and boiling points	have low melting and boiling points
have high densities	have low densities

You can investigate an element's properties to find out if it is a metal or a non-metal. *BUT, there are exceptions to these rules.*

How would you tell if your chair leg was made from metal or plastic?

Mercury

Mercury is a metal but it is liquid at room temperature. It only becomes a solid at –39 °C. Mercury conducts heat very well and expands so it has been used in thermometers. It is also very poisonous, so most thermometers don't contain mercury any more.

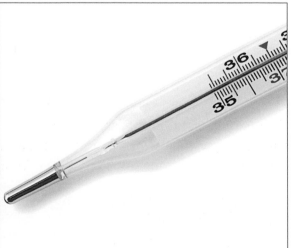

Carbon

Carbon exists naturally in several different forms we call allotropes. We are used to thinking of carbon in forms like coal, which do have the properties of non-metals. But it also exists in other forms:

▶ *Diamond* is a non-metal but it is one of the hardest substances there is. Diamond is made from a crystal arrangement of carbon atoms. It has a very high melting temperature (about 3500 °C) and is so strong it is used in drills and for cutting glass.

▶ *Graphite* is also made from carbon atoms that are arranged in sheets. It is soft and used in the 'lead' we have in the pencils we write with. Unlike most non-metals, graphite conducts electricity.

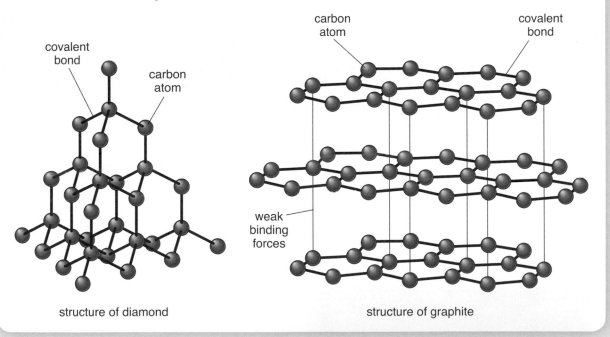

structure of diamond   structure of graphite

Sodium

Sodium is a metal but it is soft and easy to cut with a knife. Unlike most metals, it is not very dense and floats on water. However, it reacts violently with water so we usually keep it in oil.

Silicon is also an exception to the rules. It is a non-metal, and it is present all around us – for example, the sand on a beach is made of silicon dioxide. Silicon is an element we call a semi-conductor. It does not normally conduct electricity, but when it is processed and small numbers of atoms of other elements are added, we can make it conduct some of the time.

This property makes it extremely useful. Every electronic device we use, from computers to mobile phones, to microwave ovens, TVs and cars, contains 'chips' made from silicon. The element we use so we can control all these devices comes from sand!

 The compound silicon carbide has a very special property – it gives out light when electricity is passed through it. This was discovered by a scientist called Captain Henry Joseph Round. Research and write a short biography of Captain Round. See if you can find out the name of the device that he invented, which is used frequently today.

What are compounds?

A **compound** is made when atoms of different elements combine (react) chemically. Once a chemical reaction has happened, the compound cannot be changed back into its elements by using methods like filtration or distillation. The atoms combine to make molecules of compounds and can have very different properties to the elements that make them up.

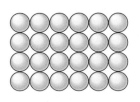 + 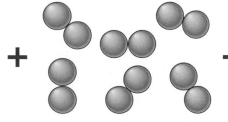 →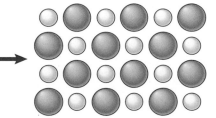

| sodium (element) | chlorine (element) | sodium chloride (compound) |

 Research online what happens when sodium, chlorine and sodium chloride are each added to water. Create a table listing the differences.

You need to remember that:

▶ Elements are made up of a single type of atom.

▶ Different types of elements can be identified by the number of protons that the atoms contain.

▶ Scientists use symbols to represent the elements.

▶ Dmitri Mendeleev listed elements with similar properties gathered together as the Periodic Table.

▶ Elements with similar properties are arranged in Groups (columns).

▶ There is a gradual change or 'trend' in the properties of the elements across a Period (row).

▶ The Periodic Table is divided into metals and non-metals.

▶ Metals are usually shiny and strong, they have high densities and are good conductors of heat and electricity.

▶ Non-metals are usually dull and brittle, they have low densities and are insulators of heat and electricity.

▶ There are some exceptions to these rules, including mercury, carbon, sodium and silicon.

▶ Compounds are made when atoms of different elements combine (react) chemically.

Next time »

Unit 7 We can use patterns of reactivity among elements to predict what will happen in a chemical reaction (page 151).

Unit 8 Compounds contain two or more different elements that are chemically joined (page 157).

Previously »

From page 116 The behaviour of particles changes the properties of matter.

From page 142 Elements are made up of a single type of atom.

Unit 7

Patterns in elements

How can we predict reactions?

The elements in the Periodic Table are arranged in groups that have similar properties. Different types of metals react differently in air. Some rust (iron), or tarnish (copper). Some don't change at all (gold) and some burst into flames immediately (sodium)! The reactivity of a metal affects what we can do with it. The reactivity describes how well a substance reacts with water, oxygen or acids. You can use your knowledge of the patterns of reactivity among elements to predict what will happen in a chemical reaction.

In this Unit, you will learn:

- ▶ about the patterns in the Periodic Table;
- ▶ how elements are classified according to their properties;
- ▶ about patterns in the reactivity of metals, known as the reactivity series;
- ▶ about what happens when metals react with acids;
- ▶ about what happens when metals react with water;
- ▶ about what happens when metals react with oxygen;
- ▶ about displacement reactions;
- ▶ how to predict what will happen in reactions using your knowledge of the reactivity series;
- ▶ how reactivity affects how easy it is to extract a metal from its ore.

Key words

corrodes	oxides	reactivity series
displacement reaction	patterns	salt
extract	Periodic Table	tarnish
Groups	predict	
hydroxides	reactivity	

How was the Periodic Table used to predict new elements?

When Mendeleev arranged the first 63 elements he knew about into a table, he noticed that the elements could be grouped according to **patterns** of their properties.

He needed to leave gaps in some columns and rows in order to keep the patterns of properties. He predicted that there should be elements to fill the gaps, ones that had not yet been discovered. He used what he had discovered about the patterns of the elements to predict the properties of the missing ones.

When these missing elements were finally discovered they closely matched Mendeleev's predictions. Also, protons and neutrons were discovered in the nucleus of atoms after Mendeleev's work. So we now order what is called the **Periodic Table** by the atomic number of the elements. In fact, although later scientists have added many more elements, Mendeleev's table looks very similar to the modern Periodic Table.

Which Groups have names?

As you can see from the diagram of the Periodic Table, the columns are divided into **Groups**. Some of these Groups have specific names.

Group	Name
Group 1	alkali metals
Group 2	alkaline earth metals
Group 7	halogens
Group 0	noble gases
between Group 2 and Group 3	transition metals

How can we predict which elements will react?

We can compare how strongly different elements react with substances like water, oxygen and acids. By carrying out these comparisons, we say we are measuring the **reactivity** of elements.

Metals can be listed in order of their reactivity, from the most reactive to the least reactive. This is called the **reactivity series**. This order turns out to be the same whether we are reacting the metals with water, oxygen or acids.

It's important to remember the order of the reactivity series. Using a *mnemonic* like this can help you remember the order of the metals:

Metal	Symbol	Reactivity
potassium	K	very reactive
sodium	Na	
calcium	Ca	
magnesium	Mg	fairly reactive
aluminium	Al	
zinc	Zn	
iron	Fe	not very reactive
lead	Pb	
copper	Cu	
silver	Ag	not reactive
gold	Au	

People **S**taring **C**an **M**ake **A**thletic **Z**ebras **I**n **L**ondon **C**opy **S**illy **G**ames

Potassium **S**odium **C**alcium **M**agnesium **A**luminium **Z**inc **I**ron **L**ead **C**opper **S**ilver **G**old

See if you can make up your own mnemonics. Make one for the names and one for the chemical symbols.

How do metals react with acids?

Metals react less strongly with acids as you go down the reactivity series. We use acids that have been mixed with water – they are dilute acids.

Metals from potassium to iron in the reactivity series will react with dilute acids to make a **salt** and hydrogen.

metal + acid → metal salt + hydrogen

The metals below iron in the reactivity series don't react with dilute acids.

Metal	Symbol	Reaction with acid
potassium	K	reacts violently
sodium	Na	
calcium	Ca	
magnesium	Mg	reacts fairly well
aluminium	Al	
zinc	Zn	
iron	Fe	
lead	Pb	no reaction
copper	Cu	
silver	Ag	
gold	Au	

Aluminium reacts slowly to make an oxide layer that then protects the metal inside.

How do metals react with water?

For reactive metals:

metal + water → metal hydroxide + hydrogen

Metals as far down as lead in the reactivity series always react with water to make hydrogen. The more reactive metals react strongly with cold water to make **hydroxides**.

For example:

sodium + water → sodium hydroxide + hydrogen

$$2Na + 2H_2O \rightarrow 2NaOH + H_2$$

For less reactive metals, the reaction with cold water is slow. So we need to heat the water to make water vapour, which makes the reaction faster:

metal + steam → metal oxide + hydrogen

The less reactive metals react slowly with water, but quickly with water vapour, to make **oxides**. For example:

magnesium + water vapour → magnesium oxide + hydrogen

$$Mg + H_2O \rightarrow MgO + H_2$$

Metal	Symbol	Reaction with water
potassium	K	reacts with cold water
sodium	Na	
calcium	Ca	
magnesium	Mg	reacts with water vapour
aluminium	Al	
zinc	Zn	
iron	Fe	
lead	Pb	no reaction with water or water vapour
copper	Cu	
silver	Ag	
gold	Au	

Aluminium reacts slowly to make an oxide layer that then protects the metal inside.

 Explain why pipes for central heating systems can be made from copper, but not from zinc.

How do metals react with air?

Most metals react with the oxygen in air to make a dull metal oxide.

metal + oxygen → metal oxide

Metals as far down the reactivity series as magnesium react very strongly with the oxygen in the air. All we need to do is heat them up and they start to burn. They react so strongly, the reactions are dangerous because they give out lots of light and heat. They burn with different colours, which is why metals like magnesium are used in fireworks.

Further down the reactivity series, to copper, metals look dull when they are left for some time in air. We say they **tarnish**; we have to polish them to make the metal shine. The reaction is the same but takes place much more slowly.

For example:

zinc + oxygen → zinc oxide

$$2Zn + O_2 \rightarrow 2ZnO$$

In fact, when iron is left in contact with water *and* air, it does more than tarnish – it **corrodes** to form brown iron oxide (rust).

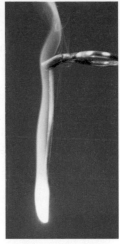

Magnesium reacting with oxygen.

 You can see why silver and gold are the metals used for making jewellery. What would happen to a ring made of potassium?

Metal	Symbol	Reaction with oxygen
potassium	K	reacts easily and burns with a bright flame
sodium	Na	
calcium	Ca	
magnesium	Mg	
aluminium	Al	reacts slowly, faster if heated
zinc	Zn	
iron	Fe	
lead	Pb	
copper	Cu	
silver	Ag	no reaction
gold	Au	

Aluminium, zinc, iron, lead and copper are all used as building materials. For example, in the past lead and copper were often used for the roofs of buildings. Copper is also used for electrical cables.

New copper.

Aged copper.

? Investigate the uses of these five metals in everyday life. What effects do their reactions with air and water have on where the metals can be used? See if you can find buildings nearby, or photographs of buildings, where these metals have been used.

What are displacement reactions?

In a **displacement reaction**, a more reactive metal pushes out (displaces) a less reactive metal from a salt. For example:

$Mg + CuSO_4 \rightarrow MgSO_4 + Cu$

Magnesium is more reactive than copper, so, in this reaction, magnesium displaces copper from its salt to make magnesium sulfate. But the reverse cannot happen, because copper is less reactive than magnesium.

We can show this in the laboratory. When magnesium metal is added to blue copper sulfate solution, the blue becomes much paler as magnesium sulfate is formed. Magnesium sulfate solution is colourless. The copper is displaced by the magnesium.

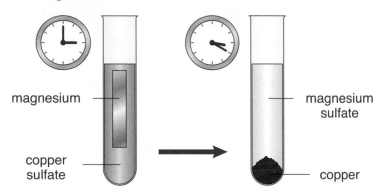

1 If you tried to displace magnesium sulfate using iron, what do you think would happen?

2 Displacement reactions are important for protecting metals like iron against corrosion. How do you think this works?

How can we predict reactions?

Just like Mendeleev, you can use your knowledge of the reactivity series to **predict** what will happen in a reaction. All you need to remember is that more reactive metals displace less reactive metals.

For example:

potassium + zinc sulfate → potassium sulfate + zinc

Potassium displaces zinc. In fact, potassium will displace all the other metals in the reactivity series because it is the most reactive.

But:

iron + magnesium sulfate → iron + magnesium sulfate

No change! This is because iron is less reactive than magnesium.

Predict what will happen, if anything, if we try to react zinc with copper sulfate.

How easy is it to extract a metal from its ore?

Many metals are found in the ground as metal ores, mixed up with other substances.

Metals that are at the bottom of the reactivity series, like copper, silver and gold, are easy to **extract**. They have been around as metals for thousands of years because they aren't very reactive. All we need to do is separate the metal from the mixtures. In fact, gold can be separated from soil and other substances simply by washing it very carefully – a kind of filtration. Unfortunately, it is very rare!

More reactive metals like potassium and sodium are not present in simple mixtures. They are so reactive they occur naturally only in compounds like oxides. It takes a lot of energy to extract the pure metal.

 Many substances are traded around the world and have a price that changes day by day. Find out what today's gold price is. Why is gold so expensive?

You need to remember that:

- ▷ Mendeleev predicted new elements from observing the properties of elements and arranging them in the Periodic Table.
- ▷ We can predict which metals will react by placing them in order of their reactivity.
- ▷ Metals react less strongly as you go down the reactivity series.
- ▷ Metals react with acids to make a metal salt and hydrogen.
- ▷ Metals react with oxygen to make metal oxides.
- ▷ Very reactive metals burn brightly in air.
- ▷ Less reactive metals tarnish slowly in air.
- ▷ Very reactive metals react with water to make metal hydroxides and hydrogen.
- ▷ Less reactive metals react with water vapour to make metal oxides and hydrogen.
- ▷ In displacement reactions, a more reactive metal forces out (displaces) a less reactive metal from a salt.
- ▷ We can get pure metals by extracting them from their ores in the ground.
- ▷ Some less reactive metals like gold and silver are easier to extract but very hard to find.

Next time »

Unit 8   Compounds contain two or more different elements that are chemically joined (page 157).

Unit 10   Oxides are made in oxidation reactions (page 167).

Previously »

From page 147 — Compounds are made when atoms of different elements react chemically.

From page 151 — We can predict which metals will react by placing them in order of their reactivity.

Unit 8

Compounds

Why are compounds important?

Compounds come in all shapes and sizes because there are millions of ways for atoms to combine. Compounds are made when elements join together in a chemical reaction. Once the atoms have combined to make a compound they cannot easily be separated. The properties of compounds are usually very different from the properties of the elements they contain.

Hydrogen and oxygen react together explosively. But together they make water!

In this Unit, you will learn:

- about compounds and molecules;
- about the different properties of compounds;
- how to use chemical formulas;
- rules for naming compounds;
- how to use chemical equations;
- some basic facts about chemical reactions;
- about some everyday reactions.

Key words

bonds	ions
compounds	molecules
covalent compound	properties
formula	symbols
ionic compound	

What are compounds?

Compounds contain two or more different elements that are chemically joined. The particles in compounds are called **molecules**, made from two or more different atoms joined together. (Remember that elements can contain molecules too, but they are made from atoms of the same element joining together.)

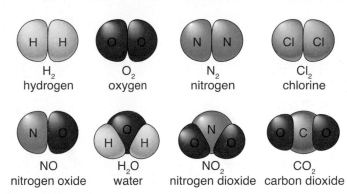

H₂
hydrogen

O₂
oxygen

N₂
nitrogen

Cl₂
chlorine

NO
nitrogen oxide

H₂O
water

NO₂
nitrogen dioxide

CO₂
carbon dioxide

Draw a table with the headings 'Elements' and 'Compounds'. Place the following substances into the correct columns: mercury, diamond, carbon monoxide, sulfur dioxide, ammonia, sodium, helium, hydrochloric acid.

What types of compounds are there?

There are two types of compounds – ionic and covalent.

An **ionic compound** is made when a metal reacts with a non-metal. For example, a molecule of sodium chloride, or table salt, is made when one atom of sodium (a metal) reacts with one atom of chlorine (a non-metal). The sodium atom gets a positive electrical charge, and the chlorine atom gets a negative electrical charge.

We call atoms that have electrical charges **ions**. The compound sodium chloride is held together by the attraction of the positively and negatively charged ions.

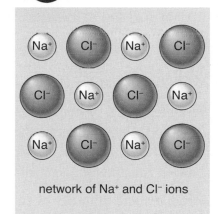

network of Na⁺ and Cl⁻ ions

A **covalent compound** is made when two non-metals react. For example, each molecule of the carbon dioxide that we breathe out is made from one atom of carbon and two atoms of oxygen. The atoms join together because they share electrons between them. These electrons whizz around the three atoms in the molecule and hold the atoms closely together. We say the electrons form **bonds** between the atoms.

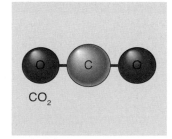

CO₂

From what you know about the elements and their patterns of properties from the Periodic Table, see if you can work out whether the following compounds are ionic or covalent: potassium chloride, carbon monoxide, sulfur dioxide, potassium iodide.

What are the properties of compounds?

The **properties** of compounds are very different from the properties of the elements they contain. Sodium is a very reactive metal and chlorine is a poisonous gas. When these two elements react they make the white sodium chloride crystals that you use to flavour food in cooking!

sodium   +   chlorine   →   sodium chloride

 Carbon and oxygen react together in different ways, they can make carbon dioxide or carbon monoxide. Find out about and describe the different properties for these elements and the two compounds they can make. Which one is poisonous? Which three are essential for life?

How do we show reactions using symbols?

We use chemical **symbols** to represent elements, just as we do in the Periodic Table (see page 143). The symbols can be put together to make a chemical **formula** to tell us what type of atoms, and how many of them, are in a compound. We can then assemble equations showing the different elements and compounds that are used and made in reactions.

Here are some formulas of compounds that show what atoms each molecule contains.

Name	Formula	Molecule is made of ...
oxygen	O_2	two atoms of oxygen
calcium chloride	$CaCl_2$	one atom of calcium and two atoms of chlorine
copper sulfate	$CuSO_4$	one atom of copper, one atom of sulfur, four atoms of oxygen
hydrochloric acid	HCl	one atom of hydrogen and one atom of chlorine

 The compound sodium hydrogencarbonate contains one atom of sodium, one of hydrogen, one of carbon and three of oxygen. Write down its formula. Find out what we call it and use it for in the kitchen!

How do we name compounds?

There are five simple rules for getting the names of compounds right!

▶ **Rule 1:** If there is a metal in the compound, it usually comes first in the name (for example, **sodium** chloride).

▶ **Rule 2:** When two elements combine, the name of the compound usually ends in -ide (for example, sodium chlor*ide*).

Compound	Elements (metals)	Elements (non-metals)	Compound name
NaCl	sodium	chlorine	**sodium** chlor*ide*
FeS	iron	sulfur	**iron** sulf*ide*
MgO	magnesium	oxygen	**magnesium** ox*ide*
$CaBr_2$	calcium	bromine	**calcium** brom*ide*

▶ **Rule 3:** When three or more elements combine and one of them is oxygen, the name of the compound usually ends in -ate.

Compound	Elements	Compound name
$CuSO_4$	copper, sulfur, oxygen	copper sulf*ate*
$CaCO_3$	calcium, carbon, oxygen	calcium carbon*ate*
KNO_3	potassium, nitrogen, oxygen	potassium nitr*ate*

▶ **Rule 4:** If two atoms of the same element combine to form a molecule, the name of the compound is the same as the element.

Compound	Molecule	Compound name
H_2	two atoms of hydrogen	hydrogen
O_2	two atoms of oxygen	oxygen
Cl_2	two atoms of chlorine	chlorine

▶ **Rule 5:** Rules 1 to 4 will usually mean you get the name of the compound right, BUT there are always exceptions to these rules! Try to learn the exceptions too – it's the only way! Here are some examples:

Compound	Elements	Compound name
H_2O	hydrogen and oxygen	water
HCl	hydrogen and chlorine	hydrochloric acid
H_2SO_4	hydrogen, sulfur, oxygen	sulfuric acid
HNO_3	hydrogen, nitrogen, oxygen	nitric acid
NH_4	nitrogen and hydrogen	ammonia

Who decides how we name chemicals?

The International Union of Pure and Applied Chemistry is the world authority that decides what names and spellings chemicals should have. They are made the same around the world so all scientists know they are talking about the same substances. For example, this is why in this book, we use 'sulfur' not 'sulphur' or 'brimstone'.

1 Have a look at some of the chemical formulas shown elsewhere in this book and see if you can name them correctly.

2 Research and describe why NH_4 is called 'ammonia'.

Some chemicals have historical names that are still widely used. For example, chalk is calcium carbonate, and brimstone is sulfur.

Find out the formulas for the following chemicals, and name them using the five rules: alumina, asbestos, Epsom salts, fluorspar, quicksilver.

You need to remember that:

○ Compounds contain two or more elements that are chemically joined.

○ The particles in compounds are called molecules.

○ Compounds can be ionic (made of charged particles) or covalent (particles share electrons).

○ The properties of compounds are usually different from the properties of the elements they contain.

○ Scientists use symbols to write chemical formulas that show us the type and number of atoms in a compound.

○ There are rules for naming compounds that tell us something about the elements they contain.

Next time ≫

Unit 9   All reactions involve the conservation of mass (page 163).

Unit 10   Types of chemical reactions include oxidation, reduction and combustion (page 167).

Previously 》》

From page 136 — Physical changes do not make new substances; chemical bonds are not made or broken.

From page 157 — Compounds contain two or more elements that are chemically joined.

Unit 9

Chemical reactions

What are chemical changes?

Unlike physical changes, chemical reactions are usually irreversible. Atoms and molecules combine in chemical reactions to make new materials. The substances cannot be converted back easily to the original atoms and molecules. They cannot be separated by physical methods like filtration and distillation (see page 124).

The atoms and molecules that react are still there after the reaction has finished. They are not destroyed. They are just rearranged. How do we know a chemical reaction has happened though? There are some tell-tale signs to look out for ...

In this Unit, you will learn:

- ▶ how reversible and irreversible are different reactions;
- ▶ about chemical reactions;
- ▶ about tell-tale signs of chemical reactions;
- ▶ about energy taken in and given out by reactions.

Key words

balanced	exothermic reactions
chemical changes	fizzing
chemical equation	heat
chemical reactions	irreversible
colour change	physical changes
combustion	precipitate
conservation of mass	product
endothermic reactions	reactants

What types of changes are there?

There are two types of changes we need to know about in chemistry – physical and chemical.

- ▶ **Physical changes** are usually reversible and no new substances are made (see page 136).
- ▶ **Chemical changes** are usually irreversible and new substances are formed.

What do chemical reactions have in common?

Atoms are combined in all sorts of ways to make different compounds but all these **chemical reactions** have some things in common. Most are **irreversible**, meaning we can't take the result of the reaction and change it back easily into what we had to begin with.

- ▶ When you strike a match and it burns, you can't strike it again.
- ▶ When you toast bread, you can't turn it back into uncooked bread – if you burn it, you can only scrape off the burnt bits!
- ▶ When you fry an egg, you can't change the fried egg into an omelette!

All these reactions are useful but they are irreversible. Other kinds of irreversible reaction are not so useful, like when steel on a car rusts.

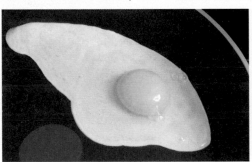 

Something else that's true of nearly all chemical reactions is that they need energy to get started.

- ▶ We put our energy into the match to make it start burning, by striking the tip on a rough surface.
- ▶ We use a toaster to convert electrical energy into heat energy that then cooks the bread.
- ▶ We have to heat the frying pan to start the egg cooking.

Most of the processes going on in our bodies are chemical reactions, and we need the energy we get from food to keep these reactions working.

? **Describe some other reactions that need energy to make them happen.**

What happens to the atoms and molecules when they react?

We can use chemical formulas to show what happens in a reaction. We write a **chemical equation** like this:

$$2H_2 + O_2 \rightarrow 2H_2O$$
reactants   *product*

The substances that react together are called the **reactants**. The compound formed by the reaction is called the **product**.

These chemical reactions are irreversible, but the numbers and types of atoms in the product stay the same as the numbers and types of atoms in the reactants. No atoms have been destroyed, they've just been rearranged to form different molecules.

If you count up the numbers of hydrogen atoms in the reactants (4), you'll see that there are still 4 hydrogen atoms after the reaction.

This is really important to remember:

mass of the reactants = mass of the products

We call this the **conservation of mass**.

? How many oxygen atoms are there before and after the reaction?

How do we write equations so they balance?

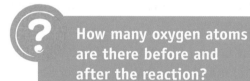

You can see in the equation for the reaction of hydrogen and oxygen to make water:

two	one		two
hydrogen +	oxygen	→	water
molecules	molecule		molecules

We say the chemical equation for the reaction is **balanced**.

This next equation *IS NOT* balanced:	This equation *IS* balanced:
magnesium + oxygen → magnesium oxide	magnesium + oxygen → magnesium oxide
Mg + O$_2$ → MgO	**2**Mg + O$_2$ → **2**MgO
reactants *products*	*reactants* *products*

Mg	O	→	Mg	O
1	2		1	1

Mg	O	→	Mg	O
2	2		2	2

You can see there are now the same numbers and types of reactant atoms as there are product atoms.

? Carbon and oxygen combine to make carbon dioxide. See if you can write the chemical equation for this reaction. Make sure it is balanced.

What are the signs of chemical reactions?

When compounds are made, there are often signs that show you a reaction is happening.

Here are some tell-tale signs to look out for:

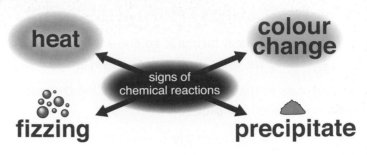

heat

colour change

signs of chemical reactions

fizzing

precipitate

What happens to energy in reactions?

We know we need energy to get a reaction started. But what happens once the reaction is under way?

Most chemical reactions involve energy changes. This energy usually takes the form of heat, but it can also be light or sound.

Exothermic reactions give out heat energy. The heat is transferred to the surroundings and the temperature rises. The surroundings can be the air, the container or water (if the reaction is between solutions).

Combustion (burning in air) is an example of an exothermic reaction. We do have to put energy in to start the reaction (like striking a match), but once the reaction gets going it gives off more heat energy than it takes in.

Think about a camp fire. We have to start the fire with some energy (like with a match, or by rubbing sticks together). Once the wood starts burning, gradually the whole pile of wood catches fire. Oxygen from the air reacts with the compounds in the wood to make carbon dioxide gas. This reaction is exothermic, so we feel the heat coming from the fire.

? We can stop camp fires by throwing thick blankets over them or covering them with water. How does that stop the chemical reaction?

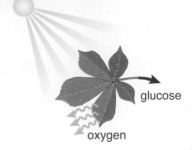

Endothermic reactions take in heat energy from the surroundings. If you measure the temperature of the mixture of reactants and products, as the reaction proceeds the temperature goes down.

Photosynthesis is an example of an endothermic reaction. Plants use energy from the Sun to convert carbon dioxide to glucose and oxygen (see page 40).

glucose

oxygen

The conservation of mass means we can work out exactly how many atoms of each element are involved in reactions.

Write balanced equations showing how you would make:

1 magnesium chloride from magnesium and hydrochloric acid;

2 potassium nitrate from potassium and nitric acid;

3 copper sulfate from copper and sulfuric acid;

4 glucose from carbon dioxide and water.

You need to remember that:

- ◗ Changes can be physical or chemical.
- ◗ Physical changes are usually reversible and no new substances are made.
- ◗ Chemical changes are usually irreversible and new substances are formed.
- ◗ All reactions involve the conservation of mass.
- ◗ Bubbles of gas, the formation of a precipitate and changes in temperature or colour are evidence of chemical reactions.
- ◗ Most chemical reactions involve an energy change.
- ◗ Exothermic reactions give out heat energy.
- ◗ Endothermic reactions take in heat energy from the surroundings.

Next time ❯❯

Unit 10   Types of chemical reactions include oxidation, reduction and combustion (page 167).

Unit 11   Acids and alkalis can react together to neutralise each other (page 175).

Previously »

From page 157   Compounds contain two or more elements that are chemically joined.

From page 162   Chemical changes are usually irreversible and new substances are formed.

Unit 10

Patterns in reactions

What are the most common reactions?

Molecules can combine in millions of different ways to make new substances, but we can detect patterns in the types of substances produced. This is because there are patterns in the types of chemical reactions that happen to make the different compounds.

For example, oxidation reactions produce iron oxide and all the other types of metal oxides that exist. Billions of years ago, primitive bacteria caused iron to be oxidised to form the red iron oxide in this banded iron rock formation.

In this Unit, you will learn:

- ▶ about types of reactions (oxidation, reduction and redox);
- ▶ about combustion and how to control it;
- ▶ about the corrosion of metals and how to prevent it.

Key words

carbon monoxide	incomplete combustion
combustion	oxidation
corrosion	oxides
fuels	redox
galvanisation	reduces
hydrocarbons	reduction

What are oxidation reactions?

In **oxidation** reactions, oxygen combines with substances to make **oxides**.

Metals react with oxygen to make metal oxides (see page 153). For example, iron corrodes in air to produce iron oxide (rust):

$$4Fe + 3O_2 \rightarrow 2Fe_2O_3$$

Another common example of oxidation is **combustion**, where a substance burns in air.

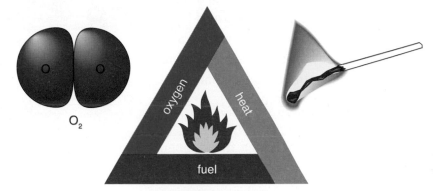

 What three things do you need to make a fire burn?

How do we use combustion reactions?

Combustion reactions are useful to us mainly because they produce lots of heat. We can use this heat in many different ways:

▶ most simply, to warm us up directly from open fires;

▶ to cook food;

▶ to drive turbines or pistons in engines, to power vehicles;

▶ to turn generators that produce electricity to power our homes and places of work.

When we use combustion in this way to do useful things, we call the substances we burn **fuels. Hydrocarbons** are a common type of fuel, which we find in nature. Gas, oil and petrol are examples of this type of fuel.

 What elements do you think make up hydrocarbons?

What reactions occur in combustion?

A fuel like natural gas (chemical name is methane, chemical formula is CH_4), burns to make carbon and hydrogen oxides. You know these as carbon dioxide and water.

methane + oxygen → carbon dioxide + water
CH_4 + $2O_2$ → CO_2 + $2H_2O$

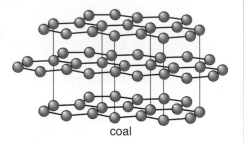

coal

Coal and petrol made from oil burn in similar ways, but produce different amounts of carbon dioxide and water. This is because methane, coal and oil are formed from molecules containing different numbers of carbon and hydrogen atoms. In fact, coal is mostly carbon, natural gas is mostly methane, and petrol contains a mix of bigger hydrocarbons like butane and octane.

gas

If a fire does not have enough oxygen, then **incomplete combustion** happens. When this happens a poisonous gas called **carbon monoxide** is formed instead of carbon dioxide:

methane + oxygen → carbon monoxide + water
$2CH_4$ + $3O_2$ → $2CO$ + $4H_2O$

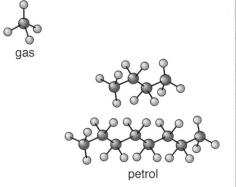

petrol

Carbon monoxide is poisonous because it binds to your red blood cells and stops them from carrying oxygen around your body. You might have a carbon monoxide monitor at home. This sounds an alarm if the combustion of gas to heat the central heating boiler or fire is incomplete. It senses the carbon monoxide being produced before it reaches dangerous amounts.

> You may well have a gas- or oil-powered oven or heating boiler at home. What practical steps can you take around your home to make sure these devices get enough oxygen to produce carbon dioxide, not carbon monoxide?

How can we control combustion?

Combustion is a fast reaction that produces a lot of heat, which means it can get out of control. With gas central heating boilers or ovens, we control the amount of fuel supplied to the flame so as to control the amount of heat produced.

When we grow new forests, we often plant trees with wide corridors that are clear of trees. If a forest fire starts, it will run out of fuel (trees) when it reaches the corridor, so the fire will be less likely to spread to other parts of the forest.

How can we stop corrosion of metals?

Rust on a car is evidence of **corrosion**. This is a type of oxidation reaction. When iron is exposed to moist air it reacts with oxygen to form iron oxide or rust.

Corrosion can be prevented in several ways. The simplest way is to coat the surface of the metal to prevent it coming into contact with water and air.

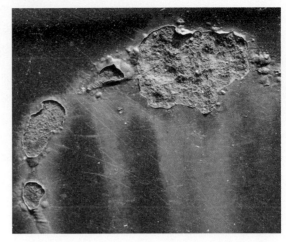

- Metal in buildings is usually painted to protect it.
- Household objects are more likely to be coated in plastic to protect them.
- Parts in machines are lubricated with oil, which helps the machine work smoothly but also protects the metal from corrosion.

A more sophisticated way of protecting against corrosion makes use of the reactivity of metals (see page 153). For example, if you coat iron with a layer of a more reactive metal like zinc, the more reactive metal (zinc) oxidises first. This prevents the iron from rusting. Coating iron with zinc is called **galvanisation**.

1 **What other metals would be suitable for protecting iron from corrosion?**

2 **Why don't we use sodium to protect iron?**

What are reduction reactions?

Reduction reactions are the opposite of oxidation reactions.

- In oxidation reactions, oxygen atoms are added to a compound.
- In reduction reactions, oxygen atoms are taken away from a compound.

For example, if magnesium oxide is mixed with carbon and heated to 2000 °C, the carbon takes an oxygen atom away to leave magnesium metal. We say the carbon **reduces** magnesium oxide.

$$MgO + C \rightarrow Mg + CO$$

But look at that equation again. The oxygen atom is also being added to the carbon atom to make carbon monoxide. So oxidation is happening as well!

- Magnesium oxide is being reduced, at the same time as ...
- Carbon is being oxidised.

This combination of reduction and oxidation happening at the same time in one reaction is very common. We call this a **redox** reaction (REDuction and OXidation).

In the example showing combustion of methane, carbon is oxidised. It's not obvious, but in fact this is also a redox reaction. The oxygen is being reduced. How is this possible?

When we look at redox reactions more closely, it's not quite as simple as just moving oxygen atoms. It's to do with how ionic and covalent compounds are made up (see page 157). The atoms in molecules are held together by electrons. Oxidation occurs when electrons are added; reduction occurs when electrons are taken away.

So with the combustion of methane, electrons move from the oxygen to the carbon. The carbon is oxidised, and the oxygen is reduced.

?

See if you can describe these redox reactions in terms of movement of electrons:

$$MgO + C \rightarrow Mg + CO$$

$$4Fe + 3O_2 \rightarrow 2Fe_2O_3$$

You need to remember that:

- ⊙ Oxides are made in oxidation reactions.
- ⊙ Oxidation often involves the addition of oxygen atoms.
- ⊙ Combustion is an oxidation reaction.
- ⊙ Combustion requires fuel, heat and oxygen.
- ⊙ Hydrocarbon fuels combust to make carbon dioxide and water.
- ⊙ Corrosion is a type of oxidation reaction.
- ⊙ Corrosion of iron can be prevented by coating the iron with paint, plastic or zinc.
- ⊙ Reduction is the opposite of oxidation.
- ⊙ Oxidation and reduction reactions that happen together are called redox reactions.

Next time »

Unit 13 Many of the chemicals synthesised in nature are combinations of the elements carbon, hydrogen, nitrogen and oxygen (page 185).

Unit 14 Fossil fuels like coal, oil and gas are burned to make energy (page 190).

Previously »

From page 122 — Some chemicals dissolve in water to form solutions; we say a solute dissolves in a solvent (water).

From page 132 — Acids and alkalis can be identified using an indicator like litmus paper.

Unit 11

Acids and alkalis

Where can we find acids and alkalis?

Acids, bases and alkalis can be found in the laboratory and at home. The strength of acids and alkalis is measured on the pH scale using an indicator solution. Weak acids are irritants (nettle venom is an acid) and strong acids are corrosive so they should be handled carefully.

Acids and alkalis can neutralise each other. If you mix an acid and an alkali together in the right proportions you get a neutral solution. Acids and alkalis react together to make salts.

In this Unit, you will learn:

- ▶ how to define acids, alkalis and bases;
- ▶ about acid and alkali strengths and the pH scale;
- ▶ how indicators work and can be used to find out pH;
- ▶ safety rules for using acids and alkalis;
- ▶ about everyday acids and alkalis and their uses;
- ▶ about neutralisation and neutralisation reactions;
- ▶ about important uses of neutralisation reactions.

Key words

acids	hydrochloric acid	nitric acid
alkalis	indicator	pH
bases	neutral	salt
chloride	neutralisation	sulfate
dilute	neutralise	sulfuric acid
hazard symbols	nitrate	Universal indicator

What is an acid?

We often use **acids** in experiments and in everyday life, but what makes a substance an acid? Here are some key features of acids.

- ▶ Acids are solutions – they work only when they are dissolved or mixed in water.
- ▶ Acids have a pH less than 7.
- ▶ Acids react with bases or alkalis to form neutral solutions (pH = 7).
- ▶ Weak acids such as lemon juice and vinegar can be found in certain foods. These acids give food a sour taste.
- ▶ Strong acids like nitric acid or sulfuric acid are used in many industrial processes, like making fertilisers and refining oil.
- ▶ Acids can corrode metals and other substances.
- ▶ Acids are harmful to some cells like skin or bacteria.

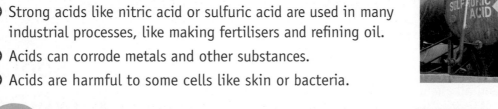

? We should never test an unknown chemical for acidity by looking for a 'sour taste'. Why not?

What is an alkali?

Alkalis are also important for us to use, and they are the 'opposite' of acids.

- ▶ Alkalis are solutions – they work only when they are dissolved or mixed in water.
- ▶ Alkalis have a pH greater than 7.
- ▶ Alkalis react with acids to form neutral solutions (pH = 7).
- ▶ Weak alkalis are found in everyday items like toothpaste and shower gel.
- ▶ Strong alkalis like bleach are used for cleaning.
- ▶ Strong alkalis can corrode metals and other substances – they are sometimes called 'caustic', which means corrosive.
- ▶ Alkalis are harmful to some cells like skin or bacteria.

? Why are alkalis like bleach and oven cleaner dangerous? Find out what precautions we can take to stay safe when we use them.

What is a base?

Alkalis are made from bases that dissolve in water. **Bases** are all substances that react with acids and can neutralise them. They are usually metal oxides, metal hydroxides or metal carbonates. Most bases do not dissolve in water, but if they do, they make an alkali.

⊳ Copper oxide is a base – it neutralises acids, but doesn't dissolve in water.

⊳ Solid sodium hydroxide is also a base, but it dissolves in water to become an alkali.

What is the pH scale?

The strength of acids and alkalis is measured using the **pH** scale.

Acids	Alkalis
Acids have a pH less than 7.	Alkalis have a pH greater than 7.
Strong acids are more corrosive than weak acids.	Strong alkalis are more corrosive than weak alkalis.
The lower the pH, the stronger the acid.	The higher the pH, the stronger the alkali.
You can **dilute** a strong acid with water but its pH stays the same.	You can dilute a strong alkali with water but its pH stays the same.

How do we measure pH?

An **indicator** is dye that changes colour depending on whether it's in an acid or an alkali. Some plants, like beetroot and red cabbage, contain natural indicators.

Universal indicator is a mixture of different dyes. Scientists use Universal indicator in the laboratory to tell how acidic or alkaline a solution is.

This colour chart shows the colour that solutions at different pHs will turn if you add a few drops of Universal indicator.

1	2	3	4	5	6	7	8	9	10	11	12	13	14

◄ increasingly acidic   increasingly alkaline ►

strong acid   weak acid   neutral   weak alkali   strong alkali

 ? If you added some Universal indicator to a glass of milk, what colour do you think it would turn?

How can we stay safe?

Strong acids and strong alkalis are very corrosive and should be handled with great care.

When you are dealing with these substances you should wear a laboratory coat, safety goggles and gloves to stop any splashes touching your skin. If a strong acid or strong alkali comes into contact with your skin, it will burn!

Containers for strong acids and alkalis are marked with **hazard symbols** to warn you about their dangers.

 If someone spilled some strong acid on a lab bench, what could they add to dilute it and stop it corroding the wood?

What are everyday acids and alkalis? @

Acids   *Neutral*   *Alkalis*

Acids and alkalis are common in everyday life.

▶ Weak acids like vinegar are used to pickle foods so that they can be stored longer.

▶ Sulfuric acid is a strong acid used in car batteries.

▶ Carbonated (fizzy) drinks are acidic and that's one reason why too much lemonade or cola can damage your teeth.

▶ You even have hydrochloric acid naturally in your stomach to help digest your food!

Water and milk are neutral.

Strong alkalis like sodium hydroxide are used in household cleaners and to make soap. Soap powder, gels for washing clothes and washing-up liquid are weaker alkalis that you often use at home.

 Why should we be careful to check car batteries regularly in case they leak? Explain why we should not throw them away in our 'normal' rubbish.

What happens in neutralisation reactions?

Acids and alkalis are chemical opposites.

▶ An alkali has a pH higher than 7. If you add an acid to an alkali, the pH decreases towards 7.

▶ An acid has a pH lower than 7. If you add an alkali to an acid, the pH increases towards 7.

If you mix exactly the right amounts of acid and alkali, you will get a **neutral** solution (pH 7) that is neither an acid nor an alkali. This type of reaction is called **neutralisation**.

Neutralisation reactions destroy acidity or alkalinity. An acid reacts with an alkali to make a substance called a **salt**, and water:

acid + alkali → salt + water

For example, hydrochloric acid is (obviously!) an acid, and sodium hydroxide is an alkali. These react together to make a salt, sodium chloride, and water:

hydrochloric acid + sodium hydroxide → sodium chloride + water
$$HCl + NaOH \rightarrow NaCl + H_2O$$

Which chemical is the alkali in this reaction? Which is the salt?

nitric acid + potassium hydroxide → potassium nitrate + water

Which acids make which salts?

Metals react with **hydrochloric acid** to form **chloride** salts:

sodium + hydrochloric acid → sodium chloride + hydrogen
$$2Na + 2HCl \rightarrow 2NaCl + H_2$$

Metals react with **sulfuric acid** to make **sulfate** salts:

zinc + sulfuric acid → zinc sulfate + hydrogen
$$Zn + H_2SO_4 \rightarrow ZnSO_4 + H_2$$

Metals react with **nitric acid** to make **nitrate** salts:

magnesium + nitric acid → magnesium nitrate + hydrogen
$$Mg + 2HNO_3 \rightarrow Mg(NO_3)_2 + H_2$$

In the chemical formula for magnesium nitrate, everything inside the brackets is multiplied by two. One molecule of magnesium nitrate contains one atom of magnesium, two atoms of nitrogen and six atoms of oxygen.

Name the acid, alkali and salt in this reaction:

$$2KOH + H_2SO_4 \rightarrow K_2SO_4 + 2H_2O$$

Why is neutralisation important? @

Neutralisation reactions have lots of uses at home and in industry, as well as in medicines and in farming.

A bee sting is an acid, so you can stop the pain by washing it with a solution of bicarbonate of soda (sodium hydrogen carbonate). This is a weak alkali used often in cooking, which neutralises the acid.

A wasp sting is an alkali, so you need to neutralise it by washing the sting with a weak acid. Vinegar will do the job.

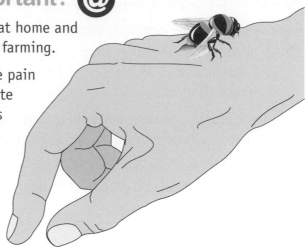

 List other chemicals that you might find at home, which you could safely put on a bee or wasp sting to stop the pain.

Have you ever had an uncomfortable burning feeling in your stomach after a meal? This is called indigestion. It happens because you have too much acid in your stomach. Medicines made from a mix of metal carbonates and hydroxides are used to **neutralise** the acid and cure the indigestion.

Plants grow best in soils that are neutral. Some soils are very acidic and not suitable for growing crops. Farmers use the alkali calcium hydroxide to neutralise the pH in acidic soils. This helps crops to grow well.

? **Copy and complete the following reaction that shows how an indigestion remedy works:**

> hydrochloric acid + magnesium hydroxide → _____ + _____

When you mix just the right amount of an acid with an alkali you get a neutral solution. Scientists do this in the laboratory using a method called titration. An acid is placed into a flask and a few drops of indicator are added to show the pH. Very small amounts of alkali can be added a bit at a time using a piece of equipment called a burette, which has a finely marked scale to measure how much alkali has been added. The colour of the indicator shows the pH of the acid changing as alkali is added. When the indicator shows that the solution in the flask is neutral, the amount of alkali used to neutralise the acid is recorded.

?

1 Which other quantities need to be measured to produce a full result for the experiment?

2 Explain why the same titration is usually repeated at least three times in an experiment.

You need to remember that:

- Acids are solutions with a pH less than 7 that will neutralise alkalis.
- Alkalis are solutions with a pH greater than 7 that will neutralise acids.
- Bases are substances that can react with acids and neutralise them.
- Most bases will not dissolve in water, but a base that does dissolve in water makes an alkali.
- The strength of acids and alkalis is measured using the pH scale.
- Universal indicator is a mixture of different dyes that we use to measure the pH of a solution.
- Strong acids and strong alkalis are very corrosive and should be handled with great care.
- Containers for strong acids and strong alkalis are marked with hazard symbols.
- Acids and alkalis are common in everyday life – they are found in household cleaning products, foods, car batteries and our bodies.
- If we mix exactly the right amounts of acid and alkali, we get a neutral solution (pH 7) that is neither an acid nor an alkali.
- In neutralisation reactions, an acid reacts with an alkali to make a salt and water.
- Neutralisation reactions can be used to treat insect stings and indigestion, and they can also improve soil for farming.

Next time »

Unit 12   Salts have a pattern of solubility that you can use to predict precipitation reactions (page 180).

Unit 14   Metal salts burn with different coloured flames and are used to make fireworks (page 193).

Previously 》

From page 167 Oxidation often involves the addition of oxygen atoms; combustion requires fuel, heat and oxygen.

From page 175 Neutralisation reactions can be used to treat insect stings and indigestion, and they can also improve soil for farming.

Unit 12

Reactions all around us

How do we know reactions are all around us?

There are patterns to chemical reactions. The most common types are neutralisation (see page 175) and oxidation and reduction (see page 169). These types of reactions have tell-tale signs that show you a reaction is happening and have lots of uses in everyday life.

For example, the organism yeast is used to help ferment chemicals to produce foods such as bread and drinks such as wine or beer.

In this Unit, you will learn:

- ▶ about colour change reactions and their uses;
- ▶ about precipitation reactions and their uses;
- ▶ about fermentation reactions and their uses.

Key words

aerobic respiration	insoluble
anaerobic respiration	opaque
antibiotics	precipitate
colorimetry	precipitation reaction
fermentation	transparent
fluorescent	yeast
indicators	

What do apples, glow sticks and invisible ink have in common?

Not much, you might think – but you'd be wrong! In fact they have coloured chemical reactions in common. **Indicators** react with acid or alkali solutions to make a coloured product. The colour of the product tells us the strength of the acid or alkali (see page 173). Lots of other chemical reactions make coloured products too.

When you bite into an apple and leave it, it goes brown. This is because a chemical in the apple oxidises in air and turns the white flesh brown.

The coloured glowing bracelets that you get at Halloween contain two chemicals that react together to release energy. This energy is used to make a dye glow in the dark. We call a chemical that glows like this **fluorescent**.

We can even use some of these reactions to make invisible ink! If you write a message on paper using lemon juice, as the juice dries you can't see the writing. But if you heat the paper by holding it near a light bulb, the writing appears. The lemon juice reacts with the paper to make a brown colour that makes the invisible ink, visible!

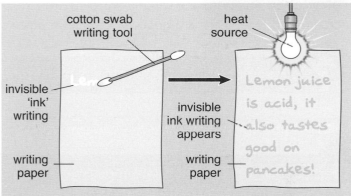

cotton swab writing tool

heat source

invisible 'ink' writing

invisible ink writing appears

writing paper

writing paper

Lemon juice is acid, it also tastes good on pancakes!

 What else could you use to write invisible messages? Design an experiment to test your ideas.

 THINKING BEYOND…

We can use a special piece of equipment called a colorimeter to measure how much of a coloured substance is in a solution. This is called colorimetry and can show how quickly a colour-change reaction is happening.

These reactions can be used to measure the amounts of chemicals like starch and proteins in substances. For example, if you look at the nutrition table on a packet of breakfast cereal, it shows how much protein, starch and fat the food contains. All these amounts can be worked out using colorimetry.

 Find out what Jan Szczepanik (1872–1926) contributed to colorimetry. What else did he invent?

What are precipitation reactions?

Solutions of substances that dissolve can change colour but they are always **transparent** – we can see through them. Sometimes a reaction between two solutions produces an **insoluble** product – a substance that does not dissolve. This is called a **precipitation reaction** and the solid is called a **precipitate**.

Solutions containing a precipitate are cloudy or **opaque** – we can't see through them.

Here is an example of a precipitation reaction:

silver nitrate + sodium chloride → silver chloride + sodium nitrate
$$AgNO_3 \quad + \quad NaCl \quad \rightarrow \quad AgCl \quad + \quad NaNO_3$$

In this precipitation reaction you see a white cloud or precipitate of insoluble silver chloride form when you mix the two soluble solutions.

Precipitation reactions are used in water treatment to remove harmful salts containing mercury and lead. This is a good way to make water safe for drinking.

 Find out what harmful effects mercury and lead can have.

 Whether precipitation happens depends on the solubility of the salt produced. Some examples are shown in the table.

Salt	Soluble	Insoluble
nitrates	all	none
sulfates	most, except ...	calcium, lead and barium
chlorides	most, except ...	copper, silver, lead and mercury
hydroxides	Group 1 metal hydroxides such as sodium and potassium are very soluble; Group 2 metal hydroxides such as calcium and magnesium are slightly soluble but might need heating	most others

You can use this information to predict whether a reaction will make a precipitate.

 If you mixed copper sulfate with sodium hydroxide, what would the products be? Would they be soluble or insoluble?

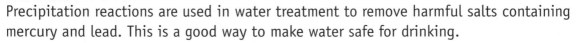

What is fermentation?

Fermentation is an example of an oxidation reaction, where sugars are converted to either gases (to make bread rise) or alcohol (to make alcoholic drinks). These reactions don't happen by themselves; we need to add simple organisms that help the reaction to happen. Fermentation is used to make beer, bread and even medicines.

How can we make bread?

Yeast is a fungus used to make bread rise. Yeast uses oxygen from air to live, for **aerobic respiration** (see page 46). Sugar (glucose) is converted to carbon dioxide and water. Eventually the yeast dies and the reaction stops.

glucose + oxygen → carbon dioxide + water

Yeast is added to the bread dough and left in a warm place to 'prove'. This means that fermentation is allowed to happen and the yeast 'eats up' the sugar to produce carbon dioxide bubbles in the dough. You need to make sure you use a large bowl for this because after a couple of hours, the dough can be twice the size it was when you left it! The bread should only be cooked after it has finished proving.

 We can also use a substance called sodium bicarbonate in cooking. When heated, it reacts with acids to produce carbon dioxide. What do you think sodium bicarbonate is used for?

Sodium bicarbonate is a base. What name do we give the process where it reacts with acids?

How can we make alcohol?

The alcohol in wine and beer is made in a similar way to rising bread, but it needs to happen away from air. Wine is produced by fermentation of fruit juice (usually grapes) and beer is made by fermentation of grain (wheat, oats, hops or malt barley). The alcohol that is made is called ethanol.

glucose + water → ethanol + carbon dioxide

The process the yeast carries out is called **anaerobic respiration** (anaerobic means 'without air'). If the reaction happens in the presence of air, the ethanol turns to vinegar, which tastes nasty in beer!

What other fermentation reactions are there?

When milk has 'gone off', it tastes sour. Milk contains a sugar called lactose. Bacteria ferment the lactose to make lactic acid, which spoils the taste. We use the same reaction deliberately to make yoghurt, which also tastes sour.

Even the makers of chocolate rely on fermentation! Cocoa beans grow in a hard outer pod that needs to be removed before the cocoa inside can be used for chocolate. Fermentation is used to make an acid that eats away the pod and makes it easier to get at the beans.

Some medicines called **antibiotics** are produced using fermentation reactions (see also page 80). Different antibiotics are made depending on whether we use bacteria or fungi in the fermentation.

 The fermentation of lactose to make lactic acid involves both reduction and oxidation. What other name can we give this reaction?

You need to remember that:

- ▶ Chemical reactions are common in everyday life.
- ▶ Oxidation reactions turn peeled apples brown in air.
- ▶ Glow sticks use chemical reactions to make a dye glow in the dark.
- ▶ Lemon juice is a natural invisible ink. You have to heat the paper to see the secret message!
- ▶ Precipitation reactions make an insoluble product when you mix two solutions.
- ▶ Precipitates make solutions cloudy or opaque.
- ▶ Salts have a pattern of solubility that you can use to predict precipitation reactions.
- ▶ Precipitation reactions can be used to treat water so that it is safe to drink.
- ▶ Fermentation reactions are used to make bread, alcohol and some medicines.
- ▶ Yeast carries out aerobic respiration to turn glucose into carbon dioxide. This is what makes bread rise.
- ▶ Without oxygen, yeast turns glucose into ethanol. This is how wine and beer are made.

Next time »

Unit 13 We have invented new materials by synthesising them in chemical reactions (page 184).

Unit 14 Metal salts burn with different coloured flames and are used to make fireworks for celebrations (page 193).

Previously »

| From page 162 | Chemical changes are usually irreversible and new substances are formed. |
| From page 167 | Hydrocarbon fuels combust to make carbon dioxide and water. |

Unit 13

Resources

Why do we make new materials?

New or synthetic materials can be very useful. Chemical reactions were used to synthesise (make) almost everything you see around you. Plastics are common synthetic materials used to make a huge variety of everyday items, from bottles to mobile phone cases, and from food packaging to CDs. Even some foods we eat are synthetic, like margarine.

Many medicines are synthetic materials and save people's lives every day. They have to be carefully tested though to make sure they are safe and effective.

All these synthetic materials depend upon a supply of natural resources that we are steadily using up. If we are to carry on making all these materials, we need to find ways to reuse them or replace the resources we use up.

In this Unit, you will learn:

- where new chemicals come from;
- about the importance of water and the Sun;
- how photosynthesis works;
- how chemicals make our metabolism work;
- why we have limited resources;
- what sustainable development means.

Key words

metabolic pathway	polymers	reuse
metabolic reactions	raw materials	sustainable development
metabolism	recycling	synthesised
monomers	renewable energy	
photosynthesis	respiration	

Where do new chemicals come from?

Some synthetic materials are entirely invented by humans. Nylon was one of the first synthetic materials. Before 1940, light and tough clothes were often made from silk. Silk is produced naturally by insects, but after World War II silk became rare and more expensive. Nylon was invented as a replacement for silk.

To create tough fibres, nylon is made from a long chain of identical smaller molecules joined end-to-end in a chemical reaction. The building blocks are called **monomers**; the chains are called **polymers**. Polymers are easy to make and have properties that can be used for very different purposes. Nylon has been used for all sorts of things – from toothbrushes and guitar strings to clothes and parachutes.

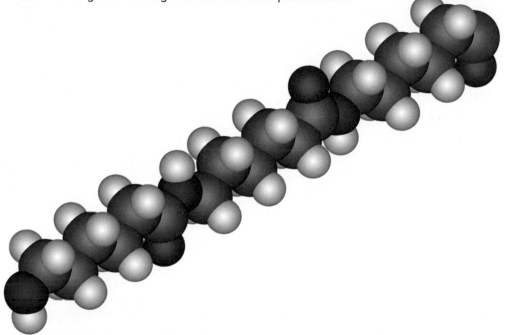

This is what three joined monomers for nylon-6 (a particular type of nylon) look like. Each coloured ball is an atom: carbon atoms are dark grey, hydrogen atoms are almost white, oxygen atoms are red and nitrogen atoms are blue. Hundreds of monomers are joined together in chemical reactions to make one polymer chain.

Some synthetic chemicals are made in nature, and we can't live without many of them:

▶ Our bodies synthesise chemicals in reactions using chemicals from foods and minerals. This enables us to grow and gives us energy. This process is called metabolism.

▶ Plants synthesise new materials in a reaction called photosynthesis, which means 'light building'. The reaction uses energy from sunlight (see page 40).

▶ The bark of a willow tree contains a chemical called salicylic acid. Humans discovered that it eased pain. Although the tree makes this chemical naturally, we have learnt how to synthesise it in factories. We make medicines from it, such as aspirin.

 Find out where your skin comes from, and how your bones are synthesised.

What is photosynthesis?

Plants depend upon the reaction called **photosynthesis** to grow. Plant leaves contain chloroplasts (these make plants green) that act like 'factories' where photosynthesis makes new materials. Sunlight provides the energy to make the reaction happen.

carbon dioxide + water → glucose + oxygen

Plants use the glucose molecules for energy and as the building blocks for all the new materials they need to grow. (There is more about photosynthesis on page 40.) The oxygen that plants make during photosynthesis provides us with what we need to survive as well.

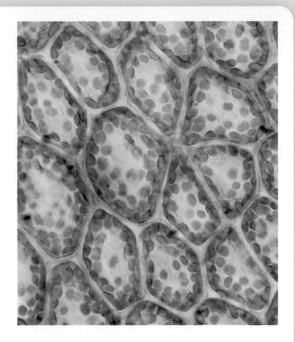

 The formula for glucose is $C_6H_{12}O_6$. See if you can balance this equation for photosynthesis.

$$? CO_2 + ? H_2O \rightarrow C_6H_{12}O_6 + 6O_2$$

What is metabolism?

Animals, including humans, are 'built' from raw materials in a complicated mix of chemical reactions. The reactions inside us are controlled by the cells from which we are made (see page 14). The raw materials we need are broken down from foods (plants and other animals).

New materials are synthesised by combining carbon atoms with other elements like hydrogen, nitrogen and oxygen in different ways. These **metabolic reactions** together form the process called **metabolism**. These reactions allow us to:

- grow;
- reproduce;
- maintain our skin, bones and organs;
- respond to our environment.

There are many different types of metabolic reaction that join up to make a **metabolic pathway**. This means that the products (new materials) **synthesised** in one reaction are used as reactants (raw materials) in the next reaction along the pathway. These reactions all work together in a certain way to produce energy and make all the right materials at the right time. Think of it like the musicians in an orchestra playing together to create a perfect piece of music. It's important that everybody plays the right notes on the right instruments at the right time or all you get is a racket!

How are our resources limited?

Just like any chemical reaction, you need reactants, or **raw materials**, to synthesise products, or new materials.

We use fossil fuels like coal and natural gas to generate electricity to make light and heat. We use oil to produce petrol to run cars. Oil is also used to make plastics and other synthetic materials. These sources of raw materials are not being replaced – it takes millions of years for fossil fuels to form.

 What do you think happens if you use all your raw materials to synthesise new materials?

What kinds of recycling are there?

Our planet provides us with a rich supply of these fossil fuels and other raw materials like plants, animals, oxygen, water and minerals. All these supplies are limited and need to be used carefully to stop them running out. This is why recycling is so important.

We naturally recycle lots of these natural raw materials. We grow plants and breed animals for food. Many of the chemicals involved are recycled naturally as part of the food chain (see page 96). The waste and dead matter decomposes, producing 'new' raw materials like minerals, water and oxygen.

Another kind of recycling that happens all the time is where oxygen produced by plants in photosynthesis is used by humans and animals in **respiration**. The carbon dioxide we produce as a waste product of respiration is then used by plants for photosynthesis.

The problem is that our sources of raw materials are limited. If we use more food than we produce, we get famines. The process of making fossil fuels takes millions of years but we have been using these fuels at a much faster rate than that. For example, more than half of the oil discovered under the North Sea has now been used.

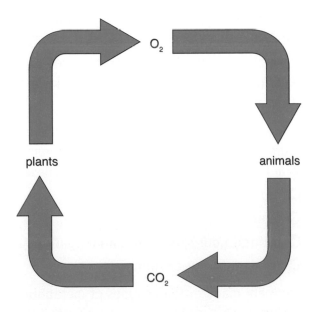

 What things can we do to make our limited supply of raw materials last longer?

Why is sustainable development important?

The resources we use for food, light, heat and making new materials are limited. An important challenge for us is to make sure that we use the resources we need without using them up, or by replacing them. This is called **sustainable development** and we can do this in several ways.

We can reduce the amount of new resources we need by **recycling** materials. More and more materials are now recycled, from plastic and paper to textiles and batteries.

We can also **reuse** objects like electrical devices, bottles and boxes. Before throwing something away, think if it could have another use! Or sell it on to someone who can make use of it.

List some materials that are collected for recycling. What are they recycled into?

Why is renewable energy important?

We have used fossil fuels as a source of energy for many years and we know these resources are running out. We can stop this happening by using less and making our supplies last longer. We can also find new **renewable energy** sources. The wind, Sun and sea are the main sources of renewable energy that are starting to be used.

The way we live makes enormous differences to the world around us. Burning fossil fuels not only uses up those resources, it also produces huge amounts of carbon dioxide gas. This is bad for the environment:

▶ it can make rain more acidic, so that it damages buildings and prevents crops from growing well;

▶ it contributes to changing our climate, through global warming.

We will learn more about acid rain and global warming, and ways to control them, on page 206.

Plastics contain long-chain molecules called polymers that are traditionally made from crude oil, which is a non-renewable resource. Many scientists are investigating how other resources can be used to make plastics.

Did you know that a plastic can be made from milk? Milk is warmed (but not boiled) and a particular amount of vinegar is added. When lumps start to appear the heat is turned off. Once the mixture has cooled, the lumps are sieved out and they can be moulded into different shapes.

The polymer is the protein in milk, called casein, which precipitates when it reacts with the acidic vinegar. Unfortunately, the polymer decomposes, so the plastic does not last long.

Research and describe three uses of plastics with a short lifespan.

You need to remember that:

- ▶ New materials are synthesised in chemical reactions.
- ▶ Some everyday materials like nylon and plastics are entirely synthesised by processes we have invented.
- ▶ Plants and animals synthesise the materials they need for growth and survival by reactions such as photosynthesis and metabolic reactions.
- ▶ Many of the chemicals synthesised in nature are combinations of the elements carbon, hydrogen, nitrogen and oxygen.
- ▶ Our supplies of raw materials like fossil fuels are limited.
- ▶ Sustainable development means recycling materials or using them carefully to prevent supplies running out.
- ▶ Wind, tidal and solar power are sources of renewable energy.

Next time ≫

Unit 14   Fossil fuels like coal, oil and gas are burned to make energy (page 190).

Unit 16   Water is recycled in the water cycle (page 205).

Previously »

From page 130 — Exothermic reactions give out heat energy, endothermic reactions take in heat energy from the surroundings.

From page 184 — Many of the chemicals synthesised in nature are combinations of the elements carbon, hydrogen, nitrogen and oxygen.

Unit 14

Making use of chemistry

How is chemistry useful?

As humans have evolved they have learnt to control chemical reactions and use them to their advantage. We use our knowledge of chemistry in making light and heat, and in preparing food so that it is safe and edible. We use chemical reactions to make medicines that save lives and make life more comfortable for millions of people every day. We can even have some fun with chemistry by making fireworks, but that's best left to the experts!

In this Unit, you will learn:

- ▷ about burning fuels for energy;
- ▷ about synthetic medicines;
- ▷ about chemistry in cooking;
- ▷ how chemical reactions are used in fireworks.

Key words

aspirin	hydrocarbons
baking powder	hydrogen
biodiesels	landfill gas
biofuels	non-renewable resources
fireworks	renewable resources
flame test	synthetic medicines
fossil fuels	

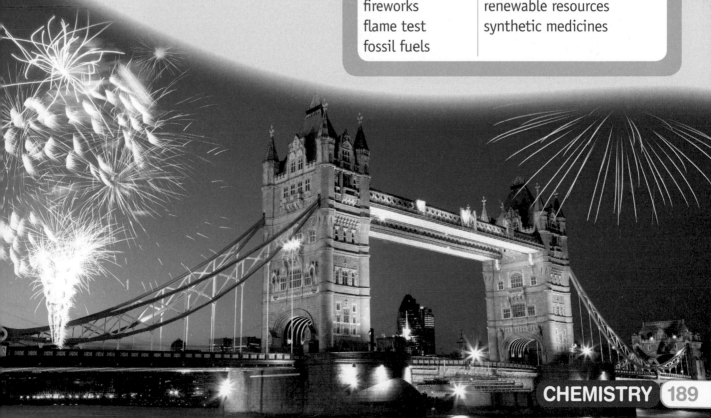

What are hydrocarbons?

Fuels are burnt to release energy we can use. There are many types of fuels, but many fuels are formed from molecules that contain just hydrogen and carbon atoms. These are called **hydrocarbons**, and a lot of the hydrocarbon fuels we use come from the remains of dead animals and plants that lived hundreds of millions of years ago (see page 167). Examples of these **'fossil fuels'** are petrol, natural gas, oil and coal.

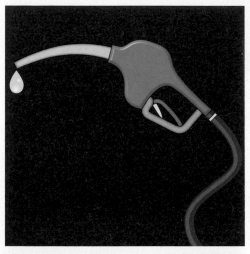 

 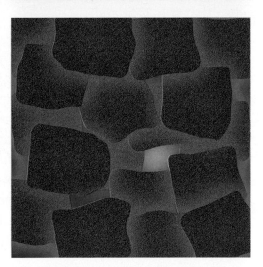

Eventually these fuels will run out, so they are called **non-renewable resources**. There is a lot of scientific effort going on to look for **renewable resources** of energy, which we can replace easily or which we can always depend upon (like the wind).

When hydrocarbons are burnt they form carbon dioxide gas. As we have burnt so much fuel over hundreds of years, we have added huge amounts of carbon dioxide to the air. Over time, this has led to global warming (see page 207). We are changing our climate, which could cause us problems across the whole world, like rising sea levels. This is another reason why we are looking for other sources of energy.

? Natural gas mostly contains methane. Methane has no smell. Find out why the natural gas we use in our homes has a smell.

How can we use pure hydrogen?

Hydrogen can be used as a fuel that is more environmentally friendly than hydrocarbons. When hydrogen is burnt, it reacts with oxygen to form water vapour, and gives out energy in the form of heat. No carbon dioxide is made.

hydrogen + oxygen → water
$$2H_2 + O_2 \rightarrow 2H_2O$$

The products of the reaction are more environmentally friendly, but hydrogen has to be stored and used carefully because it can explode.

Space rockets use hydrogen as a fuel. For example, the Space Shuttle carried a huge tank that held liquid hydrogen, but also liquid oxygen because there is no oxygen in space.

1 Find out the boiling points of hydrogen and oxygen. How were they kept as liquids in the external tank on the Space Shuttle?

2 Is the reaction between hydrogen and oxygen endothermic or exothermic? Explain your evidence.

What are biofuels?

Biofuels are a renewable source of energy, formed from the natural decay of plants, animals and our own rubbish. We are developing new ways of using our waste materials to make energy. For example, when our dustbins are emptied, a lot of our rubbish goes to landfill sites where it is buried. The rubbish starts to decompose and **landfill gas** is produced. Landfill gas is mainly carbon dioxide and methane, which can be burnt to make heat or electricity.

methane + oxygen → carbon dioxide + water + energy
$$CH_4 + 2O_2 \rightarrow CO_2 + 2H_2O$$

It is still more effective and friendly to the environment to reuse or recycle our waste (see page 186), but for the rubbish that can't be recycled, biofuels are useful products.

What sort of chemical is methane? (Hint: which elements does methane contain?)

Did you know that chip fat is also a good source of energy? **Biodiesels** are an alternative to fossil fuels. They are made from animal or vegetable fats. The fat is collected and turned into biodiesel by a chemical reaction with alcohol.

When biodiesel is burnt as a fuel it produces water and carbon dioxide, as well as heat. It makes much less carbon dioxide than hydrocarbons, so biodiesel is less environmentally damaging. Biodiesel can be used to run cars but it might make your car smell like the fish and chip shop that the fuel originally came from!

? **Research two other sources of biofuels. What are the advantages and disadvantages of producing and using them?**

How does chemistry help us produce medicines?

About 2400 years ago an ancient Greek called Hippocrates wrote about using a powder made from the bark and leaves of willow trees to treat pains and fever. He didn't know it, but he was using the medicine we now call **aspirin**. Since Hippocrates, we have worked out which particular chemical in the bark has the medical effect. We now synthesise aspirin and make pills so we don't have to eat willow bark!

If you have ever been given any medicine by your doctor, it was almost certainly made in a factory by a chemical reaction. Today we have **synthetic medicines** available to treat all sorts of diseases. We also have vaccines that can stop us getting diseases like measles, chicken pox and mumps in the first place. Most of these are now synthesised chemically, so that it is easier to make the quantities we need, and for us to take the right amounts.

What does chemistry do for cooking? @

Cooking is just chemistry! Chemical reactions are involved in making many of the foods we eat:

- ▶ making bread rise;
- ▶ making cakes light;
- ▶ making meat edible.

Yeast makes bread rise because it ferments sugar into alcohol and carbon dioxide (see page 181).

Cakes are light because of a reaction between **baking powder** (sodium bicarbonate) and cream of tartar (sodium aluminium sulfate). When a liquid is added to these two chemicals a reaction happens that releases bubbles of carbon dioxide. The bubbles are trapped in the cake mixture as it bakes, making the cake light and airy. If you forget to put the baking powder in, you get something more like a biscuit!

Most foods are cooked before we eat them. This is because it makes things softer, tastier and easier to eat. Raw meat would be very tough, not to mention not very tasty! Cooking meat changes the molecules that make it so that they are less tough. It also kills any bacteria that would make us ill.

 Investigate some other types of chemical reactions that happen in cooking.

How do we make fireworks? @

Fireworks are used to celebrate all sorts of occasions all over the world. The Chinese first used firecrackers that sparkled and sizzled in about 200 BC. (Fireworks were found accidentally by Chinese alchemists looking for a potion to give eternal life. The results of experiments can be very surprising.) Later, mixtures of sulfur-containing compounds were packed into bamboo tubes and the first fireworks were invented.

These days you can go to impressive fireworks displays with all sorts of amazing sights and sounds, but have you ever wondered how we get all the different colours?

What is the flame test?

Metal salts burn with different coloured flames. Pyrotechnicians (fire scientists) have been trying to find new and wonderful colours ever since the first fireworks were discovered. Here are some of the metal salts used to make the colours of fireworks.

This property of metal salts is also useful for working out what elements are used to make things. This is called the **flame test**.

Flame colour	Metal salt
red	strontium or lithium
orange	calcium
yellow	sodium
green	barium
blue	copper
indigo	caesium
violet	potassium

 Many fireworks also need to be launched high into the air. They contain fuels that give off oxygen. The oxygen reacts with carbon or sulfur to produce hot gases that push the firework into the air. Write equations for the combustion of:
(i) carbon and (ii) sulfur.

You need to remember that:

- As humans have evolved they have learned to control chemical reactions and use them to their advantage.
- Fossil fuels like coal, oil and gas are burned to release energy we can use.
- Fossil fuels are non-renewable sources of energy.
- Biofuels like landfill gas and biodiesels are being developed as renewable sources of energy.
- Synthetic medicines are used to prevent and cure many diseases.
- Cooking is chemistry – chemical reactions make food taste good and safe to eat.
- Metal salts burn with different coloured flames and are used to make fireworks for celebrations.

Next time ≫

Unit 16 Some human activities produce unwanted chemical reactions that damage the environment (page 203).

Unit 16 The burning of fossil fuels is helping to speed up global warming (page 206).

Previously 》》

Remember · We can group rocks based on their characteristics.

From page 173 · The strength of acids and alkalis is measured using the pH scale.

Unit 15

Rocks and weathering

What reactions form the landscape?

There are different types of rocks that are formed by different physical and chemical processes. Each type of rock can be identified by its particular properties. We use the properties of stone to construct buildings and for carving statues. Molten rock cools when it erupts from a volcano and solidifies to make a mountain. Rocks can also be made from tiny skeletons of sea creatures that lived millions of years ago. Rocks break down over long periods of time and are recycled too!

In this Unit, you will learn:

- ▶ how to describe the characteristics of groups of rocks;
- ▶ about rock formation and weathering;
- ▶ about the processes of the rock cycle.

Key words

acid rain	igneous rock	porous rocks
biological weathering	lava	rock cycle
chalk	layers	sediment
chemical weathering	lithification	sedimentary rock
compression	marble	slate
crystals	metamorphic rock	strata
deposited	minerals	transported
erosion	non-porous rocks	weathering
evaporates	onion-skin weathering	
freeze–thaw weathering	physical weathering	

What are rocks made of?

You might think that rock is just rock, but you'd be wrong! Rocks are made of mixtures of solid compounds called **minerals**. Minerals occur naturally as **crystals**.

There are three types of rock. Each type has particular properties.

What is sedimentary rock?

Sedimentary rock is usually soft and crumbly and made of grains that are stuck together. The **sediment** that makes this type of rock contains fragments of larger rocks. Sediment forms **layers** at the bottom of lakes or seas over millions of years. You can see these layers clearly in the rocks at the Grand Canyon in the USA.

Did you know that **chalk** is a sedimentary rock made from the microscopic skeletons of marine plants and animals called plankton?

 The table shows four types of sedimentary rock. Copy and complete the table for each type of rock by researching one place where it can be found and one use we have found for it.

Type of sedimentary rock	Place it can be found	Use
chalk	White Cliffs of Dover, UK	by farmers to raise the pH of acid soils
limestone		
sandstone		
shale		

What is metamorphic rock?

Metamorphic rock is made from interlocking crystals. It is usually hard, smooth and shiny. This type of rock is formed when existing rocks are affected by high temperature or pressure. **Marble** is a metamorphic rock made from limestone (calcium carbonate). It contains medium-sized crystals that don't have a particular arrangement. Marble has been used for building and sculptures for thousands of years. It's so hardwearing that the Parthenon in Athens is still standing and it's nearly 3000 years old!

Slate is a metamorphic rock that is quite different because it is made from layers of interlocking crystals that lie in one direction. This is why slate can easily be split along the line of crystals to make roof tiles.

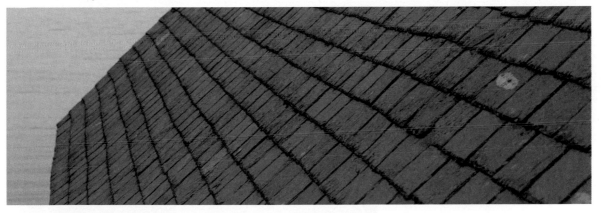

? The table shows three types of metamorphic rock. Copy and complete the table for each type of rock by researching one place where it can be found and one use we have found for it. See if you can find close-up pictures of each rock.

Type of metamorphic rock	Place it can be found	Use
slate		
marble		
gneiss		

What is igneous rock?

Igneous rock is also made from interlocking crystals that form when molten (liquid) rock cools down and solidifies. These rocks are very hard to break. Granite is a type of igneous rock that can be used as a kitchen work surface because it is hard to scratch.

The table shows three types of igneous rock. Copy and complete the table for each type of rock by researching one place where it can be found and one use we have found for it. See if you can find close-up pictures of each rock.

Type of igneous rock	Place it can be found	Use
granite		
basalt		
obsidian		

Which rocks allow water through?

The grains in **porous rocks** are rounded and don't interlock. Gaps between the grains let the water in.

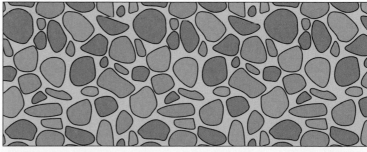

porous

The interlocking crystals in **non-porous rocks** rocks don't have any gaps between them so water can't get in.

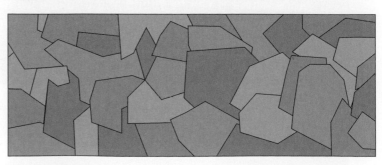

non-porous

How do rocks change over time?

Rocks gradually wear away. This is called **weathering** because it is caused mainly by changes in the weather. There are three types of weathering: physical, chemical and biological.

The other way in which rocks change is called erosion. This is where water, ice or the wind carries pieces of rock away. Humans can also cause erosion.

How does physical weathering work? @ ⇄

Physical weathering happens because of changes in temperature that break down the rock. **Freeze–thaw weathering** happens when water inside a crack freezes and expands. The pressure caused by this forces the rock apart, so the crack gets bigger and eventually the rock splits. Over thousands of years, a mountain can be broken into millions of tiny fragments.

Onion-skin weathering happens because of large changes in the temperature between the day and the night. During the day, rock expands slightly as it heats up. At night, the temperature falls and, as the rock cools, it contracts. Eventually, this can cause the outer layer of the rock to peel away like the skin of an onion.

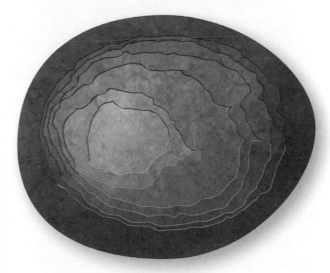

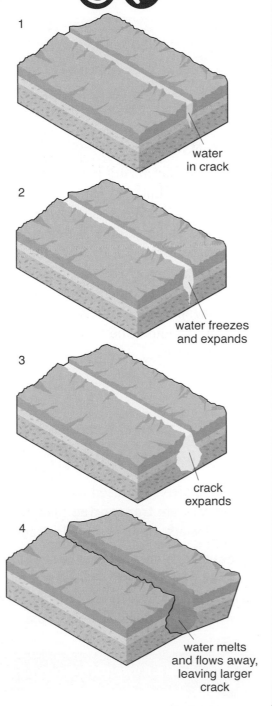

1 water in crack

2 water freezes and expands

3 crack expands

4 water melts and flows away, leaving larger crack

? Name one kind of rock that is softer and would wear away more quickly.

How does chemical weathering work?

Chemical weathering happens because rain is naturally acidic. Air contains a small amount of carbon dioxide that dissolves in rain to make a weak acid, called carbonic acid (H_2CO_3). The pH of rain is reduced further when pollutants like sulfur dioxide and nitric oxide are dissolved. It is now called **acid rain**. If acid rain falls on rocks like limestone, which contain metal carbonates, a chemical reaction occurs and the rock dissolves. You can often see this effect on carvings and statues.

 What other types of rock contain carbonates and would be vulnerable to acid rain?

How does biological weathering work?

Biological weathering is caused by animals and plants. For example, rabbits burrow underground causing weak rocks to break up and tree roots can grow into the cracks in the rocks. The crack widens as the root grows and eventually the rock splits and smaller rocks may fall away. This is one reason why trees shouldn't be planted too close to houses.

What is erosion?

Erosion is often confused with weathering, so beware! **Erosion** is when the pieces of broken rock are **transported** (moved away) – usually by wind or water, or even moving ice in glaciers. Humans can also cause erosion.

For example, a cliff next to the sea is affected by the water and the waves. Pieces of rock fall away from the cliff. These are then transported out to sea by the movements of the waves. The rocks on the sea bed are gradually worn away as they crash against each other. Slowly, smaller and smaller rocks are formed. The sand on beaches is formed in this way.

 Explain the difference between weathering and erosion.

How are rocks formed?

Rocks change from one type to another over long periods of time in a kind of natural recycling process called the **rock cycle.**

❶ Igneous rocks are formed from molten (liquid) rock called magma that is deep underground. This is what you see when a volcano erupts. When molten rock reaches the surface of the Earth it is called **lava**. The lava cools as it gets nearer the surface and crystals are formed.

The size of the crystals depends on the speed of cooling. If it cools quickly, the rock will be made of small crystals but if it cools slowly, the crystals are large. Lava is also full of volcanic gases, so igneous rock that are formed in this way, like pumice stone, are full of holes where the gas bubbles were. These rocks never contain fossils because the heat of the molten rock would destroy the plants or animals rather than preserving them.

❷ Igneous and metamorphic rocks break down into smaller particles when they are exposed to weathering and erosion. The particles are transported to another place by wind and water and form sedimentary rocks.

❸ Sedimentary rocks often contain fossils. These are the remains of dead plants or animals that were covered by sediment before they decomposed. We can use our knowledge of what animals and plants lived when to work out when the rock formed.

❹ Layers of sediment can also be formed when water that contains dissolved salts evaporates. These minerals, such as 'rock salt' (halite), are called **evaporates**.

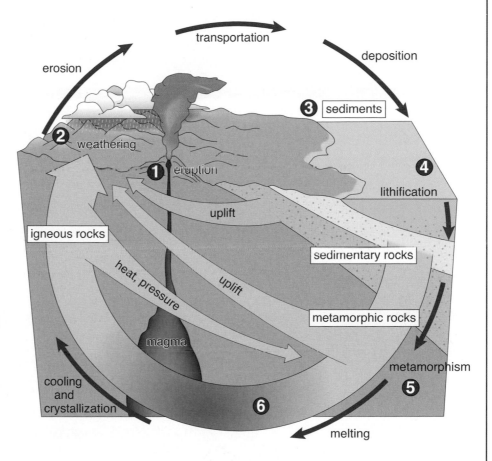

❺ Igneous and sedimentary rocks can be changed by heat or pressure. The minerals and crystals in these rocks are rearranged to form new, metamorphic rocks. Metamorphosis means 'changing from one thing to another'. You occasionally find fossils in metamorphic rock, but they are deformed (changed) by the same heat and pressure that cause metamorphosis. If the heat or pressure changes are too high, the fossils are completely destroyed.

❻ Metamorphic rocks, deep underground, can melt. If this molten rock cools, it becomes igneous rock and the whole rock cycle starts again!

 Explain why it is pointless to search for new sources of fuels like oil or gas in granite mountains.

As sedimentary rocks form, particles are deposited (laid down) over long periods of time. These layers of sediment are called strata. As time goes by, more strata form, so the oldest layers are at the bottom of the rock. These oldest layers have all the water squeezed out by compression – the weight of the layers above causes high pressure. This process is called lithification.

Lithification makes the particles of sediment stick together like cement, leaving solid minerals within the layers. Dead plants and animals that settle along with the sediment form hard fossils or liquid oil due to the same compression.

? Draw a diagram showing how sedimentary rocks form. Use your diagram to explain how the strata can give us clues about the age of rocks or fossils. What other methods can we use to work out the age?

You need to remember that:

- ◉ Rocks are made from minerals that may form crystals.
- ◉ There are three main types of rocks: sedimentary, metamorphic and igneous.
- ◉ Sedimentary rocks are formed over millions of years when mineral particles collect at the bottom of lakes or seas.
- ◉ Metamorphic rocks are formed when other types of rock are changed by heat or pressure.
- ◉ Igneous rocks are formed when molten rock from inside the Earth cools.
- ◉ Fossils form when dead plants and animals settle into the layers that form sedimentary rocks.
- ◉ Weathering occurs when rocks wear away due to physical, chemical or biological processes.
- ◉ Erosion occurs when pieces of rock are carried away by the wind, water, ice or humans.
- ◉ The rock cycle shows how the formation, weathering and erosion of rocks link together.

Next time »

(Unit 16) Soil is a mixture of rock fragments, humus, water, air and living things (page 204).

(Unit 16) Acid rain is caused by pollution and damages the environment (page 206).

Previously »

From page 190   Non-renewable fossil fuels like coal, oil and gas are burned to release energy we can use.

From page 200   Weathering occurs when rocks wear away due to physical, chemical or biological processes.

Unit 16

Chemistry and the environment

Why are soil and the environment important?

The surface of the Earth is covered in rocks and mountains but is also covered in soil. Soils are different in different areas, but why? It all depends on the plants, animals and rocks in the environment. All these factors work together to make the soil we need to grow crops and feed animals. We need water too, and like rock, nature recycles water so we don't run out!

The environment depends on a natural balance of all these reactions. This balance is upset by many human activities. The effects on the world we live in can be dramatic! It's important to understand how these things happen so that they can be prevented.

In this Unit, you will learn:

- about the types and properties of soil;
- how soil is formed;
- about the water cycle;
- how chemical reactions and pollution affect the environment.

Key words

acid rain	humus
climate	organic materials
condenses	pollutants
evaporates	precipitation
global warming	transpiration
greenhouse effect	water cycle
greenhouse gases	weather

What is soil?

Plants need soil to grow but what is soil made from?

Soil is a mixture of:

- decaying **organic materials** (plant and animal), called **humus**;
- fragments of weathered rock;
- water;
- air;
- living things like earthworms, bacteria and fungi.

The organic matter in soil is decomposed by bacteria and fungi to release minerals that can be used by new plants. Earthworms help improve the quality of the soil by dragging the organic material from the surface down to the lower layers.

Soil provides plants with water and nutrients for growth. Plants take these up by their roots that are anchored in the soil.

What types of soil are there? @

Soils have different properties in different areas. This affects how good the soil is for growing plants so it's very important for farmers to know about soil quality. Soil quality is affected by:

- The amount of humus. Plants grow best in soil that contains a lot of humus.

- The type and size of the weathered rocks. This can affect how well the soil drains away rain water.

- The type of minerals. Some soil has a lot of clay, so it is sticky when you dig it. Other soil can have a lot of iron. This type of soil looks quite red. The type of mineral can also affect the pH of the soil. For example, if soil contains a lot of the base, calcium oxide (lime), it will be very alkaline. Farmers can add a type of acid to the soil to change the pH to suit the type plants they are growing.

Sand, loam and clay soils.

Iron-rich desert soil.

 Describe some ways in which you could improve the quality of soil.

What is the water cycle? @ ⇄

Have you ever thought about where the rain comes from or where the water in rivers goes? Water never stops moving and is constantly recycled. This process is called the **water cycle** and without it we'd run out of water very quickly!

When rain or snow falls, this is called **precipitation**. Rain and melted snow run off the surface of the ground and fill the lakes and rivers, which eventually flow into the sea. Water **evaporates** when the temperature is high enough. Water is released by plants too in a process called **transpiration**. As the water vapour rises into the sky it makes clouds. When the water vapour cools down, it **condenses** and falls as rain (or snow if it's cold enough) and the whole cycle begins again.

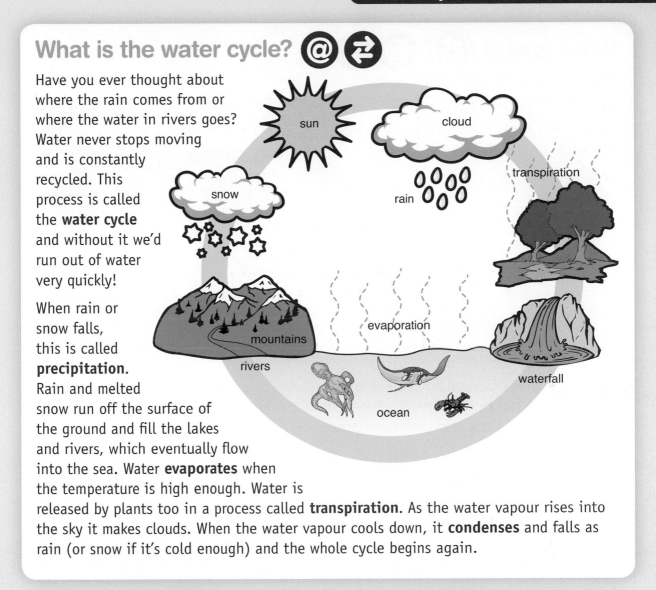

sun

cloud

snow

rain

transpiration

mountains

rivers

evaporation

ocean

waterfall

How do chemical reactions affect the environment? @ ⇄

People have a dramatic effect on the environment. Carbon dioxide is produced by animals when they breathe. Plants use the carbon dioxide for photosynthesis and produce oxygen. The balance of this cycle has been upset by human activities such as cutting down forests and burning fossil fuels. Fewer trees means less oxygen and burning fossil fuels like coal, oil and natural gas, produces different types of gases that pollute the atmosphere. **Pollutants** change the way plants and animals live and may even alter the landscape around us.

Chemical reactions can have good and bad effects on the planet. Draw up a table listing six chemical reactions we use every day or in industry, and list one good and one bad effect of each.

What is acid rain?

Pollution can make rain even more acidic.

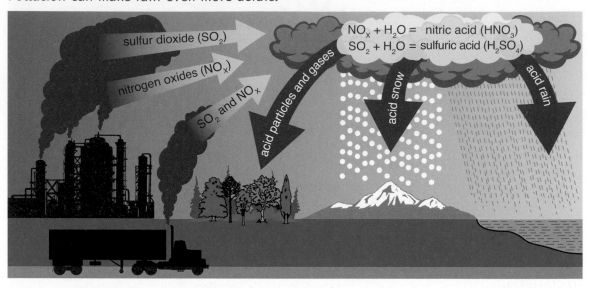

sulfur dioxide (SO_2)

nitrogen oxides (NO_x)

SO_2 and NO_x

acid particles and gases

$NO_x + H_2O =$ nitric acid (HNO_3)
$SO_2 + H_2O =$ sulfuric acid (H_2SO_4)

acid snow

acid rain

Sulfur dioxide is produced by burning fossil fuels that also contain small amounts of sulfur. Car exhaust fumes contain nitric oxide. These gases dissolve in rain to make sulfuric acid and nitric acid. These are strong acids that lower the pH of the rain.

Acid rain has many damaging effects on the environment:

- ► rivers, lakes and streams become more acidic so plants and animals can't live in them;
- ► strong acids speed up chemical weathering of rocks, buildings and statues;
- ► soil becomes acidic so trees and plants can't grow;
- ► acid rain damages trees by destroying the waxy coating on leaves.

Being environmentally friendly means finding ways to reduce or prevent the effects of pollution like acid rain. How can this be done?

Governments all over the world are working to reduce the amount of pollutants produced by industrial processes that involve burning fossil fuels. Sulfur dioxide can be removed from oil and natural gas before they are burnt. Power stations can have filters called 'scrubbers' that remove the sulfur dioxide from the exhaust gases.

? Gases produced by power stations in the UK tend to affect the environment of countries to the east and north of the UK. Explain why this is.

What is the greenhouse effect?

The greenhouse effect is a natural process that helps living things to survive on Earth. A layer of carbon dioxide and other **greenhouse gases** like methane surrounds the Earth. The Sun heats the Earth up and this layer of gases acts as a blanket that reflects the heat back to Earth to keep the heat in. This **greenhouse effect** happens normally and without it the world would be a *much* colder place! So, normally, the greenhouse effect on Earth is a good thing.

Sun

carbon dioxide and other gases in the atmosphere trap heat, keeping the Earth warm

Earth

What is global warming?

Normally, the Earth's temperature on average stays about the same from year to year. Over many hundreds or thousands of years, we know that the average temperature rises or falls very slowly. We know this because we can examine rocks, fossils, ice and plants and tell how warm the Earth was when they formed.

In the last hundred years or so, scientists have noticed that the Earth's average temperature is rising more quickly than we think has happened before. **Global warming** is the name we give to this process. We think that this is because the mixture of greenhouse gases is changing, so that the greenhouse effect is getting stronger.

How might we be causing global warming?

One of the main gases that helps make the Earth warmer is carbon dioxide. As we burn fuels and cut down large areas of forests, the proportion of carbon dioxide in the air increases.

The air we breathe is an interesting mix of gases.

Gas	Percentage of the air (approximate)
nitrogen	78.1%
oxygen	20.9%
argon	0.95%
carbon dioxide	0.04%
other gases like helium, neon, methane, hydrogen	0.01%

 Add up the percentages in the table and make sure they total 100.0%.

It only takes small changes in the amount of carbon dioxide compared to nitrogen or oxygen to change how much heat is reflected back to Earth by the greenhouse effect. So we think that our burning of fossil fuels to make carbon dioxide has been a big factor in causing global warming.

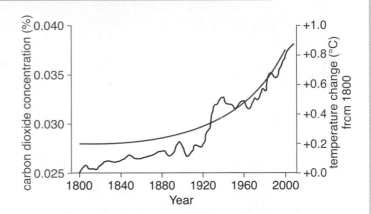

 Describe some of the effects that global warming is having on our planet.

What is climate change?

It's important to remember that **weather** means the rainfall, temperature and sunshine that we get on any one day in a particular place. The **climate** is something different – it is the average of many days or years of these measurements, over a wider area. We can measure over time that our climate has been changing, and generally getting warmer in the last 150 years or so. But just because our climate is changing, does not mean that every day of weather will be warmer and drier!

 People often complain that their summer weather has been wetter and colder, so they think global warming isn't happening. Write an explanation to them of why global warming is happening, and the difference between climate and weather.

You may have heard some people saying that global warming is a natural process and that we are not causing it. The problem is that the atmosphere is huge and it is impossible to measure every small part of it all the time. So we have to add together billions of measurements and take averages. This makes it very difficult to be absolutely certain that any one thing is a cause of global warming.

The amount of heat the Sun gives out changes from year to year and over longer periods of time, so this is also affecting the Earth's temperature. It is also possible that the Earth has heated up in this way millions of years ago. Of course, humans were not around to measure it then, so we can only make our best guess about what the temperature was based on evidence from old rocks, ice, fossils and plants.

One thing is for certain: humans are burning fuels and cutting down trees much faster than has happened ever before. So we are fairly sure we are increasing the amount of carbon dioxide in the atmosphere faster than happens naturally. And unless nature has a way of balancing out this increase, we are changing the world around us.

? Investigate some of the possible effects of global warming. You could talk about:
- sea levels;
- effects on ice at the Earth's poles;
- extreme weather events.

You need to remember that:

- Soil is a mixture of decayed organic material called humus, rock fragments, water, air and living organisms like bacteria and fungi.
- Soil provides plants with water and nutrients for growth.
- Organic matter is decomposed by bacteria and fungi.
- Earthworms improve the quality of soil by dragging organic material to lower layers.
- Soils have different properties in different areas.
- Soil quality depends on factors like the amount of humus, the type of rock fragments, the amount of water and the pH.
- Water is recycled in the water cycle. Water evaporates to form clouds and condenses to form rain and snow (precipitation) which falls back to the ground where it can evaporate again.
- Acid rain is caused by pollution and damages the environment.
- The greenhouse effect is where some gases in the atmosphere keep the Earth warm.
- We have measured the average temperature of the Earth and it is rising faster than normal. We call this global warming.

Introducing Physics

The science of physics is the investigation of matter and energy – it's all about how things work. Those 'things' can be as small as particles called electrons, or as big as the entire Universe! To some people, physics seems like something that doesn't happen to them every day. But in fact, physics and physicists affect all of us, every second of every day. For example, the World Wide Web was invented because of a physics experiment, by the physicist Tim Berners-Lee.

Why do energy and matter, matter?

This book talks about a wide range of different topics:

- ▶ forces
- ▶ energy
- ▶ sound
- ▶ electricity
- ▶ machines
- ▶ light
- ▶ magnetism
- ▶ astronomy

To start with, these may seem like separate topics but, the more you study the subject, the more you will discover how they all fit together.

For example, what have magnets got to do with electricity? In Unit 6, you will learn how to make a magnet using electricity. If you continue to study physics, you will learn how to make electricity using a magnet.

Physics can help us to see the wonder of everything around us.

- ▶ Microscopes can show us the tiniest particles of matter.
- ▶ Telescopes, spacecraft and particle accelerators reveal the nature of the Universe and tell us how everything started.
- ▶ Did you know that the Sun burns up 4 200 000 000 kg of matter every second? This is about the same as the mass of everyone living in the UK!

What do physicists do?

Physics is not just fascinating, it's useful too. There are many jobs that require an understanding of physics.

- ▶ Engineers use physics when they design, make, operate and maintain machinery.
- ▶ Electronics has brought us radio, television, phones and computers.
- ▶ In hospitals, doctors use radioactivity, ultrasound and X-rays to see inside patients.
- ▶ Athletes use equipment and clothing designed in laboratories.

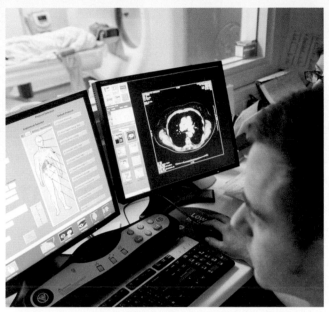

A medical physicist watches as a patient has an X-ray scan.

What will you see?

In this book, we will explore and investigate matter and energy, and how it all works. We will look at:

- ▶ What forces and energy are, and how we can find and use them.
- ▶ What sound and light are made from, and how they behave.
- ▶ How electricity and magnetism work, and what we can use them for.
- ▶ How we live on a planet, orbiting a star, in a galaxy of billions of stars, in a Universe of billions of galaxies.
- ▶ How scientists create theories and laws to explain how the Universe works.
- ▶ How we can predict things, and carry out experiments to test if we are right.

In 1964, physicists produced a theory explaining why everything has mass. In 2012, this particle explosion at CERN revealed what we think is the 'Higgs boson', a particle that confirms this theory.

Previously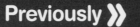

Remember | When things speed up, slow down or change direction, there is a cause.

Unit 1

Describing movement

How can we describe how an object moves?

All day long, we move around. We see other people moving. Cars, trucks and planes move.

Beyond the Earth, planets orbit the Sun. And the whole Solar System itself is moving through space at about 250 kilometres each second!

In this Unit, you will learn:

- ▷ how to measure time and distance;
- ▷ how to calculate speed;
- ▷ how to draw graphs to represent movement;
- ▷ the meaning of 'accelerating'.

Key words

accelerating	gradient
average speed	light gate
distance	speed
distance–time graph	time

How can we record movement?

If you move while someone takes a photo of you, the photo may be blurred. The faster you move, the more blurred it will be.

Some types of speed camera take two photos of a car, one quickly after the other. A fast car moves a greater distance in the time between the two photos.

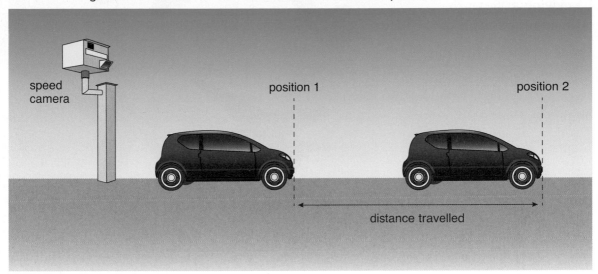

In the lab, we can use a ticker timer to record the movement of a car or trolley.

▶ The timer marks dots on the tape at regular intervals.

▶ If the car is going fast, the dots will be far apart.

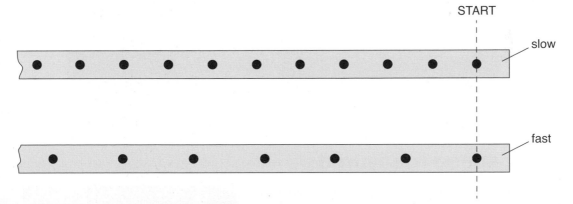

Photography helped scientists to understand how things move. Our eyes aren't quick enough to see what's going on, but lots of photos taken in quick succession show us how objects move and change. Science often makes progress when new instruments and techniques are invented.

? **Find out what Eadweard Muybridge's photographs revealed about how horses gallop.**

What is speed?

The **speed** of an object tells us how fast it is moving. The speedometer of a car shows its speed – it might be moving at 50 km/h (kilometres per hour).

Speed is defined like this:

$$\text{speed} = \frac{\text{distance travelled}}{\text{time taken}}$$

or simply,

$$\text{speed} = \frac{\text{distance}}{\text{time}}$$

The units of speed are:

m/s (metres per second)

Speed can also be measured in these other units:

km/h (kilometres per hour)
mph (miles per hour)

Put these things in order, from slowest to fastest:
- a space rocket
- a snail
- a fast car
- an aircraft
- a sprinter
- a toddler

How is speed measured?

To find how fast an object is moving, we measure two quantities:

- the **distance** it moves (in m);
- the **time** it takes (in s).

Then we calculate speed using $\text{speed} = \frac{\text{distance}}{\text{time}}$

For example, if a car travels 320 m in 20 s:

$$\text{speed} = \frac{\text{distance}}{\text{time}} = \frac{320}{20} = 16 \text{ m/s}$$

A bird flies 320 m in 40 s. What is its speed?

How do we measure distance and time?

Imagine that you want to find the speed of someone running on the school field.

▶ Mark points A and B, about 100 m apart. Measure the distance from A to B using a tape measure.

▶ Use a stopwatch. Start the watch when the runner passes point A, stop it when they pass point B.

Now you can calculate their **average speed** over this distance. (It's the average because their speed may have varied during the run.)

Some speed cameras work in the same way:

▶ a car passes over two detectors buried in the road;

▶ an electronic timer starts as the car passes over the first detector;

▶ the timer stops as it passes over the second detector;

▶ a computer calculates the car's speed.

If the car is travelling too fast, the camera takes a photograph of it.

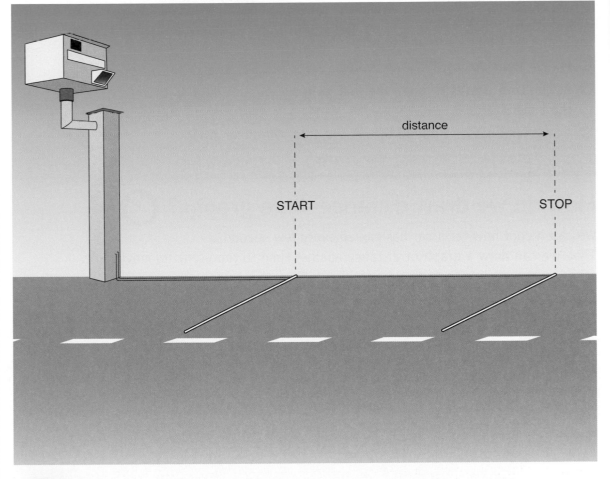

 A car takes 4.0 s to travel 50 m. Calculate its speed. If the speed limit is 13 m/s, is it travelling too fast?

How do we measure speed in the lab?

You can find the speed of a moving trolley using a ticker timer.

- ◐ Choose two marks on the tape. Measure the distance between them.
- ◐ Calculate the time interval between the two marks. To do this, you need to know that each gap on the tape represents 0.02 s.

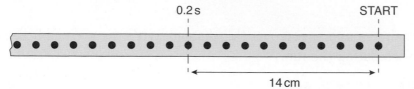

0.2 s   START

14 cm

 A trolley moves 14 cm in 0.2 s. Calculate its average speed.

Alternatively, you can use two light gates. A **light gate** has an invisible beam; when the beam is broken, an electronic timer starts or stops.

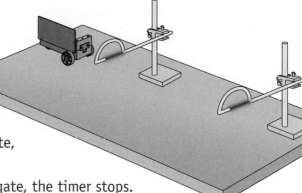

- ◐ Fix an 'interrupt card' to the trolley.
- ◐ As the card passes through the first gate, the timer starts.
- ◐ As the card passes through the second gate, the timer stops.

How do we draw distance–time graphs?

We can record how far a car has moved every few seconds.
Then we can draw a graph of distance against time to represent its movement.

A **distance–time graph** has:

- ◐ distance on the y-axis
- ◐ time on the x-axis.

Time (s)	Distance (m)
0	0
4	24
8	48
12	72
16	96
20	120

distance (m)

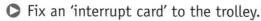

time (s)

 How far had the car travelled after 10 s? How long did it take to travel 90 m?

What do distance–time graphs tell us?

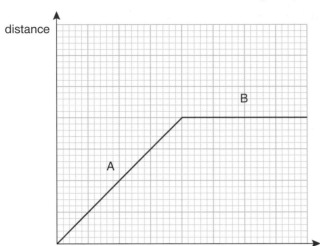

distance

B

A

time

▶ **Section A:** The graph is sloping upwards. The distance is increasing at a steady rate. The car is moving at a steady speed.

▶ **Section B:** The graph is flat (horizontal). The distance is not increasing. The car is stationary. It has stopped; it is not moving.

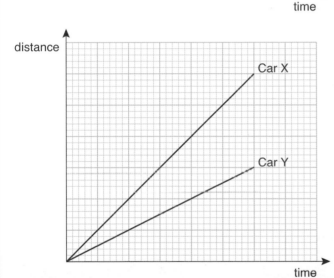

distance

Car X

Car Y

time

The steepness of the graph tells us how fast something is moving.

▶ The graph for Car X is steeper than the graph for Car Y.

▶ Car X is travelling faster than Car Y. Its speed is greater.

The steepness of a graph is called the **gradient**. The gradient of a distance–time graph tells us about a moving object's speed.

? Sketch a distance–time graph for a car that travels fast at first, then at a slower speed, and then stops.

Sketch graphs are a good way of showing how two quantities are related – distance and time, for example. It's easier to see the relationship from a graph than to read a sentence, or to look at a table of data, or to make sense of an equation.

Look in some newspapers and magazines – you will often see graphs used as a way of communicating information.

? Find two graphs and interpret the information in words.

What does 'accelerating' mean?

If a driver wants to go faster, they push down hard on the accelerator pedal. The car's speed increases – it goes faster.

'**Accelerating**' means 'going faster' or 'speeding up'. 'Decelerating' means 'slowing down'.

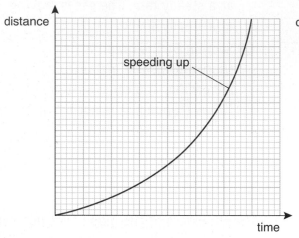

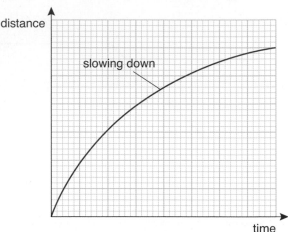

This graph is for a car accelerating. The distance–time graph gets steeper – its gradient increases.

This graph is for a car which is slowing down. The distance–time graph becomes less steep – its gradient decreases.

You need to remember that:

- ◗ To determine the speed of a moving object, we measure distance travelled and time taken:

$$speed = \frac{distance}{time}$$

Quantity	Unit
distance	m or km
time	s
speed	m/s or km/s

- ◗ A distance–time graph can represent an object's movement.
- ◗ A steep gradient indicates a high speed.
- ◗ We say an object is 'accelerating' when its speed is increasing.

Next time ≫

Unit 2 Forces appear whenever two objects interact (page 220).

Unit 2 If forces on an object are unbalanced, it will start moving, speed up or slow down (page 225).

Previously »

Remember — Pushes and pulls are examples of forces.

From Page 218 — An object's speed is the distance it travels every second; if its speed increases, it is accelerating.

Unit 2

Forces

Why are forces important?

We use forces all the time. We push things and pull things. We lift things and throw things. We squash things and break things.

To understand all of these actions, we use the idea of forces.

In this Unit, you will learn:

- what forces are;
- how to represent forces;
- how to measure forces;
- about important forces including friction, drag, gravity and upthrust;
- the effects of forces.

Key words

air resistance	interact
balanced forces	lubrication
contact force	mass
drag	newton (N)
force	newtonmeter
forcemeter	unbalanced forces
friction	upthrust
gravitational field	weight
gravity	

Where do forces come from?

If you push or pull something, you are exerting a **force** on it.

▶ A horse can pull a cart.

▶ A shark can push its teeth into you.

All of these things involve forces. However, it's important to understand that it isn't only living things that can exert forces.

▶ If you drop a heavy book on your foot, you will feel the force of the book on your foot.

▶ If you sit on a chair, you do not fall on the floor. The chair pushes up on you to stop you falling.

Things can exert a force even when they aren't touching.

▶ A magnet can attract a piece of steel without touching it.

▶ The Sun's gravity pulls on the Earth across 150 million kilometres of empty space.

It may seem like magic, but it isn't! Forces appear whenever two objects **interact**.

The Earth's gravily pulls on this astronaut, preventing him from disappearing off into space.

How can we measure forces?

You can pull a heavy object along the floor. If you pull it using a **forcemeter**, the meter will show you the size of the force you are using.

A forcemeter measures forces in newtons. The **newton (N)** is the unit of force.

Another name for a forcemeter is a **newtonmeter**. Inside the forcemeter is a spring. The spring stretches as you pull it. The bigger the force, the more the spring stretches.

Using a forcemeter to measure the force pulling a piece of wood.

What are contact forces?

When two objects touch, each one exerts a **contact force** on the other.

For example, if you lean against the wall, you push on the wall. That is a contact force.

At the same time, the wall pushes back on you. The force of the wall stops you from falling over.

We can draw these forces as arrows.

- ▶ The arrow shows the direction of the force.
- ▶ The labels tell us the two objects involved.

If you put a book on a table, the book pushes down on the table and the table pushes up on the book.

force of wall on hand

force of hand on wall

Draw a diagram with force arrows to show the two contact forces involved when a book is on a table. Label the arrows correctly.

What are the effects of friction?

When two objects touch each other, another force may appear – **friction**. For example, if you try to push a heavy box along the ground, friction may make it difficult for you.

- ▶ Your push is trying to move the box to the right.
- ▶ Friction acts to the left.

Your pushing force must be bigger than the friction force; then the box will move.

pushing force on box

force of friction on box

What causes friction? @

Friction appears when one surface tries to slide over another. The force of friction acts along the surface.

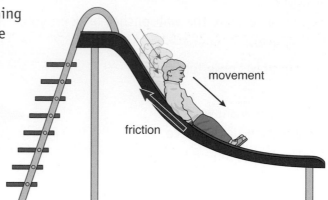

movement

friction

For example, imagine that you are coming down a slide in the playground. You are moving down the slide; friction acts up the slide, slowing you down.

Friction is used in the brakes of cars and bicycles. When a cyclist applies the brakes, a rubber pad presses on the rim of the wheel. The force of friction slows the turning of the wheel.

Friction is greater when the two surfaces are rough. Rough surfaces rub against each other. You can reduce friction in two ways.

▶ Rub or polish the surfaces to make them smoother.

▶ Add a substance such as oil so that the surfaces slide over each other more easily. This is called **lubrication**.

 Where is oil used to reduce friction? Give some examples.

Is friction always a problem? @

Friction can be a problem in machines. Oil is used to lubricate machines. Otherwise parts may wear away.

Friction can make it difficult to move objects. This can be overcome by putting the object on rollers, for example.

However, friction can be useful, too. When we walk, our feet push backwards, and the friction of the ground pushes us forwards.

Imagine walking on an icy surface. You can't get a grip because there is little or no friction. We need friction if we are to walk on a smooth surface.

backward push of foot on ground

forward push of friction on foot

Think about some different sports and the equipment used in them.

? List some examples where it is important that the equipment is smooth, and other examples where the equipment must be rough.

What causes weight?

Everything on Earth has **weight**. Weight is the force that pulls everything downwards. It is the force that makes things fall when you drop them.

Weight is caused by the Earth's **gravity**. Because the Earth has an enormous mass, it pulls on everything in its **gravitational field**. To escape from the Earth's gravitational field, you would have to go far, far out into space.

We can show an object's weight by drawing a force arrow, pointing downwards. The arrow points towards the centre of the Earth.

We can measure an object's weight by hanging it from a forcemeter.

Remember: weight is a force, so it is measured in newtons (N).

Using a forcemeter to measure weight.

What is the difference between mass and weight?

Don't get confused between *mass* and *weight*.

● An object's **mass** tells us how much matter it is made of.

● An object's weight tells us the force of gravity on it.

If you travel out into space, your weight will become less.

● If you go to Mars, your weight will be about one-third of your weight on Earth.

● If you go to the Moon, your weight will be about one-sixth of your weight on Earth.

However, your mass will stay the same. You are still made of the same amount of matter as on Earth.

But there is a connection between mass and weight. Your weight is caused by the pull of the Earth.

● The Earth pulls on every kilogram of mass with a force of about 10 N.

● So you can calculate your weight by multiplying your mass by 10.

weight (in N) = 10 × mass (in kg)

? Calculate the weight of a girl of mass 50 kg.

Can liquids and gases exert forces?

If you jump into a swimming pool, you will float.

▶ Your weight pulls you downwards.

▶ The water pushes back upwards.

The upward force of water on you is called **upthrust** (see also page 243).

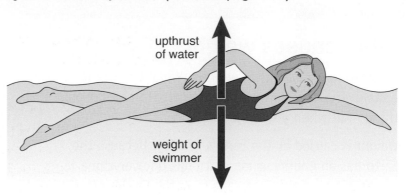

upthrust of water

weight of swimmer

There is upthrust in air, too, but it has a smaller effect than in water. The upthrust of the air makes a hot air balloon rise from the ground.

There is another force if you try to move through water or air.

▶ If you try to move through water, the force of **drag** will slow you down.

▶ When an aircraft flies through the air, the force of **air resistance** slows it down.

Drag and air resistance are a bit like friction, but they happen in fluids (liquids and gases).

▶ A shuttlecock used in badminton is designed so that there is a lot of drag as it moves through the air. Otherwise it would fall too quickly.

▶ A shark has a streamlined shape so that it can move quickly through water – and catch its prey.

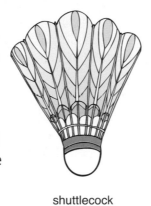

shuttlecock

shark

? Draw the outlines of two cars, one more streamlined than the other.

THINKING BEYOND...

Think about what you have experienced in a swimming pool.

? Describe what it is like if you try to wade through the water.

Explain why it is difficult to reach the bottom at the deep end.

How do forces change the way things move?

To work out how forces will make an object move, we must only think about *the forces acting on the object*. In these examples, a longer arrow means a bigger force.

▶ The forces on this object cancel out. These are **balanced forces**. The object does not move.

▶ The pushing force is cancelled out by the force of friction. Again, the forces are balanced. The object does not move.

▶ The pushing force is greater than the force of friction. These are **unbalanced forces**. The object starts moving to the right.

upthrust

weight

friction   push

friction   push

▶ Only one force acts on the ball. It falls downwards. It gets faster as it falls – it accelerates.

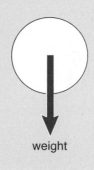

weight

▶ The drag of the air pulls upwards on the parachutist. The drag force is greater than his weight and so he falls more and more slowly – he decelerates.

air resistance

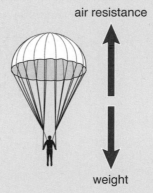

weight

If the forces on an object are balanced, it will remain still (or carry on moving at a steady speed). If the forces are unbalanced, it will start moving, speed up or slow down.

1 Just before he lands, are the forces on the parachutist balanced or unbalanced? Explain your answer.

2 A cyclist brakes in order to stop at a red light. While she is slowing down, are the forces on the bicycle balanced or unbalanced? Explain your answer.

You need to remember that:

- ▶ Forces appear when two objects interact with each other.
- ▶ We measure forces using a newtonmeter (a forcemeter).
- ▶ The unit of force is the newton (N).
- ▶ We represent forces using force arrows.
- ▶ The force of friction can arise when two objects touch each other.
- ▶ Friction is the force that enables us to walk.
- ▶ We can reduce unwanted friction by using lubrication.
- ▶ The weight of an object is a force caused by the pull of the Earth's gravity.
- ▶ On the Earth's surface:
    weight (in N) = 10 × mass (in kg)
- ▶ The force pushing upwards on objects in water is called upthrust.
- ▶ When objects move through liquids or gases, they experience drag.
- ▶ When the forces on an object are balanced, its motion does not change.
- ▶ Unbalanced forces cause the motion of a body to change – it speeds up or slows down.

Next time ▶▶

Unit 3   Forces can be made to turn things using levers (page 227).
Unit 5   Pressure tells us about how a force is spread out over an area (page 240).

Previously »

| From Page 220 | The unit of force is the newton (N). |
| From Page 225 | Unbalanced forces cause the motion of a body to change. |

Unit 3

Levers

Why are levers useful?

Perhaps you have used a teaspoon to prise off the lid of a tin of golden syrup. You are using the spoon as a lever. When you press down on a door handle, you are using a lever. When your foot pushes down on a bicycle pedal, you are pressing on a lever.

There are even levers in your body. Many of the bones in your body work as levers.

A lever is a device that allows us to apply forces more conveniently, or to make a small force into a bigger force.

In this Unit, you will learn:

- ▶ the different classes of levers;
- ▶ how levers change forces;
- ▶ how to calculate the moment of a force;
- ▶ how to use the Principle of Moments.

Key words

anticlockwise moment	machine
clockwise moment	moment
effort	newton metres (Nm)
engineer	pivot
fulcrum	Principle of Moments
levers	turning effect
load	

What is a lever?

Levers are usually long, thin and stiff (but they don't have to be). When children play on a see-saw, they are using a lever.

In the picture, the man is pushing down on one end of the see-saw. The children are being pushed up at the other end.

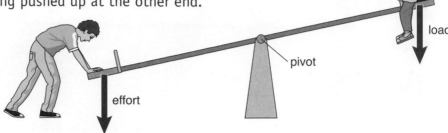

The see-saw is balanced on a **pivot** half way along its length. As the man pushes down, the see-saw turns about the pivot and the children go up. Another word for pivot is **fulcrum**.

The man is trying to make the children move upwards. Their weight, pushing downwards, is called the **load**. The man's force pushing on the see-saw is called the **effort**.

Where can we see levers at work?

For any lever, you should be able to identify these three things:

- the pivot (about which the lever turns);
- the effort *E* (the force someone is applying to the lever);
- the load *L* (the force which is being moved).

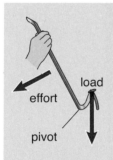

A crowbar is used to lift a large load at one point.

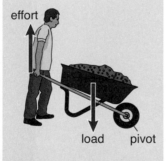

A wheelbarrow can carry a heavy load.

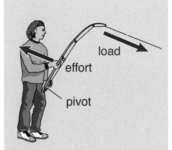

An angler holds the end of the rod still and pulls on it part way up.

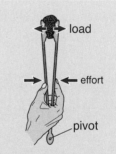

Tongs are like a pair of levers joined at one end.

There are dozens of levers at work in your body. Your bones are the levers, your joints are the pivots and your muscles provide the forces.

? **Find out some examples of levers in the body. Make cardboard models to show how they work.**

How do levers change forces?

The picture shows how a child can balance a heavy adult on a see-saw.

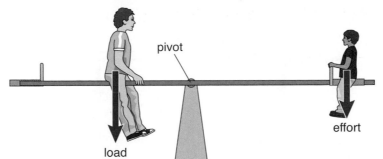

The adult's weight is the load. For the see-saw to be balanced, the adult must sit closer to the pivot.

The child's weight is the effort, pushing down on the see-saw. The child is lighter than the adult.

From this we can see that a small force further from the pivot can have the same effect as a big force closer to the pivot. The further a force is from the pivot, the greater is its **turning effect**.

How can we calculate the turning effect of a force?

The bigger the force, the greater its turning effect.

Also, the further the force acts from the pivot, the greater its turning effect.

So we can calculate a quantity called the **moment** of the force like this:

   moment = force × distance from pivot

The diagram represents the adult and child on the see-saw.

There are two forces pushing down on the see-saw. We can calculate the moment of each force.

For the child:

   moment = 500 × 2.2 = 1100 N m

For the adult:

   moment = 800 × 1.3 = 1040 N m

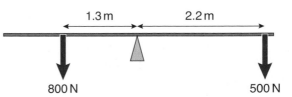

The child's moment is greater than the adult's, so the child will go down and the adult will go up.

Units: moment is measured in **newton metres (N m)**.

Quantity	Unit
force	N
distance from pivot	m
moment	N m

 Calculate the moment of a force of 4 N acting 0.50 m from a pivot.

How can we balance a see-saw?

In this diagram, the people on the see-saw have moved so that it is balanced.

We can check that it is balanced by calculating the moment of each force.

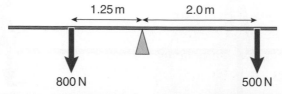

1.25 m

2.0 m

800 N

500 N

Adult: moment = 800 × 1.25 = 1000 N m

The weight of the adult is tending to make the see-saw turn anticlockwise. We say that this is an **anticlockwise moment**.

Child: moment = 500 × 2.0 = 1000 N m

The weight of the child is tending to make the see-saw turn clockwise. We say that this is a **clockwise moment**.

So the two moments are turning the see-saw in opposite directions, and they are equal in size. We can write:

clockwise moment = anticlockwise moment

and we know that the see-saw will be balanced. This is called the **Principle of Moments**:

For an object to be balanced, the clockwise and anticlockwise moments acting on it must be equal.

 If the child moved further from the pivot, would the see-saw turn clockwise or anticlockwise?

How can we use the Principle of Moments to calculate an unknown force?

We can use the Principle of Moments to work out the force that is needed to balance a lever.

In the diagram, what force F will balance the lever? The force F is turning the see-saw clockwise. Because we want the see-saw to be balanced, we can write:

clockwise moment = anticlockwise moment

$$F \times 1.5 = 60 \times 2.0$$

$$F = 60 \times \frac{2.0}{1.5} = 80 \text{ N}$$

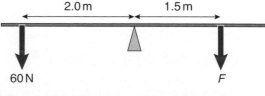

2.0 m

1.5 m

60 N

F

So a force of 80 N is needed. (Check that this makes sense: the force F is closer to the pivot so it must be greater than the 60 N force.)

 If the 60 N force was 1.0 N from the pivot, what value of F would be needed to balance it? Draw a diagram before doing the calculation.

How can we use the Principle of Moments to calculate an unknown distance?

We can use the Principle of Moments to work out where a force must be applied to balance a lever.

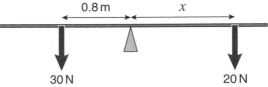

In the diagram, how far from the pivot should the 20 N force be applied to balance the 30 N force? (This distance is labelled x.)

The 20 N force is turning the see-saw clockwise. To balance the see-saw:

   clockwise moment = anticlockwise moment

$$20 \times x = 30 \times 0.8$$

$$x = \frac{30 \times 0.8}{20} = 1.2 \text{ m}$$

So the 20 N force must be applied at 1.2 m from the pivot. (Check that this makes sense: the 20 N force is smaller than the 30 N force so it must be applied further from the pivot to balance the lever.)

 If the 30 N force was 1.0 m from the pivot, where would the 20 N force have to be applied to balance it? Draw a diagram before doing the calculation.

Why are levers called 'machines'?

A lever is an example of a simple **machine**. A machine is anything that can be used to make it easier to do something that involves forces.

For example, a ramp is also a simple machine. You might not be able to lift a heavy load straight upwards, but you can push the load up a ramp or slope.

A pulley system is a machine that makes it easier to lift heavy loads.

So machines can change the size of a force, allowing you to lift heavier loads. They can also change small movements into bigger ones. In this way, we can do things that we would otherwise find difficult.

In everyday life, the word *machine* may mean something much more complicated – a bicycle, for example. A bicycle is a lot of simple machines – levers, wheels, pulleys and so on – combined to make a more complex machine. Similarly, a washing machine is a combination of simpler machines all operated by an electric motor.

What is 'mechanical engineering'?

An **engineer** uses ideas from science to make things that do work for us.

There are many branches of engineering. Mechanical engineers use forces and their effects to construct machines. They design and make complex machines, such as cars, and structures, such as motorways to carry those cars.

Some mechanical engineers focus on shrinking machines to make them as small and as portable as possible. The vibrating alarm in a mobile phone is a tiny machine that shakes the outer casing.

This humanoid robot is a product of engineering know-how. There are lots of levers and other simple machines involved in its design.

We are now designing 'nanomachines', which are so small that hundreds of them could fit inside the full stop at the end of this sentence.

All these things require an understanding of machines and the forces that make them work.

THINKING BEYOND...

There are many branches of engineering – mechanical, civil, aeronautical, electrical, electronic ...

? Choose one type of engineering and find out what it involves. Explain how this branch of engineering affects your life.

You need to remember that:

- ◐ A lever is an example of a simple machine.
- ◐ A lever turns about a fixed point, called the pivot or fulcrum.
- ◐ A force on the lever, called the effort, results in a force acting on the load.
- ◐ A force on a lever has a turning effect, which is greater for a bigger force, and greater the further it acts from the pivot:

    moment of force = force × distance from pivot
- ◐ Moment is measured in newton metres (N m).
- ◐ For a balanced lever, the Principle of Moments says:

    clockwise moment = anticlockwise moment

Next time 》

Unit 5　Hydraulic machines can increase the size of a force (page 244).

Previously »

| Remember | We measure an object's mass in kilograms (kg). |
| From Page 223 | The weight of an object is a force caused by the pull of the Earth's gravity. |

Unit 4

Density

What does 'density' mean?

The idea of density helps us to compare different materials.

In everyday speech, we might say, "Steel is heavier than wood," or "Plastic is lighter than glass." In science, we say, "Steel is denser than wood."

Aircraft are often made of aluminium because it is a strong, light metal.

In this Unit, you will learn:

- ▶ the meaning of 'density';
- ▶ how density is measured;
- ▶ what density tells us about floating and sinking;
- ▶ how scientists use standard units when they make measurements.

Key words

density	SI units
mass	volume
particles	

What does 'density' mean?

Aircraft are made mainly of metals, for strength. A steel aircraft would be too heavy to fly, so aircraft are often made of aluminium. This is because aluminium is a lighter metal than steel.

We say that the density of aluminium is less than the density of steel.

To compare aluminium and steel we need to make a fair test. We take the same volume of each metal and measure its mass.

The two cubes shown are the same size.

▶ The two cubes have the same volume.

▶ The steel cube has more mass than the aluminium cube.

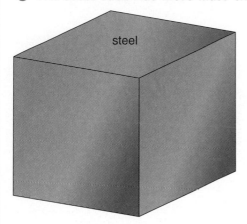

steel

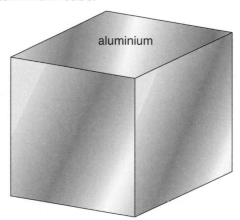

aluminium

The steel cube has more mass in the same volume. The density of steel is greater than the density of aluminium.

How is density defined?

Density is defined like this:

$$\text{density} = \frac{\text{mass}}{\text{volume}}$$

The units of density are:

g/cm³
(grams per centimetre cubed)

kg/m³
(kilograms per metre cubed)

The table gives the densities of some different substances.

Substance	Density in g/cm³	Density in kg/m³
air	0.0013	1.3
wood (pine)	0.50	500
ethanol	0.79	790
water	1.00	1000
concrete	2.4	2400
aluminium	2.7	2700
steel	7.9	7900
lead	11.3	11300

 Which has the greater density, water or wood?

How is density measured?

To find the density of a substance, we take a sample of the substance and measure two quantities:

▶ its **mass** (in g or kg);

▶ its **volume** (in cm³ or m³).

Then we calculate density using:

$$\text{density} = \frac{\text{mass}}{\text{volume}}$$

For example, a block of glass is measured:

mass of glass = 52 g

volume of glass = 20 cm³

$$\text{density of glass} = \frac{\text{mass}}{\text{volume}} = \frac{52}{20} = 2.6 \text{ g/cm}^3$$

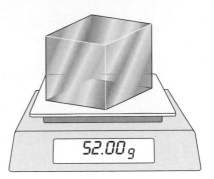

 An ice block has a mass of 460 g. Its volume is 500 cm³. Calculate the density of ice.

How is mass measured?

Find the mass of a sample by placing it on a balance. Remember, mass is measured in g or kg.

For a liquid, find the mass of the empty container. Then add the liquid and find the new mass. Remember to subtract the mass of the container.

How is volume measured?

For a regular solid, measure the sides and calculate the volume.

For a liquid, use a measuring cylinder.

For an irregular solid, submerge it in water. Calculate the increase in volume.

If you walk around a supermarket, you will see many products labelled with their mass or volume.

● Solid products: usually the mass is given, in g or kg.

● Liquid products: usually the volume is given, in ml or l.

Take care! The label may say 'weight in grams' – in science, we call that mass, not weight.

? Find out what it means when the symbol e appears beside the mass or volume.

Why do some things float?

We can use the idea of density to work out if something will sink or float in water.

● Anything less dense than water will float.

● Anything denser than water will sink.

It is useful to remember:

density of water = $1.0 \, g/cm^3$ = $1000 \, kg/m^3$

People are less dense than water, so we float.

A diver must use weights to sink in water.

? The density of oak (wood) is $600 \, kg/m^3$. Will a piece of oak float in water?

Why are some materials denser than others?

A gas such as the air has a low density. The **particles** of the air are far apart – there is a lot of empty space between them.

The pictures show the particles of some solids.

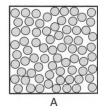 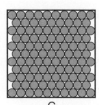

A   B   C

A and B have the same arrangement of particles, but B's particles have more mass than A's. So B is denser than A.

The particles of B and C are identical, but C's particles are squashed more closely together. So C is denser than B.

What are scientific units?

Scientists use standard units when they measure things. Then it is easy to share results.

These units are described as **SI units**. 'SI' stands for *Système Internationale* (International System). Each unit has a name and an abbreviation.

Quantity	SI unit
mass	gram, g; kilogram, kg
length	metre, m
time	second, s
force, weight	newton, N

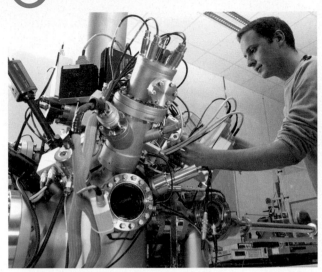

In the UK, the National Physical Laboratory devises new methods of making accurate measurements.

THINKING BEYOND…

The newton is an example of an SI unit named after a famous scientist of the past. It's one way science commemorates its heroes. You could find out some more.

Of course, Isaac Newton never measured a force in newtons!

? Write a short biography of Newton and explain why the unit of force is named after him.

What prefixes are used with SI units?

For large quantities, we use bigger units. For example:

  1 kilogram = 1000 grams   1 kg = 1000 g

The prefix 'k' stands for kilo. It makes the unit 1000 times bigger. We call this a factor.

For small quantities, we use smaller units. For example:

  1 millimetre = 1/1000 metre   1 mm = 0.001 m

Prefix	Stands for	Factor
μ	micro	1/1000 000
m	milli	1/1000
c	centi	1/100
k	kilo	1000
M	mega	1000 000

? What unit is represented by ms?

You need to remember that:

▷ To determine the density of a substance, we measure the mass and volume of a sample.

▷ Then we calculate:

$$density = \frac{mass}{volume}$$

Quantity	Unit
mass	g or kg
volume	cm^3 or m^3
density	g/cm^3 or kg/m^3

▷ Density of water = $1.0 \, g/cm^3$ = $1000 \, kg/m^3$

▷ An object with a density less than the density of water will float.

▷ Scientists use standard SI units like the metre, kilogram and second when making measurements.

Next time »

Unit 5   Pressure increases with depth in a fluid, because of the weight of the fluid (page 239).

Previously »

From Page 220 Forces appear when two objects interact with each other.

From Page 231 A machine is anything that can be used to make it easier to do something that involves forces.

Unit 5

Pressure

Why is 'pressure' important?

When divers go down into deep water, they experience the pressure of the water, pushing in on them from all around. The deeper they go, the greater the pressure.

At great depths, divers must use small submersible craft with hard casings that can withstand the pressure – otherwise they could be crushed to death.

In this Unit, you will learn:

- the meaning of 'pressure';
- how to calculate pressure;
- how fluids create pressure;
- how boats float because of upthrust;
- how pressure is used in hydraulic machines.

Key words

atmospheric pressure	pascal (Pa)
barometer	pistons
fluids	pressure
hydraulic machine	upthrust

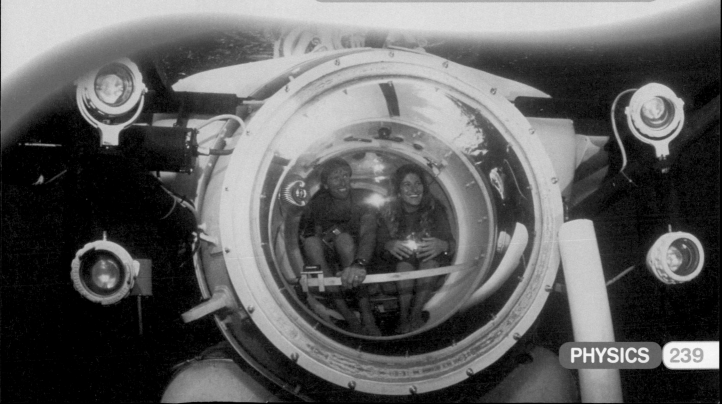

What does 'pressure' mean?

If you push on a drawing pin, it will go into a cork board. You have to press hard enough – you have to apply enough **pressure**.

If you do not press with enough force, the pin will not go into the board. Increasing the pressing force increases the pressure so that the pin will go into the board.

When the pin is sharp, your pushing force is concentrated on a small area. If the pin is blunt, it will be more difficult to push in. Your force is spread over a bigger area and the pressure is less.

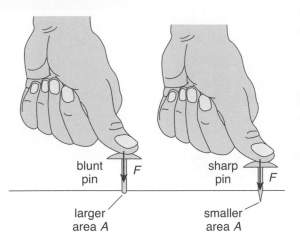

blunt pin F sharp pin F

larger area A smaller area A

This tells us that the pressure P created by a force depends on two things:

● the size of the force F – a bigger force gives greater pressure;

● the area A the force presses on – a smaller area gives a greater pressure.

Who needs high or low pressure?

Pins and needles have sharp points so that the force pushing them into a board or through some fabric is concentrated on a small area – the pressure is high. If you are stitching fabric by hand, unfortunately the high pressure of the needle may also puncture your finger!

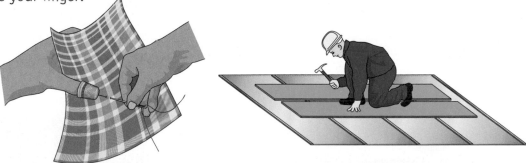

Often, we want the pressure of a force to be low. A thimble helps to spread the force when a needle pushes against it, giving low pressure and protecting your finger. People working on a glass roof need to spread their weight over a large area to avoid the pressure from their hands and feet damaging the glass.

Camels have wide feet so that their weight is spread over a large area. Then the pressure on the desert sand will be low and they won't sink into it.

Explain why a drawing pin has a sharp point at one end and a wide head at the other end.

How is pressure defined?

Pressure is defined like this:

$$\text{pressure} = \frac{\text{force}}{\text{area}} \qquad P = \frac{F}{A}$$

Quantity	Symbol	Unit
force	F	newton (N)
area	A	metre squared (m²)
pressure	P	**pascal (Pa)** newtons per metre squared (N/m²)

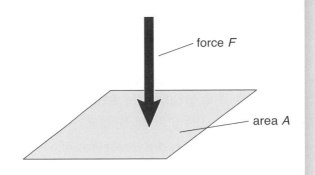
force F

area A

THINKING BEYOND...

You can think of pressure as a way of describing how concentrated a force is – a big force concentrated on a small area gives a high pressure. In a similar way, density tells you how concentrated the mass of an object is.

That's why both are calculated by dividing – compare the equations:

$$\text{pressure} = \frac{\text{force}}{\text{area}} \qquad \text{density} = \frac{\text{mass}}{\text{volume}}$$

Calculating pressure tells you how the force is shared over the area; density tells you how mass is shared over volume.

? Imagine a cube 2 cm × 2 cm × 2 cm with mass 0.1 kg and weight 1 N. What is its density? What pressure does it exert on the table where it rests?

How is pressure calculated?

To calculate the pressure exerted by a force, you need to find out how many newtons of force are pressing on each square metre. In the diagram, 8 N are pressing on 4 m², so 2 N are pressing on each m². The pressure is 2 N/m², or 2 Pa.

Using the equation for pressure:

$$\text{pressure} = \frac{\text{force}}{\text{area}}$$

$$= \frac{8}{4} = 2 \text{ Pa}$$

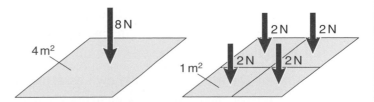
8 N, 4 m², 2 N, 2 N, 1 m², 2 N, 2 N

? If a force of 400 N presses on a surface of area 2 m , what will be the pressure, in Pa?

How do liquids exert pressure?

Think of the water in a swimming pool. There are tonnes of water; and the weight of the water presses down on the bottom of the pool. That creates pressure. The greater the depth of water in the pool, the greater the pressure.

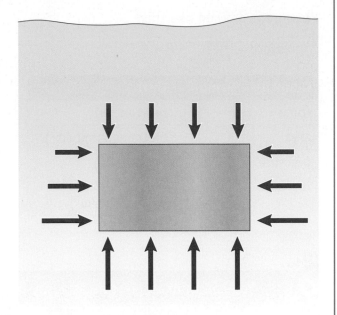

If we zoom in on the molecules of the water, they are moving around all the time (see page 117). The molecules bounce off each other and any object that is in the water. Each bounce causes a tiny force, and all the many tiny forces add up to create a constant pressure. So any object in water will be pressed on by the water from all directions.

? Look at the picture. Explain why the pressure on the upper surface of the object is less than the pressure on its lower surface.

How do gases exert pressure?

Gases can exert pressure, too. When you turn on a gas tap, the pressure of the gas pushes it out into the room.

The air around us exerts pressure. We can understand why gases such as the air exert pressure if we think of the molecules that make up the gas. The molecules are moving around rapidly.

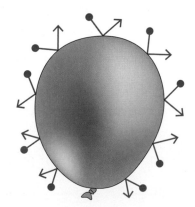

Look at the balloon in the picture. The air molecules around it collide with the surface of the balloon, and bounce off it. Each collision causes a tiny force on the balloon. The many tiny forces add up to make the pressure on the balloon.

The pressure of the atmosphere is known as **atmospheric pressure**. This is measured using a **barometer**. Meteorologists measure changes in atmospheric pressure to help predict the weather.

If you climb a high mountain, the pressure is less. There is less air above you, pressing downwards.

On a weather map, isobars are lines drawn to show where the pressure is high and where it is low. The wind spirals round from high pressure to low pressure, rather like water spiralling round as it drains from a washbasin. @

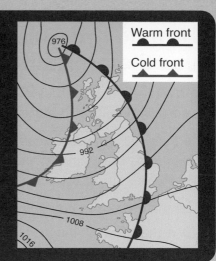

? Look online at a weather map of Europe that shows isobars, for example from the BBC. Identify the areas of low and high pressure. What weather can we expect when the pressure is high?

How does pressure in a fluid create upthrust? @

Liquids and gases are **fluids** – substances that can flow. Water and air are fluids.

When an object is placed in a fluid, it experiences pressure on it on all sides. Pressure acts in all directions in a fluid, not just downwards. There is something unusual that happens to objects in a fluid though.

Think about a submarine surrounded by water. The diagram shows that the pressure on the bottom of the submarine is greater than the pressure on the top, because the bottom is deeper in the water than the top. The result is a force pushing upwards on the submarine – this is the **upthrust**.

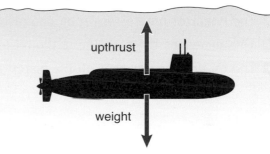

With a boat on the surface of the water, the upthrust of the water balances the weight of the boat. The upthrust of water keeps the boat afloat. If you add more weight to the boat, it sinks deeper in the water until the upthrust balances the weight again.

With a submarine, you need to control its weight to stop it floating to the surface.

The diagram shows a submarine in the sea. There are two forces on the submarine:

- ▶ its weight pulls it downwards;
- ▶ the upthrust of the water pushes it upwards.

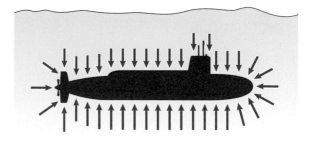

If the upthrust is greater than the submarine's weight, it floats upwards.

? A submarine can take water into its tanks so that its weight increases. Draw a diagram of the forces on the submarine when it is sinking. Which force is greater?

How do hydraulic machines use the pressure of a fluid?

A **hydraulic machine** uses the pressure of a fluid to transmit a force from place to place.

You may have noticed that tractors and diggers have shiny metal rods that move to push and lift. These rods are **pistons**. They come out of cylinders.

The picture shows how a piston works.

▶ A fluid (oil) is pumped into the cylinder.

▶ The pressure of the oil pushes on the piston so that it moves upwards.

In a digger, the piston moves a lever that raises the scoop.

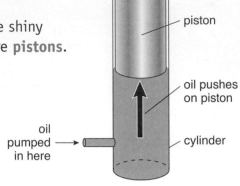

rod is pushed upward

piston

oil pushes on piston

oil pumped in here

cylinder

How do hydraulic machines increase the size of a force?

The picture shows how a car jack works.

▶ The operator presses down on one piston, which fits inside a narrow cylinder.

▶ This increases the pressure of the oil in the whole system.

▶ The oil presses upwards on the piston in the large cylinder, lifting the car.

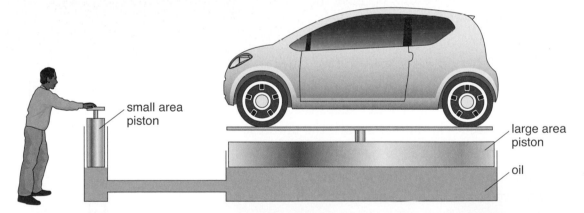

small area piston

large area piston

oil

The pressure in the two cylinders is the same. However, the force on the bigger piston is greater because it has a much greater area. In this way, a small force on a small piston is changed into a large force on a big piston.

It may seem as though we are getting 'something for nothing'. However, the small piston must be pushed a long way down in order to lift the large piston a small distance.

 If the area of the large piston is five times the area of the small piston, how many times bigger will the force on the large piston be?

You need to remember that:

◐ Pressure tells us about how a force is spread over an area:

$$\text{pressure} = \frac{\text{force}}{\text{area}} \qquad P = \frac{F}{A}$$

Quantity	Symbol	Unit
force	F	newton (N)
area	A	metre squared (m²)
pressure	P	pascal (Pa) newtons per square metre (N/m²)

◐ Pressure in a fluid (a liquid or gas) is caused by the particles of the fluid moving around and colliding.

◐ Pressure acts in all directions in a fluid.

◐ Pressure increases with depth in a fluid, because of the weight of the fluid above.

◐ The higher pressure at the bottom of a boat compared to the top causes upthrust.

◐ A boat floats because the upthrust balances the weight of the boat.

◐ Pressure can be transmitted and increased by a fluid; this is used in hydraulic machines.

Next time 》

Unit 11 We hear because sound waves cause air molecules to press against our eardrums (page 276).

Previously »

From Page 220   Forces appear whenever two objects interact.

From Page 225   Unbalanced forces cause the motion of a body to change.

Unit 6

Magnets

How do magnets work?

Magnets are interesting things – they can attract or repel each other without touching.

It is very difficult to explain *how* magnets work, but you can learn a lot about what magnets can do without knowing a lot of advanced scientific ideas.

We use magnets every day without really thinking about it. They are great for holding letters and notes to metal fridge doors – but did you know there is a magnet inside the fridge that helps keep the door closed tightly?

In this Unit, you will learn:

- about magnetic and non-magnetic materials;
- how magnets attract and repel each other;
- how we represent magnetic fields;
- how electromagnets work.

Key words

attracts	magnetic material
compass	magnetic pole
core	north pole
electromagnet	permanent magnet
magnet	repels
magnetic field	solenoid
magnetic field lines	south pole

Which materials are magnetic?

A bar **magnet** is an example of a **permanent magnet**. It will remain magnetic for a long time.

A bar magnet can attract pieces of iron and steel. Any material that is attracted by a magnet is called a **magnetic material**. The table below gives some examples.

 How could you show that a magnet's attraction can work through a non-magnetic material – for example, through paper?

Magnetic materials	Non-magnetic materials
iron	copper
steel (most types)	stainless steel
nickel	aluminium
ferrite (used for fridge magnets)	paper

What are the forces between two magnets?

A bar magnet has two ends; one is its **north pole**, the other is its **south pole**.

If two magnets are placed so that their ends are close together as shown, they may attract or repel.

▷ A south pole **attracts** a north pole; a north pole attracts a south pole.

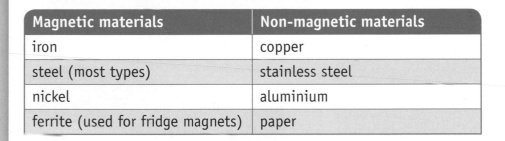

▷ A north pole **repels** another north pole; a south pole repels another south pole.

We summarise this as 'Like poles repel, unlike poles attract.'

'Like poles' means two of the same type. 'Unlike poles' means two of the opposite type.

The magnetic force between two poles is stronger if they are closer together.

 Will two south poles attract or repel each other? Draw a diagram to show this.

What are the poles of a magnet?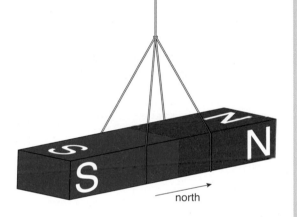

If a bar magnet is hung so that it is free to rotate, it will turn until one end points towards the north – this end is called the magnet's north pole.

The other end points south, of course, and is called the south pole. This is how a **compass** works.

The magnet turns because it is in the Earth's magnetic field. There is a lot of iron and nickel inside the Earth's core and they make it behave like a giant magnet, with one **magnetic pole** close to each geographical pole.

 A magnet's north pole is attracted towards the north. What kind of magnetic pole (north or south) must there be in the north?

north

 **THINKING BEYOND...**

Something scientists don't know: does a north pole always come with a south pole? Every magnet we have discovered, no matter how large or how small, appears to have both poles together. Some scientists think that they may be able to discover particles that are just north poles or south poles. But we haven't found any of these 'magnetic monopoles' yet.

 If there was a magnetic monopole that could move freely near the Earth, what do you think would happen to it?

What is a magnetic field?

A magnet can attract magnetic materials near to it, without touching them. We say that there is a **magnetic field** around the magnet.

We can show up a magnet's field using iron filings. We draw **magnetic field lines** to represent the pattern.

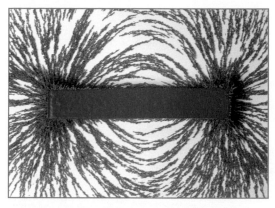 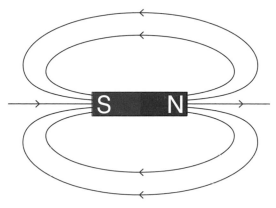

- The lines come out of the north pole and go into the south pole.
- The arrows on the lines show the direction of the field, from a north pole to a south pole. A compass will point in this direction.
- Where the field lines are closer together, the field is stronger.

 The magnetic field of a bar magnet is strongest at its poles – true or false? Explain how you can tell.

What is the field surrounding two magnets?

The magnetic field surrounding two magnets depends on whether they are attracting or repelling.

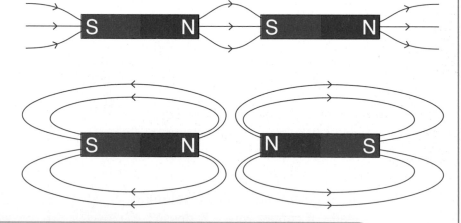

 Draw the magnetic field pattern for two south poles, repelling each other.

How are magnets and magnetic materials used?

Magnets and magnetic materials are used in:

- ◉ compasses (for showing direction);
- ◉ fridge magnets;
- ◉ the stripe on a credit card that contains stored information;
- ◉ magnetic memories such as computer hard disk drives;
- ◉ loudspeakers, headphones and some microphones;
- ◉ electric motors and generators.

The disc in a computer hard drive is coated on both sides with a magnetic material. This is the drive's memory. A pattern of tiny magnetised areas is used to store digital information.

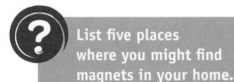

? List five places where you might find magnets in your home.

What is an electromagnet?

An **electromagnet** is another way of making a magnetic field.

- ◉ A coil of wire is connected to a battery or a power supply.
- ◉ A current flows in the coil.
- ◉ A magnetic field appears all round the coil.

One end of the coil is a north pole, the other end is a south pole. The magnetic field of the electromagnet is the same shape as the field of a bar magnet.

If the current is reversed, so that it passes through the coil in the opposite direction, the field will be reversed – the north pole will be at the other end.

The coil of wire is sometimes called a **solenoid**. It is usually made of copper wire – it doesn't have to be a magnetic material.

When the current is switched off, the coil stops being magnetic. The field disappears.

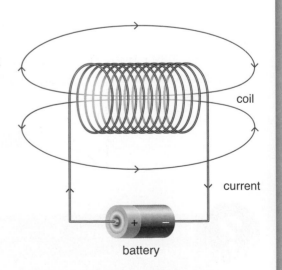

coil

current

battery

Electric current and magnetism are closely related. The connection between electricity and magnetism was first discovered by Hans Christian Oersted in 1820. He noticed that, when he switched on an electric circuit, the needle of his compass moved.

Oersted made his observation during a public lecture. The audience watched as he repeated it several times to make sure that what he saw was really true.

 Plan an investigation to test whether three different electrical items are also magnetic when they are switched on and when they are switched off.

How can an electromagnet be made stronger?

An electromagnet can be made stronger in three ways:

1. Use a coil with more turns of wire.

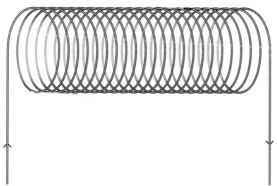

2. Put a bigger current into the coil.

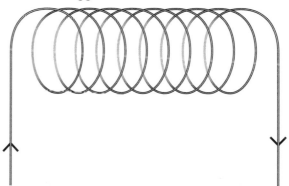

3. Add an iron **core** to the coil.

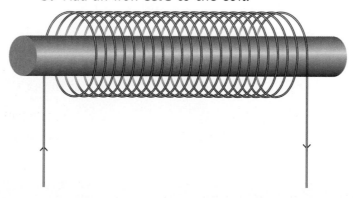

 Each of the electromagnets shown has the same current. Put them in order, from strongest to weakest.

How are electromagnets used? ⇄ @

Electromagnets have many uses because they can be turned on and off easily, and because the direction of the magnetic field can be reversed.

- ▶ Electric bell – an electromagnet moves a striker backwards and forwards very quickly, producing the ringing sound.
- ▶ Electric motor – the electric current passing through the coil causes a rotor or axle to rotate and generate turning forces or *moments* (see page 229).
- ▶ Loudspeakers and headphones – the electric current passing through the coil causes a magnetic 'piston' to vibrate and produce sounds (see page 270).
- ▶ Brain scanner – we can map the electric currents inside our brains using a person-sized electromagnet, to show whether our brains are healthy.
- ▶ Particle accelerators – we can 'bend' beams of electrically charged particles such as electrons and protons, and speed them up or slow them down, using huge electromagnets.

A scrapyard crane uses an electromagnet to lift steel. The steel falls off when the current is switched off.

You need to remember that:

- ▷ Some materials, such as iron, nickel and most types of steel, are magnetic.
- ▷ A magnet creates a magnetic field around itself.
- ▷ Magnetic field lines come out of the magnet's north pole and go into its south pole.
- ▷ We can show the direction of magnetic field lines using a compass.
- ▷ Like poles repel; unlike poles attract.
- ▷ The Earth is a large magnet because its core contains iron and nickel.
- ▷ An electromagnet is a coil with an electric current flowing through it.
- ▷ The greater the current and the more turns on the coil, the stronger the electromagnet.
- ▷ An iron core makes an electromagnet stronger.

Next time »

Unit 7 In electricity, like charges repel; opposite charges attract (page 254).

Unit 8 An electric current in a circuit causes electromagnets to work or motors to turn on (page 261).

Previously »

From Page 221 — The force of friction can arise when two objects touch each other.

From Page 247 — In magnets, like poles repel; unlike poles attract.

Unit 7

Static electricity

What happens when an electric current stops moving?

If you have long, straight hair, try brushing it a lot. Does it start to stand on end? Does the brush attract the hair? (This works better if you use conditioner and it's a dry day.)

Perhaps you have heard tiny crackling sounds when you take your clothes off? (This works better with synthetic fibres such as polyester or nylon.)

These are effects of static electricity. A Van de Graaff generator is used for showing the effects of static electricity in the lab.

Take care! It's easy to get static electricity mixed up with magnetism. They are two completely different things.

In this Unit, you will learn:

- ▶ how objects can be charged with static electricity;
- ▶ how electric charges affect each other;
- ▶ how we can explain the effects of static electricity.

Key words

electric charge	neutral
electrons	neutrons
friction	positive charge
insulators	protons
lightning	static electricity
negative charge	

How can we charge things up with static electricity?

A toy balloon is made of rubber. Blow one up and rub it on a jumper or other item of clothing.

This will give the balloon a charge. Hold it near your hair. Can you feel your hair being attracted to the balloon?

Touch the balloon on the wall. Will it stick?

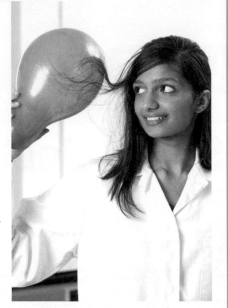

When two different materials are rubbed together, they may become charged. The best materials for this are **insulators** – materials that will not conduct electricity. The charge 'sticks' to the surface and does not move away.

Good insulators include plastics and fabrics such as wool and cotton.

It is the force of **friction** that causes the two materials to become charged. We say that they have gained an **electric charge**.

An object with no overall electric charge is described as **neutral** (uncharged).

Can electric charges repel as well as attract?

The picture shows two plastic balls, hanging on threads. Each ball has been charged by rubbing it with a woollen cloth.

The balls are repelling each other. Each one exerts a force on the other, so that they move away from each other.

▷ Sometimes, charged objects attract each other.

▷ Sometimes they repel each other.

This suggests that there are two types of electric charge. They are known as **positive charge** and **negative charge**.

When two objects made from insulators are rubbed together, they become charged. They gain opposite charges – one positive, the other negative. The charges they gain depend on the materials they are made of.

For example, when a polythene rod is rubbed with a woollen cloth:

▷ the polythene rod gains a negative charge;

▷ the woollen cloth gains a positive charge.

 When an acrylic rod is rubbed with a cotton cloth, the rod gains a positive charge. What type of charge will the cloth have? Explain your answer.

What are the forces between electric charges?

The first diagram shows that a positive charge and a negative charge attract each other. We say, "Opposite charges attract."

The second diagram shows that two positive charges repel each other. We say, "Like charges repel."

 Draw a diagram to show two negative electric charges and the forces between them.

Occasionally, you may come across a very tall man married to a very short woman. People say, "Oh yes, opposites attract!"

In fact, psychologists have found that people are generally attracted to people with similar characteristics to themselves, and they are happier that way.

In science, we always test an idea before we accept it.

 'Opposites attract' is a handy way of remembering how magnetic poles or electric charges behave. Find out how people remember the colours of the rainbow and the names of the planets.

So what is electric charge?

Electric charge is a fundamental property of matter.

Matter is made up of particles – atoms and molecules. And these particles are made up of still smaller particles – **protons**, **neutrons** and **electrons**.

Protons have positive charge and electrons have negative charge. Neutrons have no charge – they are neutral.

Since all electrons have negative charge, they will all repel each other. Because all protons have positive charge, they will repel each other but attract electrons.

It is the electrical attraction between protons and electrons that holds an atom together.

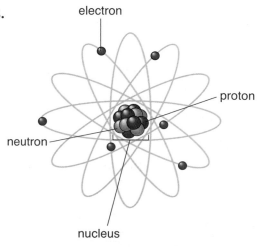

electron

proton

neutron

nucleus

How do objects become charged?

When one object is rubbed against another, friction drags electrons from one material on to the other.

▶ Some electrons are easily pulled off an atom because they are on the outside of the atom.

▶ The material that gains electrons ends up with a negative charge (because electrons are negative).

▶ The material that loses electrons ends up with a positive charge.

(Some materials hold onto their electrons more strongly than others. The materials that hold electrons more strongly are the ones that get a negative charge when rubbed.)

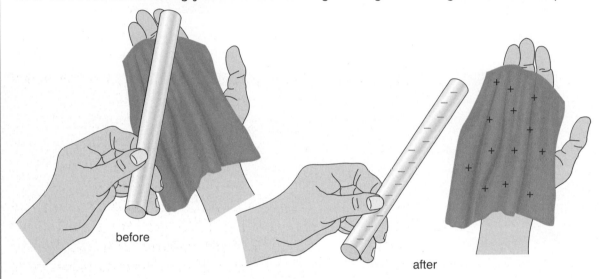

before

after

When you comb your hair, both your hair and the comb are neutral at the start. As you comb, electrons are rubbed off your hair and on to the comb.

 Explain why your hair and the comb attract each other.

Why is it called static electricity?

When a plastic rod has a negative charge, it has gained electrons. Those electrons do not move.

The word *static* is another word for *stationary*, meaning 'not moving'. So **static electricity** involves electric charge that is not moving.

Usually, when we think of electricity, we think of things like electric lights or electric motors. These involve electric currents, where electric charge is moving.

Static electricity often involves materials that are electrical insulators. Electrons cannot easily move in these materials, so they keep their electric charge.

What is lightning?

A thundercloud has a large static electric charge. The ground is usually positively charged and the cloud is usually negatively charged. When lightning flashes, we are seeing the charge escaping from the cloud and 'striking' the ground. The 'flash' of **lightning** is a giant electric current.

In fact, when we video lightning strikes and replay them in slow motion, we can see that every strike is made up of lots of individual flashes faster than our eyes can see. That is why lightning can appear to 'flicker'. There can be up to 20 flashes making up one strike of lightning!

Some of the earliest electrical experiments involved flying a kite in a thunderstorm. When the kite was struck by lightning, an electrical current came down the kite string.

Don't try this! A Swedish scientist called Georg Richmann was killed in 1753 when experimenting during a thunderstorm.

? List some places where you have seen signs warning of the dangers of electricity.

You need to remember that:

▶ When two different materials are rubbed together, they may become electrically charged by friction.

▶ One material will have a positive charge, the other a negative charge.

▶ Like charges repel, opposite charges attract.

▶ Materials become charged when electrons are transferred from one material to the other.

▶ Electrons have negative charge.

▶ Lightning is a giant electric current between a thundercloud and the ground.

Next time ≫

Unit 8   An electric current is a flow of electric charge (page 263).

Previously »

| Remember | You can make simple electric circuits using batteries, wires, bulbs and other components. |
| From Page 255 | Electrons have negative charge. |

Unit 8

Electric current

How do electric circuits work?

We use electricity every day. Sometimes it comes from batteries, sometimes from the mains.

Whenever you switch on a light, the electricity you use comes from a power station. More fuel must be burned and the generators must work harder.

In this Unit, you will learn about what happens in the wires of an electric circuit.

In this Unit, you will learn:

- ▶ about conductors and insulators;
- ▶ how to draw circuit diagrams;
- ▶ how electric current is measured;
- ▶ how current flows in circuits.

Key words

ammeter	electron
amp (A)	in parallel
circuit symbol	in series
component	insulator
conductor	switch
electric charge	terminal
electric current	

What makes a complete circuit?

If you want a light to keep shining, it must be part of a complete circuit.

When we make circuits in the lab, we connect everything together using metal wires. The wires are covered with plastic so that one metal wire cannot touch another.

▶ A metal is a **conductor**.
  Metals conduct electricity.

▶ A plastic is an **insulator**.
  Plastics do not allow electricity
  to pass through them.

A **switch** has two pieces of metal.

▶ When they touch, the switch is
  'closed' and the circuit is complete.

▶ When they do not touch, the switch
  is 'open' and the circuit is broken.

This switch is in the open position.

 Explain why the lamp in the photograph is not shining.

How do we represent an electric circuit?

A switch is a **component** in a circuit, represented by the **circuit symbol** ___•⁄ ___. Scientists and engineers use circuit symbols to represent a large variety of components in a circuit. Because they use the same symbols, everyone can understand a circuit diagram – and so can a computer.

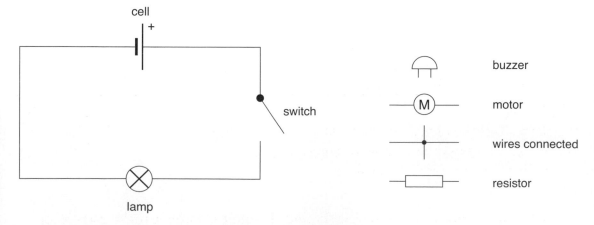

In a circuit diagram, the connecting wires are represented by lines.

 Draw a circuit diagram with a cell (a single 'battery'), a buzzer and a switch.

You are learning about some of the basic building blocks of electric circuits. A computer circuit has many millions or billions of components.

To make such complex circuits, engineers build sub-circuits which do particular jobs – for example, adding two numbers together, or storing a digit of information. Then they build bigger circuits from these sub-circuits, and so on, up to the giant circuits of the complete computer.

Research what other symbols are used for more complicated circuit diagrams. Your list should include: diode, resistor, transistor and capacitor.

@

What is a series circuit?

In the circuit shown, all the components are connected end-to-end, one after another. We say that they are connected **in series**.

You can trace round the circuit with a finger. Start at the end of the cell labelled '+'. Eventually you will get back to the cell, without having to choose between different routes to follow. The circuit never divides.

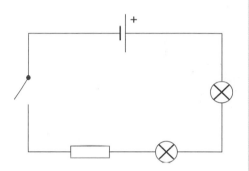

 Name the components in the circuit, in order, starting from the cell.

How do we measure electric current?

When a circuit is complete, we can see things happening – lamps light up, motors turn, and so on. We say that there is an **electric current** in the wires.

To detect the current, we add an **ammeter** to the circuit. The current must flow through the ammeter to make it work. It must be connected in series.

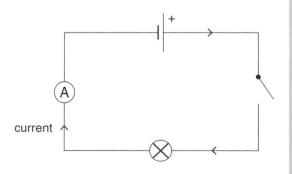

The ammeter shows how much current is flowing. The unit of current is the ampere, or **amp (A)** for short.

 Draw the symbol for an ammeter.

Scientists rely on instruments when they make measurements. An ammeter is used to measure electric current.

A ruler is a very simple instrument but, like every other instrument, we need to be sure that it is correctly calibrated – that is, that it gives correct readings. If your 30 cm ruler is 1 mm short, it will give slightly incorrect measurements.

The ammeters that you use in school were calibrated when they were manufactured, but their readings may not be as accurate now.

? **Describe how you would check whether two ammeters give the same reading.**

How does current vary round a circuit?

The circuit shown has three ammeters in it.
All three show the same current.

- ▶ The current flows from the positive end of the cell.
- ▶ It flows through one lamp and then the next.
- ▶ It flows back to the negative end of the cell.

The ammeters show that electric current doesn't get used up as it goes round a circuit. It has the same value at all points around a series circuit.

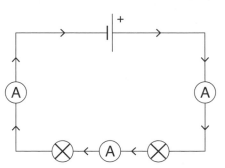

What is a parallel circuit?

In a series circuit, all of the components are connected end-to-end. The current flows through them one after another.

The diagram shows another way to connect components. They are side-by-side. We say that they are connected **in parallel**.

When the switch is closed, a current can flow in the circuit.

- ▶ When the current reaches point X, it divides.
- ▶ Some current flows through one lamp.
- ▶ The rest of the current flows through the other lamp.
- ▶ The two lots of current join up again when the wires meet at point Y.

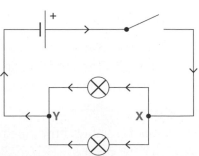

? **If the switch in this circuit is opened, what will happen?**
Explain your answer.

So what is electric current?

An electric current is a flow of **electric charge**. A current can flow in a metal wire because metals contain lots of **electrons** that are free to move about inside the wire.

Every electron has a negative charge so, when electrons move, charge is moving and this is an electric current.

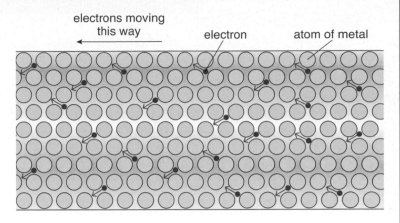

electrons moving this way   electron   atom of metal

A cell or battery has two ends or **terminals**.

▶ The positive terminal, labelled +, attracts electrons.

▶ The negative terminal, labelled –, repels electrons.

When there is a complete circuit, electrons are attracted by the positive terminal of the cell and repelled by the negative terminal. This makes them travel round the circuit, so that there is a current in the wire.

Electrons are particles. They cannot disappear or get used up, and they cannot 'leave' the wires or components. This explains why the current is the same all the way round a series circuit.

You need to remember that:

▶ A complete circuit is needed for a current to flow.

▶ A circuit diagram shows how components are connected together.

▶ Standard symbols are used to represent components in a circuit.

▶ Components connected end-to-end are in series.

▶ Components connected side-by-side are in parallel.

▶ The current is the same all round a series circuit.

▶ Current is shared between components in a parallel circuit.

▶ Electric current is a flow of electric charge.

Next time 》

Unit 9   You can connect cells in series to make a battery that will make a bigger current flow around a circuit (page 265).

Unit 9   Potential difference is a measure of how much energy electrons can transfer in a circuit (page 267).

Previously ≫

From Page 261   Electric current is a flow of electric charge in a complete circuit.

From Page 262   The current is the same all round a series circuit.

Unit 9

Voltage and resistance

What are cells and batteries for?

Every circuit needs a cell, a battery, a power supply or mains electricity to make it work. These have two purposes:

▶ they push the current round the circuit;

▶ they provide the energy for the components in the circuit.

When a lamp lights up, its energy is coming from the battery. Without the current, the energy would not reach the lamp.

In this Unit, you will learn:

▶ how voltage is measured;

▶ how cells combine to make a battery;

▶ how current depends on voltage;

▶ why lights come on straight away;

▶ what electrical resistance means.

Key words

battery	transfer
cell	volt (V)
potential difference	voltage
potential energy	voltmeter
resistance	

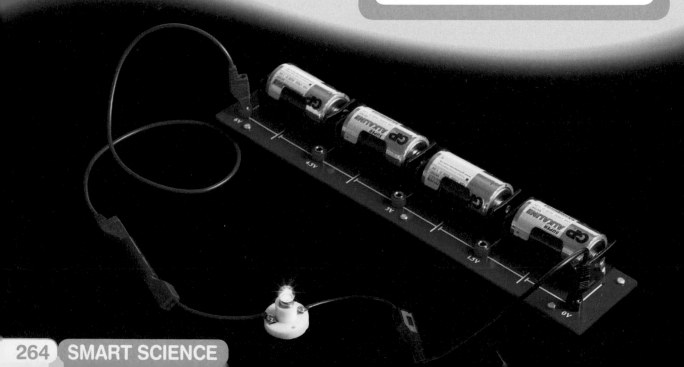

How do we measure voltage?

A **cell** is a source of energy to push electric current round a circuit and make components work. **Voltage** is a way of measuring the amount of energy a cell can provide. You may have seen cells labelled with their voltages, such as '1.5 V' or '9 V', where the unit is the **volt (V)**.

A **voltmeter** is used to measure voltage. If you want to check the voltage of a cell, connect a voltmeter across it.

▶ Plug connecting wires into each of its terminals.

▶ Connect the wires to the two terminals of the cell.

The voltmeter is connected *across* the cell, so we say that it shows the voltage *across* the cell. Another name for voltage is **potential difference**.

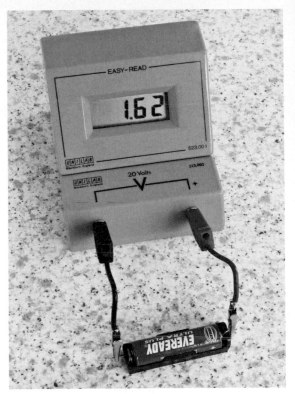

What happens when cells are connected together?

Two or more cells can be connected together to make a **battery**.

(In everyday life, we often call a single cell a *battery*.)

In a battery, the cells are connected together in series. Usually, they are joined so that the positive terminal of one is connected to the negative terminal of the next.

For cells in series, the voltages add up. So two 1.5 V cells give a total of 3.0 V.

1.5 V	3.0 V	4.5 V	1.5 V

You can see from the fourth diagram that, when one cell is reversed, its voltage must be subtracted.

Draw diagrams to show two different ways in which four 1.5 V cells could be connected together in series to give 0 V.

When a new idea comes along, we may need a new word for it.

Sometimes scientists make up new words for their discoveries and inventions. *Transistor* was made up from *transfer* and *resistor*.

At other times, they borrow a word and give it a new use. The word *cell* was used for the rows of small rooms used by monks in a monastery. When Robert Hooke saw rows of identical spaces in a piece of cork, he called them 'cells'. Then scientists learned to make powerful batteries by combining a number of simple electrical 'cells'.

? The word *lens* is the Latin word for a lentil. Find out why this word was chosen by scientists to mean a piece of glass shaped so that it can focus light.

What happens if we increase the voltage in a circuit?

If you use one cell to light a lamp, it may glow dimly. If you use two cells, it will be brighter. This tells us two things:

○ the lamp is brighter because there is more current in the circuit;

○ the lamp is brighter because it is being supplied with energy more quickly.

The diagram shows how you could connect an ammeter and a voltmeter in the circuit to make measurements.

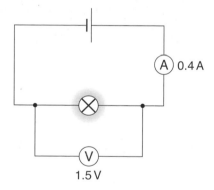

1.5 V

3.0 V

○ The ammeter will show that the current is roughly twice as much when there are two cells.

○ The voltmeter will show that the voltage across the lamp is twice as much when there are two cells.

So a bigger voltage makes a bigger current flow.

It can help to think that the voltage of the cell tells us about the 'push' it gives to make the current flow in the circuit. When there are two cells in the circuit, the current is 'pushed' by both cells and so it is bigger.

? Is the voltmeter in the diagram connected in series or in parallel with the lamp?

What does 'potential difference' mean?

A cell pushes electric charge around a circuit. We can picture a cell giving energy to the electrons at its negative terminal.

Then the electrons flow round the circuit. They **transfer** their energy to the components in the circuit, say to produce light (in a bulb) or sound (in a buzzer).

Finally, they return to the other terminal of the cell.

The potential difference of the cell tells us how much energy the electrons can transfer in the circuit, from when they leave the cell to when they return to it. They have been given a potential to transfer energy. The bigger the potential difference across the terminals of the cell, the greater this **potential energy** of the electrons.

The mains voltage is about 230 V. This means that the mains provides a lot of potential energy to the electrons, and so they can deliver lots of energy quickly to a circuit.

It's important to take care when using language in science. For example, you might hear someone say, "He got 2000 volts of electricity through him."

But it isn't voltage that goes through someone when they get a shock, it's current. It would be better to say, "He got 2000 volts across him so that a big current went through him."

Voltage is *across* something; current goes *through* something.

 Look at some electrical appliances. Find the label on each which tells you the voltage needed to make it operate. List the appliances and their voltages. Can you also find out the current that passes through them when they are operating?

What does 'resistance' mean?

Some components in a circuit let current flow more easily. They have low **resistance**. Other components may have high resistance – it takes a high voltage to make even a small current flow through them.

When a current flows through a component with high resistance, it loses a lot of potential energy. Its energy is transferred to the component, which gets hot.

It is important that connecting wires have low resistance. Otherwise energy would be wasted in them.

Resistance isn't always a bad thing. The filament of a light bulb must have resistance. Then the current will transfer energy to it and the bulb will get hot and light up.

You get an electric shock when a voltage makes a current flow through you. Current can flow easily through your insides because there is a lot of water inside you and water has quite low resistance. If the current is big enough, it can make the water boil inside the cells of your body – that's nasty!

To get inside you, the current must pass through your skin. Dry skin has higher resistance than wet skin and may be enough to protect you from a fatal shock.

Wet skin is a good conductor. That's why you have to be especially careful with electricity in the bathroom.

? Look around a bathroom. Explain how you are protected from electricity when you are in there.

You need to remember that:

- ▶ Voltage (potential difference) is measured in volts (V), using a voltmeter.
- ▶ The voltages of cells add up when they are connected in series.
- ▶ The greater the voltage of a cell, the greater the current it will push around a circuit.
- ▶ Potential difference is a measure of how much energy electrons can transfer in a circuit.
- ▶ The resistance of a component is a measure of how much energy is needed to make a current flow through it.

Next time »

Unit 14   We use fuels and renewable energy sources to generate electrical energy (page 292).

Unit 16   Batteries are sources of electrical energy. The electrical energy is transferred from stored chemical energy (page 300).

Previously »

| Remember | Sounds travel away from sources, getting fainter as they spread out, and they are heard when they enter your ears. |

| From Page 220 | Forces appear when two objects interact with each other. |

Unit 10

Sound

What are sounds?

Sounds are what we hear with our ears. A dog barking, a cat purring, a musician playing, a friend speaking.

Sounds are an important way in which we learn what's going on around us. And musical sounds can give us a lot of pleasure.

In this Unit, you will learn:

- ▶ how sounds are produced;
- ▶ the difference between loud and soft sounds;
- ▶ the difference between high sounds and low sounds.

Key words

amplitude	pitch
frequency	syrinx
hertz (Hz)	vibration
larynx	vocal folds
loudness	

What are vibrations?

We can't see sounds, but we can sometimes see what is making the sound.

If you hold a ruler halfway over the edge of a table and flick the end, you can hear it making a springy, wobbly noise. You can also see the end moving up and down very fast. This repeated, up-and-down, movement is what we call a **vibration**.

The vibrating ruler causes a sound wave in the air, and this is what we hear. To learn more about sound waves, see page 274.

We can see vibrations in other ways too. The photograph shows the wave patterns in water produced by a tuning fork.

How can a guitar make musical sounds?

All musical instruments vibrate to make sounds. They do this in different ways.

A guitar is a stringed instrument. It has six strings of different thicknesses. You pluck the strings to make different notes.

- If you pluck the string harder, the note will be louder – it has a greater **loudness**.
- The thickest string makes the lowest notes – they have a low **pitch**.
- If you press on the string to shorten the length that vibrates, the pitch will be higher.

 Describe how a violin produces sounds.

How do other instruments work?

A flute is a wind instrument. When you blow across the mouthpiece, the air inside the tube of the flute is made to vibrate.

- If you blow harder, the note will be louder.
- If you hold down different keys on the flute, the pitch of the note – how high or low it is – changes.

With an electronic keyboard, pressing a key sends an electric current back and forth through the loudspeaker. This makes the loudspeaker vibrate, and a sound is made. Each key makes a note with a different pitch.

A keyboard can be programmed to sound like different instruments. The electric current is shaped by electronic circuits to give a sound which can be a good imitation of the real instrument.

? A mobile phone can make a range of different sounds electronically. List some other devices that can do this. How realistic are they?

How do birds make sounds?

A bird has a special organ in its windpipe, called the **syrinx**. As a bird breathes, air passes over the syrinx and makes it vibrate.

The bird uses muscles to control the shape of the syrinx and the amount of air going past it. In this way, the bird changes the pitch and loudness of the sounds it makes.

The syrinx is at the point the windpipe splits into two to connect to the lungs. Some birds can control each side of the syrinx separately, which means they can make two different sounds at the same time!

How do humans make sounds?

Of course, we don't need a musical instrument to make our own sounds. Like birds, we can control how air moves through our windpipe and mouth to change the sounds we make.

Unlike birds, we don't have a syrinx, so we can't make two sounds at the same time. Instead, we have an organ higher up in our windpipe called the **larynx**. This contains two membranes called **vocal folds** (commonly known as 'vocal cords').

We use muscles to change the shape and size of the vocal folds, and this is how we make sounds of different pitch.

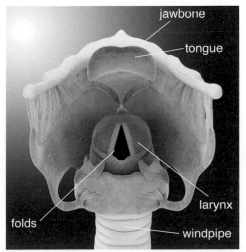

jawbone
tongue
larynx
folds
windpipe

? Describe the differences between how a human and how a bird produce sounds.

How loud is that sound?

To make a sound louder, we must make its vibrations bigger.

We can use a microphone and an oscilloscope to show the patterns of different sounds. The microphone turns the sound into an electrical signal in a wire; the oscilloscope shows the signal on its screen.

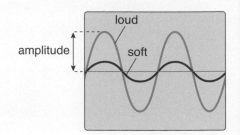

On the screen, we see the wave pattern of the sound's vibrations. The louder the sound, the greater the **amplitude** (height) of the wave. The source of the sound has to vibrate back and forth more to make a louder sound.

How high is that sound?

An explosion in a film is a sound of low pitch. A bird singing makes sounds of high pitch. The oscilloscope screen shows that a note with a high pitch vibrates more times each second. It has a higher **frequency**.

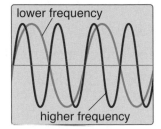

To measure the frequency of a note, we need to find how many vibrations there are each second. The scientific unit for frequency is the **hertz (Hz)**. A sound that vibrates 100 times per second has a frequency of 100 hertz (100 Hz).

 Draw up a table of six different sounds and research what frequencies they include.

You need to remember that:

- Sounds are produced by vibrations.
- Differences in the loudness of sounds are measured using the quantity 'amplitude'.
- Differences in the pitch of sounds are measured using the quantity 'frequency', using the unit 'hertz', Hz.
- Strings on a guitar vibrate to produce musical sounds.
- Birds produce sounds using an organ called the syrinx.
- Humans produce sounds using an organ called the larynx.

Next time »

Unit 11   The vibrations of a sound need something to travel through, called a medium (page 274).

Unit 11   We hear sounds because the sound waves cause our eardrums to vibrate (page 276).

Previously »

| From Page 270 | Sounds are produced by vibrations. |
| From Page 272 | Differences in the pitch of sounds are measured using the quantity 'frequency', using the unit 'hertz', Hz. |

Unit 11

How sound travels

In space, no one can hear you scream!

This was the advertising slogan for the film *Alien* – and it is absolutely true!

Astronauts have to use radios if they are going to speak to each other when they are out in empty space.

In this Unit, you will learn:

- ▶ why sounds cannot travel through empty space;
- ▶ how sounds travel as sound waves;
- ▶ how fast sounds travel;
- ▶ how we hear sounds.

Key words

infrasound	sound wave
insulation	ultrasound
medium	vacuum
noise	

What can sounds travel through?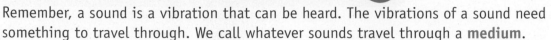

Remember, a sound is a vibration that can be heard. The vibrations of a sound need something to travel through. We call whatever sounds travel through a **medium**.

The medium for most sounds we hear is air. If you pluck a guitar string, vibrations travel through the air to your ears. You hear the note of the guitar.

Air is a gas. Sounds can also travel through solids and liquids. If you put your ear to a table and tap the table, the sound reaches your ear through the wood.

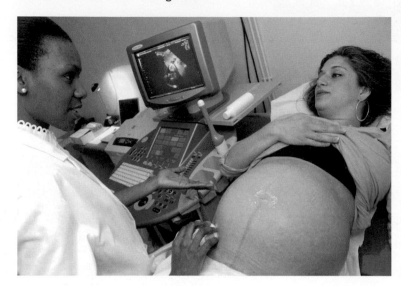

In an ultrasound scan, vibrations pass into the mother and are reflected by the baby. The reflected sound waves are turned into a picture so we can see how well the baby is growing.

In space, there is no air. Space is a **vacuum** – there is no medium at all. This means that sound cannot travel through space.

What is a sound wave?

When an object vibrates, it causes the air nearby to vibrate. The vibrations spread outwards through the air until they reach our ears.

Think of a vibrating guitar string. As it vibrates, it pushes on the molecules of the air so that they move back and forth. These molecules push on molecules further way, so that they also vibrate.

If we could see the molecules of the air, we would see that they form a regular pattern, squashed close together in places and spread out in between. This pattern, moving through air, is called a **sound wave**.

air molecules move
back and forth

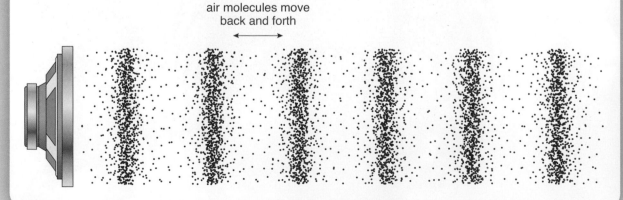

The idea of 'waves' is very important in physics. Sound waves, light waves, waves on the sea ... It's even possible to show that particles such as electrons and neutrons sometimes behave like waves.

? All waves can be reflected. Describe how you would demonstrate that sound waves can be reflected.

How fast do sound waves travel?

A sound wave is simply air molecules vibrating and knocking into each other.

Molecules in the air are moving all the time at about 400 metres per second (m/s). Sound waves travel through air at a slightly slower speed – about 330 m/s.

Light travels much, much faster than sound – at about 300 000 000 m/s!

This is why, during a thunderstorm, we see a lightning flash before we hear the clap of thunder. They happen at the same time, but the lightning flash reaches our eyes almost instantaneously. The sound of the thunder may take several seconds to reach us.

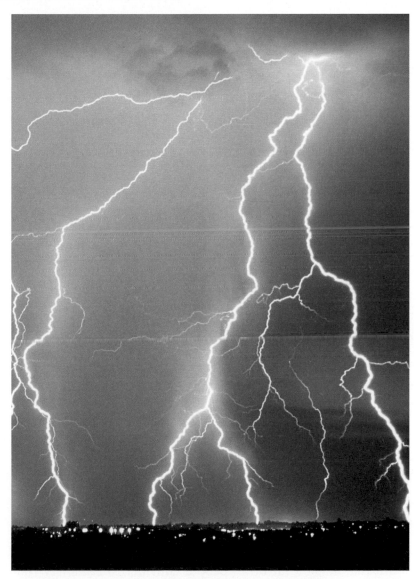

?
1 How many times faster is light than sound?
2 How long does it take the sound of thunder to travel 5 km?

How do we hear?

If a friend talks to you, a sound wave travels from their vocal folds to your ear.

What happens inside your ear?

▶ The vibrations of the air press on your eardrum, so that it also vibrates.

▶ This causes the three small bones to vibrate, and they press on the cochlea.

▶ This sends electrical signals along nerves to your brain, which you recognise as sounds.

As we grow – and even before we are born – we learn how to tell apart sounds of different pitch and loudness. Eventually we learn how these sounds combine to make speech.

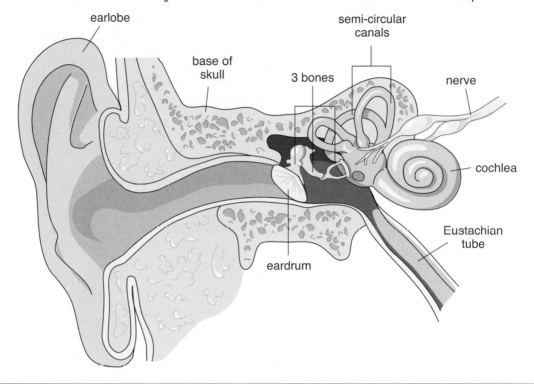

Why are there sounds we don't like?

Sound is really important to us as a way of understanding the world.

We choose some sounds to give us warnings: a smoke alarm or a police siren, for example.

Other sounds are annoying: the loud noise of a drill as it hits a wall or a road, or the buzz of a wasp.

Any unwanted sound is called **noise**. We don't all agree about noise. For example, you might like music that other people consider to be noise. Thankfully, science has nothing to tell us about what music we should or shouldn't like!

? **Describe how the pitch and loudness of a police siren change in order to attract the most attention.**

Why do some machines make noises? @

Any machine with moving parts will cause vibrations. As we know, vibrations are what cause sound waves.

An important part of designing machines is to make sure that they don't cause unwanted sounds.

A good example is a car. Many parts of a car vibrate. For example, the wheels and tyres vibrate as they roll over rough road surfaces. Designers work hard to reduce the loudness of this noise, by putting thick layers of soft material around the frame of the car. This material is called **insulation**.

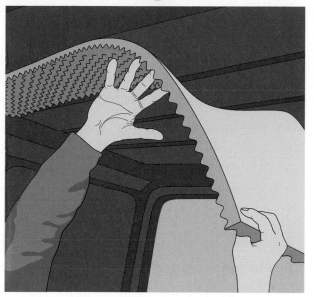

What sounds can we hear?

We cannot hear very faint sounds. We cannot hear very low-pitched sounds, or very high-pitched sounds.

Hearing tests show that people can usually hear a wide range of frequencies of sounds, between about 20 Hz and 20 000 Hz.

- Sounds which have frequencies above 20 000 Hz are called **ultrasound**.
- Sounds which have frequencies below 20 Hz are called **infrasound**.

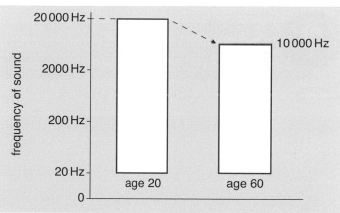

As we get older, it becomes harder to hear high-pitched sounds. By the time you reach the age of 40, you may not be able to hear sounds with frequencies above about 15 000 Hz. At 60, the limit might be 10 000 Hz.

THINKING BEYOND...

You could estimate your teacher's age by measuring the highest frequency they can hear.

? How accurate would this be?

What causes poor hearing?

Our ears contain very delicate bones. They are very sensitive so that we can recognise a wide range of sounds.

Some people have poor hearing, perhaps because the delicate bones in the ear do not move properly, or because the cochlea is damaged, or because the signals do not transmit to the brain.

They may have worked in noisy environments, or they may not have protected themselves properly at concerts. Some diseases can also lead to hearing damage.

How can we protect our hearing?

Some things we can do to protect our hearing are obvious. One example is wearing ear protectors when doing loud jobs such as drilling or using machinery.

You may not notice your ears being damaged when it happens. Only later on do you notice your ears 'ringing' or that you can't hear certain sounds. If that ever happens to you after a concert or listening to headphones – it's too loud!

Once our hearing is damaged, it is very difficult to fix. So look after your hearing and turn the volume down. Your ears will thank you.

 What precautions should you take when listening to a portable music player with headphones?

You need to remember that:

- A sound wave needs a medium to travel through.
- The speed of sound in air is about 330 metres per second (m/s).
- Sound waves cause your eardrum to vibrate, which moves bones inside your ear that cause an electrical signal to be sent to your brain.
- Humans can hear sounds of between 20 Hz and 20 000 Hz.
- Our ears are easily damaged by too much loud noise, so we can protect them by reducing the loudness of sounds.

Next time ⟫

Unit 12 Light travels in straight lines at 300 000 000 m/s (page 281).

Unit 16 Sound waves are a way of transferring energy (page 302).

Previously »

Remember — There are many sources of light, including the Sun, and darkness is the absence of light.

From Page 275 — The speed of sound in air is about 330 metres per second (m/s).

Unit 12

Light

Why is light important to us?

Our sight is the sense that gives us most information about our surroundings. Sight depends on light.

You are using light in order to read this book – even though the letters are in black, which is the absence of light! Without light, the pages would look entirely black and you wouldn't be able to read a word.

In this Unit, you will learn:

- ▶ where light comes from;
- ▶ how light travels;
- ▶ how light interacts with different materials;
- ▶ how light is reflected.

Key words

absorb	ray
angle of incidence	reflect
angle of reflection	reflected ray
image	scatter
incident ray	shadow
Law of Reflection	sources of light
mirror image	translucent
normal	transparent
opaque	virtual image
parallel	

Where does light come from?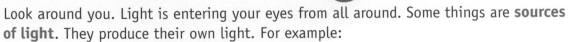

Look around you. Light is entering your eyes from all around. Some things are **sources of light**. They produce their own light. For example:

- ▶ flames such as candles and fires – hot things glow;
- ▶ the Sun and the stars, which are giant balls of hot gas;
- ▶ light bulbs, lasers, TVs and computer screens – these use electricity to produce light;
- ▶ insects and fish that glow in the dark – some chemical reactions produce light.

We see these sources when light from them enters our eyes.

How do we see other things?

There are many things that we see which do not produce their own light – other people, for example.

We see them because they **reflect** light into our eyes. There must be another source of light, shining on the object, if we are to see it.

The diagram shows how we see a picture in an art gallery.

- ▶ Lamps shine on the picture.
- ▶ Light reflects from the picture to our eyes.

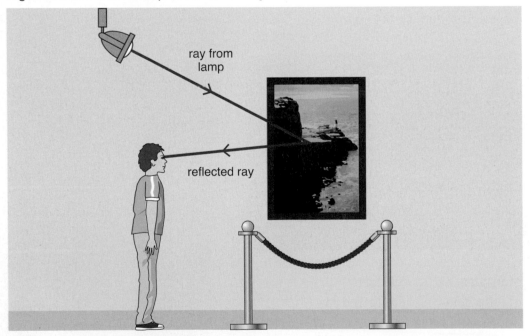

? People used to think that we see things because feelers come out of our eyes and touch everything around us. Suggest why they thought we couldn't see when our eyes are shut. Give a better explanation, using the scientific ideas given above.

How does light travel?

When we want to show the path of light, we draw a straight line called a **ray**. Light travels in straight lines.

This explains how shadows form. A **shadow** is a place where no light falls, as a result of light rays being blocked by an object.

We can work out where shadows will be by drawing rays of light spreading out from the source.

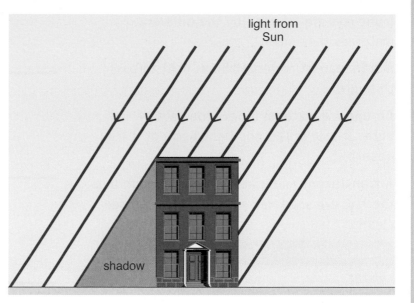

light from Sun

shadow

Light travels very fast – faster than anything else we know. Light travels at a speed of

  300 000 000 m/s, which is the same as 300 000 km/s

That means the sunlight reflecting off the International Space Station orbiting overhead takes just 1/800 of a second to reach us!

Light travels more slowly if it goes into a transparent material such as water or glass.

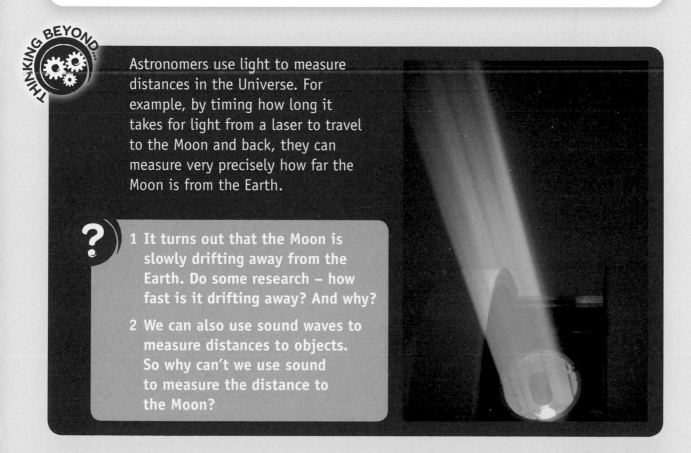

THINKING BEYOND...

Astronomers use light to measure distances in the Universe. For example, by timing how long it takes for light from a laser to travel to the Moon and back, they can measure very precisely how far the Moon is from the Earth.

?

1 It turns out that the Moon is slowly drifting away from the Earth. Do some research – how fast is it drifting away? And why?

2 We can also use sound waves to measure distances to objects. So why can't we use sound to measure the distance to the Moon?

What happens when light meets an obstacle?

Light rays are affected by the different materials they meet.

A **transparent** material allows light to pass through.

An **opaque** material blocks the path of light. It may reflect the light back, or it may **absorb** it.

A **translucent** material lets light through but the rays are scattered so that we do not see clearly.

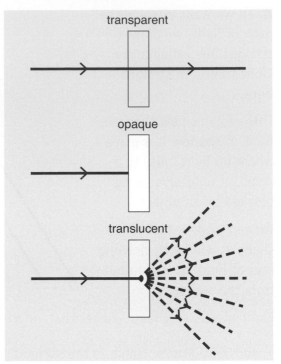

Transparent	Opaque	Translucent
water	wood	frosted glass
ice	steel	waxed paper
glass	paper	
Perspex (acrylic)		

Look around you and list six materials that you can see under the headings *transparent*, *translucent* and *opaque*.

How is light reflected?

When light strikes an opaque material, it may reflect off it. An example is the page you are looking at.

How the light reflects depends on the surface of the material.

▶ If the surface is rough, it will **scatter** light in all directions.

▶ If the surface is smooth, **parallel** rays of light (all travelling in the same direction) will still be parallel after they have reflected off it.

This is how a mirror works. A mirror has a surface that is very flat and very shiny, so that almost all of the light that falls on it reflects off without being scattered. That is why we can see a clear reflection in a mirror – an **image**.

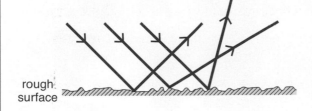
rough surface

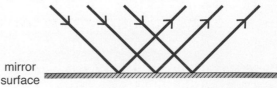
mirror surface

What is the Law of Reflection?

When a ray of light strikes a mirror, it reflects off at the same angle. The diagram shows this.

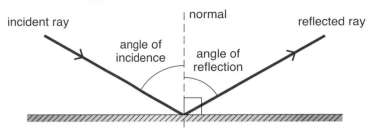

This is how you draw your own diagram to show reflection:

1. find the point where the **incident ray** reaches the mirror;
2. draw the **normal** to the mirror at this point – at right angles to the mirror;
3. the **angle of incidence** is measured between the incident ray and the normal;
4. the **angle of reflection** is measured between the **reflected ray** and the normal;
5. the **Law of Reflection** says that these two angles are equal:
   angle of incidence = angle of reflection

How does an image form in a mirror?

When you look in a mirror, you see a **mirror image** of yourself. This is often called a 'reflection'. It looks as though it is behind the mirror.

The diagram shows how you can see an image of a candle flame in a mirror.

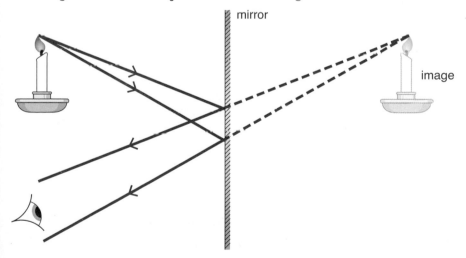

To draw this diagram:

1. draw two rays coming from the flame and reaching the mirror;
2. draw the two reflected rays, making sure they obey the Law of Reflection;
3. draw dashed lines to show where the reflected rays would meet, behind the mirror.

The reflected rays *appear* to come from a point behind the mirror. This is where the image is.

There isn't really any light coming from behind the mirror. This type of image is called a **virtual image**.

What use are mirrors?

Plane (flat) mirrors allow us to see ourselves – for example, at the hairdresser's. They can also allow us to see around corners – for example, at dangerous road junctions.

Curved mirrors can produce an image that is bigger than the original object (magnified) or smaller. Curved mirrors are used:

- ▶ as car rear-view mirrors – so we can see a wide view behind us;
- ▶ for security mirrors in shops and buses – so the shop owner or bus driver can see all the inside of the shop or bus;
- ▶ to gather light in big astronomical telescopes – the bigger the mirror, the more light can be collected from very dim and distant stars and galaxies.

 Give three examples of ways in which you use mirrors. For each example, say if it is a plane or a curved mirror.

You need to remember that:

- ▶ We see objects when light from them enters our eyes.
- ▶ Some things are sources of light (they produce their own); we see others because they reflect light or absorb it.
- ▶ A shadow is an area where no light reaches.
- ▶ Light travels in straight lines, at very high speed.
- ▶ Rough surfaces scatter light.
- ▶ Transparent materials let all the light through.
- ▶ Opaque materials block all the light.
- ▶ Translucent materials let only some of the light through.
- ▶ The Law of Reflection:

    angle of incidence = angle of reflection
- ▶ A mirror reflects light to form a virtual image.

Next time ⟩⟩

Unit 13 We can 'bend' light using refraction, because light travels at different speeds in different materials (page 287).

Unit 16 Light travelling is a way of transferring energy (page 303).

Unit 19 We use light to observe the Universe (page 317).

Previously >>

From Page 281   Light travels in straight lines at 300 000 000 m/s.

From Page 283   A mirror reflects light to form a virtual image.

Unit 13

Bending light

If light travels in straight lines, how can we bend it?

You can use a mirror to make a ray of light turn a corner. That's one way to bend light.

Another way is to use refraction – this is the bending of light that you can see in the photograph, making the drinking straw look as though it is broken.

In this Unit, you will learn:

- ▶ how and why a ray of light is refracted;
- ▶ how refraction is used;
- ▶ how refraction breaks up white light into a spectrum;
- ▶ how colours are changed by colour addition and colour subtraction.

Key words

angle of incidence	incident ray
angle of refraction	lens
colour addition	normal
colour subtraction	primary colours of light
dispersion	refracted ray
filter	refraction
focus	spectrum

When does refraction happen?

The photograph shows a ray of green light passing through a glass block.

- ▶ The ray starts out in air.
- ▶ It bends at the point where it enters the glass.
- ▶ It bends again at the point where it leaves the glass.

This bending is called **refraction**, and it happens when a ray of light passes from one transparent material into another. Notice that the ray doesn't bend *inside* the glass; it only bends at two points, where it enters the glass and where it leaves it.

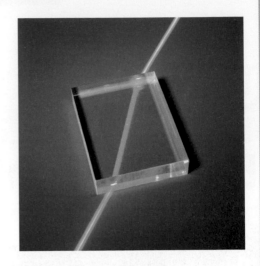

 Turn the photograph into a drawing. Use a ruler to draw the shape of the glass block. Use your ruler again to draw the three sections of the ray.

Which way does a ray bend?

We can take a close look at the point where the ray enters the glass.

- ▶ We draw the **normal** at the point where the ray enters the glass. The normal is a line at 90° to the surface of the glass.
- ▶ The **angle of incidence** is the angle between the **incident ray** and the normal.
- ▶ The **angle of refraction** is the angle between the **refracted ray** and the normal.

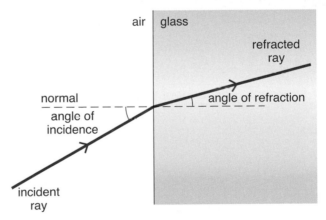

You can see that, as the ray enters the glass, it bends *towards* the normal.

Now take a close look at where the ray leaves the glass and returns to the air.

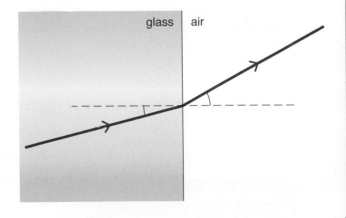

You can see that, as the ray leaves the glass, it bends *away from* the normal.

Why does refraction happen?

Light travels at different speeds in different materials.

Refraction happens because light travels more slowly in glass than in air.

Light slows down as it goes from air to glass, and this makes it bend towards the normal.

Approximate speed of light	
in air	300 000 km/s
in water	225 000 km/s
in glass	200 000 km/s (depends on the type of glass)

Light speeds up as it goes from glass to air, and this makes it bend away from the normal.

THINKING BEYOND...

In order to make more sense of why light bends when its speed changes, you would need to have a picture of how light travels as waves.

Waves on the sea change direction, just as light waves change direction when they enter glass. In deep water, they can travel in any direction. However, as they approach land, they swing round until they are parallel to the beach.

? Find out and explain why water waves behave like this.

Why does a stick look bent in water?

The diagram shows a stick, half in water.

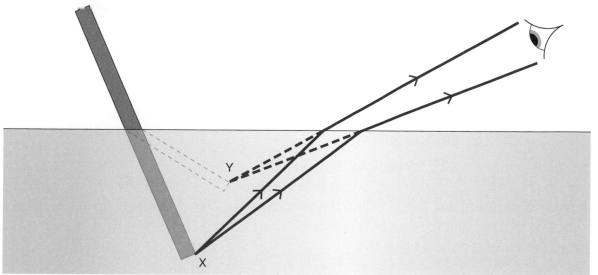

◯ Rays from the tip X of the stick bend as they leave the water.
◯ To our eye, they seem to be coming from a different place, point Y.

So it looks as though the stick is bent.

How can we use refraction?

Perhaps you have used a **lens** (a magnifying glass) to concentrate sunlight on to a piece of paper, making it burn. A lens is a cleverly shaped piece of glass that refracts parallel rays of light so that they all meet at a point.

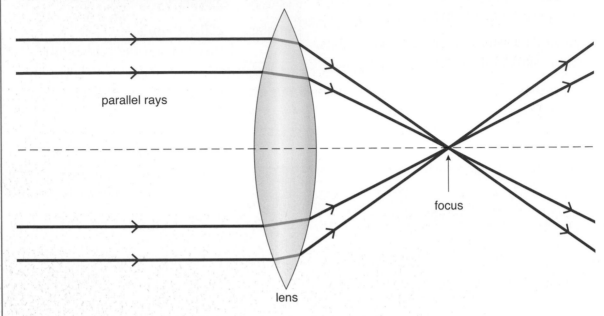

parallel rays

focus

lens

Check the diagram:

- ▶ each ray bends towards the normal as it enters the lens;
- ▶ each ray bends away from the normal as it leaves the lens.

This double-bending makes all of the rays meet at one point, the **focus** of the lens.

 How are lenses used in everyday life? Give at least two examples. @

What is 'white light'?

We all know what the colour 'white' looks like. This book is printed on white paper.

Sunlight is described as 'white light'. However, if it passes through a glass prism, it is split into all the colours of the rainbow. This is called the **spectrum** of white light. The colours come in this order:

red   orange   yellow   green   blue   indigo   violet

You can remember this as a name: Roy G Biv.

Separating white light into a spectrum is called **dispersion**.

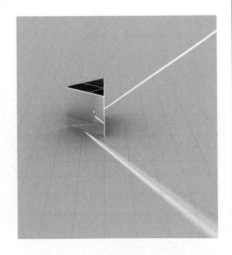

Why does dispersion happen?

The spectrum shows that white light is made up of a mixture of different colours.

Dispersion happens because, when white light enters glass, it slows down and bends. Because some colours of light travel more slowly in glass than others, they bend more.

You can see from the diagram that violet light bends most. Red light bends least.

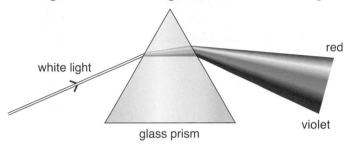

white light

red

violet

glass prism

What happens if we mix two or more colours of light?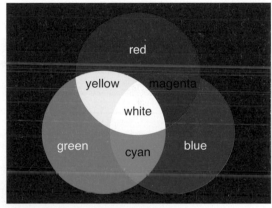

You might be surprised to know that, if you mix red and green light, you get yellow! It is not the same as mixing paint or ink.

We say that the three **primary colours of light** are red, green and blue. The chart shows the colours produced when two or three of the primary colours are mixed together.

Mixing colours like this is called **colour addition**.

red

yellow magenta

white

green cyan blue

 If you look closely at a computer or TV screen each tiny dot (or pixel) is made up of three segments – green, red and blue. How does this allow us to see colours such as yellow and white?

How does coloured glass work?

Coloured glass acts as a **filter**, which 'takes out' other colours of light. To understand what happens when white light strikes a piece of red glass, we have to think about how the different colours of the spectrum are affected:

  ▶ only red light passes through the glass;
  ▶ all the other colours of the spectrum are absorbed by the glass.

Similarly, green glass lets green light through, and so on.

Why are pieces of coloured glass or plastic called 'filters'? Think of a filter that lets through water but doesn't let sand pass through (see page 124). Coloured glass lets through some colours of light but not others.

? To make your own filters, find some pieces of clear, coloured plastic, such as sweet wrappers. Try taking photographs through different colours. What changes do you see?

Why do red things look red?

A book with a red cover looks red, at least when white light shines on it. Remember that white light is made up of all the colours, from red to violet.

▶ The ink on the book reflects red light to your eye.

▶ The ink absorbs all the other colours.

Because some colours are taken away from the white light, this is called **colour subtraction**.

The book will also look red when red light shines on it, because it will reflect all the red light. But if green light shines on it, no red light is reflected, so the book looks black.

 What colour will a blue book look under white light? And under red light?

You need to remember that:

▶ A light ray is refracted (it bends) when it passes from one transparent material to another.

▶ Refraction happens because light travels at different speeds in different materials.

▶ Light travels faster in air than it does in glass.

▶ A ray bends towards the normal when it slows down.

▶ A ray bends away from the normal when it speeds up.

▶ A lens uses refraction to focus parallel rays of light to a single point.

▶ Dispersion is the splitting of white light into a spectrum by a prism.

▶ The primary colours of light are red, green and blue.

▶ The colour of an object depends on the colour of light it reflects to our eyes.

Next time »

Unit 18 During a lunar eclipse, the Moon can appear red because the light from the Sun is refracted through the Earth's atmosphere (page 315).

Unit 19 Astronomers use telescopes with lenses to observe light from great distances (page 317).

Previously ≫

From Page 225 Unbalanced forces cause the motion of an object to change.

From Page 264 Every circuit needs a cell, a battery, a power supply or mains electricity to make it work.

Unit 14

Energy resources

Why is 'energy' important?

The idea of 'energy' is an important one in all areas of science. Animals and plants need a source of energy. Chemical reactions involve energy changes. We use electricity to move energy from place to place.

In this Unit, we look at sources of energy. In Unit 15, we look at how energy moves around as heat and, in Unit 16, we describe energy changes.

In this Unit, you will learn:

▷ about the energy stores that people use;

▷ the difference between renewable and non-renewable energy resources.

Key words

energy resources	nuclear fuels
food	photosynthesis
fossil fuels	renewable energy
non-renewable fuels	solar cells

Where do we get our energy from?

Human beings, like all animals, get energy from **food**.

Plants make their own food, using the energy of sunlight, through the process of **photosynthesis** (see page 40).

Food and sunlight are **energy resources**, from which we can get the energy to do things. Through food chains (see page 96), all the food that animals eat comes originally from plants. So we are dependent on sunlight as the ultimate source of all energy we need to live.

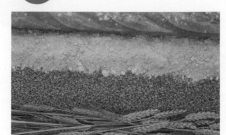

Wheat needs sunlight to grow. The grain is milled to make flour, which is baked into bread.

What other energy resources do we use? @

Food provides the energy that our bodies need to stay alive and to do things. But lots of the things we do make use of other energy resources.

- ▶ We burn wood, coal or gas for cooking our food and heating our homes.
- ▶ Cars, trucks and planes use the energy of **fossil fuels**, and so do many power stations that generate electricity.
- ▶ A windmill makes use of the energy of the wind to grind corn or to generate electricity.
- ▶ A nuclear power station uses **nuclear fuels** such as uranium to generate electricity.

Where does the energy of fossil fuels come from?

Coal, oil and gas are fossil fuels. They are extracted from under the ground.

1. Long ago, trees grew. Their trunks stored energy from sunlight.
2. The trees died and sank in boggy ground.
3. Over millions of years, the tree remains became compressed and gradually changed to become coal.

When we burn coal, we are making use of energy that came from the Sun long, long ago.

Oil and gas formed in a similar way from the remains of tiny sea creatures that lived millions of years ago. Their energy also came from sunlight, stored in the microscopic plants they ate.

An artist's impression of a forest in the carboniferous age, when coal-bearing rocks were formed.

 The carboniferous age was millions of years ago, before the time of the dinosaurs. Find out how long ago it was.

Why are fossil fuels 'non-renewable'?

Fossil fuels are stores of energy. We burn them to release their energy.

The chemical reaction of burning takes oxygen out of the atmosphere. The fuel and oxygen react to produce carbon dioxide and water vapour:

fossil fuel + oxygen → carbon dioxide + water + energy released

Once we have burned a fossil fuel, we cannot get it back again. We can go and find some more, but eventually all the supplies will be used up.

Because it takes millions of years for fossil fuels to be made, they are not being replaced in the ground. This is why they are called **non-renewable fuels**.

 Study the equation above. Look up the equation which summarises photosynthesis (see page 40). What difference can you see between these two equations?

Which energy resources are renewable?

Wood is another fuel that we burn to release its energy. When we chop down a tree for its wood, we can always plant another to replace it. Many kinds of trees only take a few years to grow, so wood is a **renewable energy** resource.

Similarly, we can generate electricity using the energy of the wind. We can extract energy from the wind today, and we know that there will be more in the future. We will never use up the wind.

Hydroelectricity uses the energy of water stored behind a dam to turn generators to produce electricity. When it rains in the future, the dam will fill up again.

The wind makes waves on the sea, and the movement of the waves can also be used to generate electricity.

Plants, wind, sea and rain get their energy from sunlight, so once again all the renewable energy resources depend on the Sun.

We can also use sunlight directly to heat water, or to generate electricity using **solar cells**. There is no sunlight at night, but the Sun will rise again tomorrow and provide us with energy for billions of years to come.

The amount of carbon dioxide in the atmosphere has increased greatly because we have burned large amounts of fossil fuels.

Most scientists who have studied the Earth's climate believe that this is causing the Earth to warm up. As a result, our climate is changing.

To reduce the effect of this, we should use renewable energy resources and leave the fossil fuels in the ground.

? Find out how engineers are designing cars that do not depend on fossil fuels (petrol or diesel). Make a poster showing how this will change motoring in the future.

You need to remember that:

▶ All the energy animals and plants use comes originally from sunlight.

▶ We use many different energy resources as sources of energy.

▶ Fossil fuels are non-renewable energy resources – once used, we can never get them back.

▶ Wind, water, solar and wave energy are renewable energy resources – they are naturally replaced after we use them.

Next time »

Unit 15 Heat energy can travel by conduction, convection or radiation (page 296).

Unit 16 Useful forms of transferred energy include electrical energy, light energy and kinetic energy (page 302).

Previously »

From Page 267 An electric current flowing through a component with high resistance makes it hot.

From Page 292 We use many different energy resources as sources of energy.

Unit 15

Heat

How does energy move around?

If your food is too hot, you can wait and it will cool down – you can blow on it if you want, but that isn't necessary.

Your food cools because energy is escaping from it. In a similar way, a cube of ice will melt because energy from the surroundings enters it and warms it up. These are both examples of energy moving around as heat.

The photo shows how we use heat energy to cook a pizza in an oven.

In this Unit, you will learn:

▶ how heat energy moves from place to place;

▶ how evaporation cools us down.

Key words

absorber	heat
conduction	heat energy
conductors	infra-red radiation
convection current	insulators
emitter	medium
evaporation	temperature
fluids	

What is 'heat energy'?

If you have a hot drink, it will soon cool down. Energy escapes from the drink to its surroundings, which are cooler – they are at a lower **temperature**.

You can try to keep the drink hot by putting it in an insulated cup with a lid, or even in a thermos flask. But eventually it will cool down.

A 'thermogram' uses different colours to show things that are at different temperatures. Left on its own, energy will always move from a hotter place to a cooler place.

Energy moving from a hotter place to a cooler place is known as **heat energy**, or simply **heat**.

There are three ways in which heat energy travels:

⊙ conduction ⊙ convection ⊙ radiation

How does conduction work?

Heat can move through solid objects. We call this movement **conduction**.

To understand conduction in a solid, we think of the particles in a solid rod.

1. The particles at the hot end of this rod have more energy – they vibrate more.

2. They bump into their neighbours, sharing their energy with them.

3. These then share energy with their neighbours, and so on.

4. Eventually, the energy from the hot end reaches the cold end.

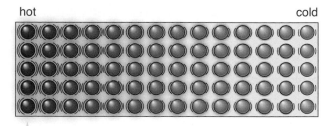

In metals, electrons are free to move about inside the metal. These electrons also help to transfer energy from the hot end to the cold end.

⊙ Metals are good **conductors** of heat.

⊙ Non-metals are generally poor conductors; we call them **insulators**.

Heat can also conduct through liquids.

You can stir a hot drink using a teaspoon. The spoon could be made from metal or plastic. What difference would you expect to notice between these, and why?

How does convection work?

Convection happens in liquids and gases; these are **fluids** – substances that can flow.

People often say, 'Hot air rises.' They are talking about a **convection current**.

1. A fluid such as air or water is heated.
2. It expands and so becomes less dense than the surrounding cooler fluid.
3. It floats upwards; colder fluid flows in to replace it.
4. In turn, this colder fluid is heated, expands and rises.
5. Meanwhile, as the hotter fluid gets further away from the heat source, it cools and sinks back down, ready to be heated again.

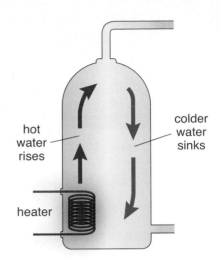

hot water rises

colder water sinks

heater

In this way, the convection current carries energy away from the area that is being heated. This is used in our houses, where a heater is placed in one part of a room. The heat energy is carried all round the room by convection currents in the air.

A hot drink may be sold in a cup with a lid. Explain how the lid helps to stop the drink from cooling down too quickly.

How does radiation work?

Conduction and convection require a **medium** – a solid, liquid or gas whose particles can carry the energy. But we get energy from the Sun; this shows that heat energy can also travel through a vacuum (empty space).

The Sun is very hot. As well as the light we see by, it produces large amounts of infra-red (heat) radiation. We say it is an **emitter** of heat.

Infra-red radiation is similar to light, but it is invisible. When infra-red radiation falls on the surface of an object, the object takes in the energy and gets hotter. We say the object is an **absorber** of heat.

In fact, every object produces infra-red radiation all the time like the mobile phone in the picture. That's why the Earth cools down at night – radiation is escaping into space. The next day, radiation from the Sun warms the Earth again.

- Dark, matt surfaces are good absorbers and emitters of radiation.
- Light, shiny surfaces are poor absorbers and emitters of radiation.

On a sunny day, currents of warm air rise from the ground as it is heated by the Sun. These currents are called 'thermals', and many birds such as eagles and vultures use them as an easy way to soar high into the sky.

? Draw a diagram to show how thermals are produced on a sunny day.

Why does evaporation cool us down?

If you get wet, water evaporates from your body and you may start to feel cold.

Evaporation is the process by which a liquid changes to a gas at a temperature below its boiling point (see page 136). For example, puddles disappear after a rain shower – they evaporate, they don't boil.

- When water evaporates, particles (molecules) of the water escape into the air.
- Some water molecules have more energy than others (they move around faster), and these are the ones that escape most easily.
- This leaves the molecules that have less energy, and so the water gets cooler.

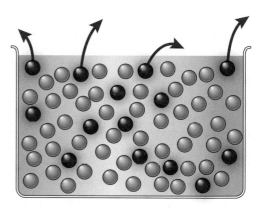

Some molecules have more energy (red) than others (blue).

Dogs pant to make water evaporate from their tongues. This cools them on a hot day.

? Explain why hot water evaporates more quickly than cold water.

You need to remember that:

- Energy travelling from a hotter place to a colder place is called heat energy.
- Heat energy can travel by conduction, convection or radiation.
- All objects emit (give out) and absorb (take in) heat.
- Dark, matt surfaces are better at absorbing and emitting heat than light, shiny surfaces.
- When we are wet, the water evaporates from our skin and makes us feel cooler.

Next time >>

Unit 16 Energy can transfer in many other ways such as sound, light or electrical energy (page 302).

Previously »

From Page 265 — Voltage is a way of measuring the amount of energy a cell can provide.

From Page 296 — Energy travelling from a hotter place to a colder place is called heat energy.

Unit 16

Energy changes

How can we tell where energy is?

You can sit and look at a lump of coal for hours on end and what will happen? Nothing.

How can you tell that it is a store of energy? You have to set fire to it. Then you will see it produce light and feel it produce heat. Light and heat are forms of energy, so coal must be a store of energy.

The energy in coal has been there for perhaps 300 million years. When it burns, that energy is released in just a few minutes.

In this Unit, you will learn:

- ⊙ how to recognise different stores of energy;
- ⊙ how energy can change from one form to another;
- ⊙ how energy tends to escape when we use it;
- ⊙ the meaning of 'conservation of energy'.

Key words

chemical energy	light energy
elastic energy	nuclear energy
electrical energy	Principle of Conservation of Energy
gravitational potential energy (GPE)	Sankey diagram
heat energy	sound energy
joules (J)	thermal energy
kinetic energy (KE)	transfer

How do fuels store energy?

Coal is mostly carbon. When it burns, it combines with oxygen from the air and its store of energy is released:

carbon + oxygen → carbon dioxide + energy released

This is a chemical reaction. We say that coal is a store of **chemical energy**.

All fuels that we burn are stores of chemical energy. This includes coal, oil, gas, wood, candle wax and charcoal.

Nuclear fuels such as uranium or plutonium are different. Their energy is released in a nuclear reaction. They are stores of **nuclear energy**.

How do batteries store energy?

Batteries are usually made of metal, with chemical substances held inside as a liquid or paste. When the battery is part of a complete circuit, a chemical reaction happens inside the battery. An electric current flows, carrying **electrical energy**.

This shows that a battery is a store of chemical energy. Eventually, the chemicals are used up and the battery is 'flat' or 'dead'.

Rechargeable batteries can take electrical energy from the mains supply. This reverses the chemical reaction and the original chemical substances are formed again.

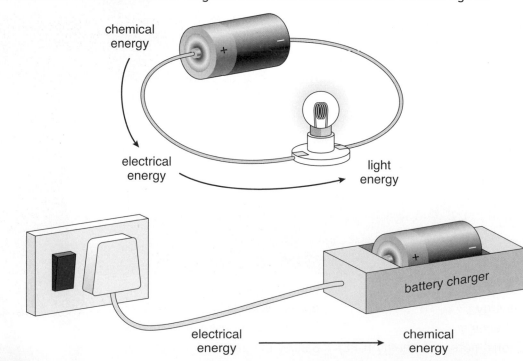

 Name some electronic devices that use rechargeable batteries.

What other ways are there of storing energy?

Stretch a rubber band and it stores energy. You can use that energy to catapult a pellet across the room. A stretched rubber band is a store of **elastic energy**. So is a stretched or squashed spring.

The elastic energy stored in a stretched spring can be used to make a clock work or to make a toy train run.

Raised objects also store energy. For example, you lift a hammer; then you let it fall on the head of a nail. When the hammer is raised, it is a store of **gravitational potential energy (GPE)**.

Think about jumping on a trampoline. A trampoline has a stretchy surface.

▶ When you press down on the trampoline, it stretches and stores elastic energy.

▶ Then it throws you back up in the air, giving you GPE.

Do hot objects store energy?

It takes energy to heat things up – for example, to boil some water. So hot objects are stores of energy.

The energy of a hot object is called **thermal energy**. It is different from the other stores of energy, because it escapes very easily.

Energy can escape from a hot object by conduction, convection and radiation (see page 296). To stop it escaping, we can insulate the object – but we can never completely stop the energy from escaping.

For example, hot food soon cools down as its energy escapes into the surroundings.

 If you heat water, it turns to steam. Which stores more thermal energy, the water at 100 °C or the steam at 100 °C? Explain your answer.

Thermal energy is stored energy. The hotter an object is, the more thermal energy it stores. Heat energy is different, because heat is energy moving from a hotter place to a cooler place. You can think of it like this: heat energy moves, thermal energy stays in one place.

? Write a paragraph describing a walk on a cold day. Explain how heat energy leaves your body and how you can try to prevent your store of thermal energy from decreasing.

Do moving objects have energy?

It takes a lot of energy to get a spacecraft into space. A rocket burns lots of fuel to do this.

When the spacecraft is in orbit around the Earth, it travels at about 8 km/s. That's fast.

The spacecraft has **kinetic energy**, or **KE**. (The word *kinetic* means *moving*.) Any moving object has kinetic energy.

▶ The faster an object moves, the greater its kinetic energy.

▶ The greater an object's mass, the greater its kinetic energy.

How can energy move around?

We have already seen (in Unit 15) how energy can **transfer** (move) from hotter places to colder places. That's **heat energy**.

Electric circuits are a good way to transfer energy from place to place. For example, the chemical energy stored in a battery can be transferred to a buzzer. We say that electrical energy is being transferred.

The buzzer makes a sound that spreads out into the room. That's **sound energy**.

Similarly, a circuit can light a lamp. **Light energy** is produced by the lamp.

? Lamps get hot when they are switched on. Name the two types of energy leaving the lamp.

How can energy change its form?

We make use of lots of devices that change energy.

Energy can keep changing between different forms. On a trampoline:

1. you push down on a trampoline as you land so that it stretches (elastic energy);

2. it pushes you up, so that you start moving (kinetic energy);

3. you go up in the air (gravitational potential energy);

4. then you fall back down, getting faster (kinetic energy) – and so on.

Device	Energy in	Energy out
buzzer	electrical	sound
solar cell	light	electrical
car (petrol)	chemical	kinetic

Why do we say 'energy is conserved'?

Energy is measured in units called **joules** (**J**).

The diagram shows the energy changes in a light bulb every second. This is called a **Sankey diagram**.

This is what it shows:

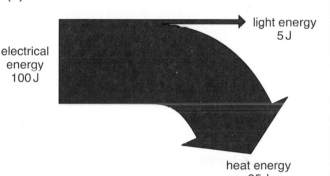

electrical energy 100 J

light energy 5 J

heat energy 95 J

◐ the bulb receives 100 J of energy – this is electrical energy;

◐ it gives out 5 J of light energy and 95 J of heat energy.

You can see from these figures (and from the diagram) that the bulb gives out as much energy as it receives.

◐ No energy disappears.

◐ No energy is created.

This is what we mean when we say 'energy is conserved'. The total amount of energy before a change is equal to the total amount after the change:

total energy before = total energy after

This is known as the **Principle of Conservation of Energy**. It is always true.

Notice too with the light bulb that much more energy is given out as heat than as light. Sometimes the heat energy is described as 'wasted' energy. Wasted energy does not disappear; it simply isn't doing the job we want.

An energy-saving light bulb takes in 60 J of electrical energy but gives out 45 J of light energy. Draw a Sankey diagram to show this. How much energy is given out as heat energy?

Does energy get used up?

You might find it a bit surprising that there is always as much energy after a change as before. What's going on? Think about a child on a swing.

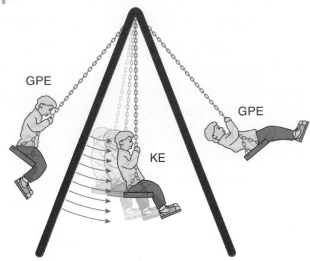

GPE

GPE

KE

1. They start off high up – they have gravitational potential energy (GPE).

2. They swing down – they have kinetic energy (KE).

3. They swing back up again – they have GPE again.

If it's a well-oiled swing, they will go back to the same height they started from. So they will have just as much energy as when they started.

However, as they swing, energy is changing back and forth between GPE and KE. So energy can change form but never disappear.

Of course, no swing is perfect. There will be some friction. So some of the energy gets changed to heat. Then the child won't swing back to the same height each time – they get lower and lower as energy is wasted as heat. Someone has to put in more energy, by pushing the swing.

What happens if the child falls off the swing? Describe the changes in energy.

It can seem a bit odd that we say that we need energy to do things, but that it never gets used up – the total amount is always constant.

The point is that we usually start with energy in a useful form and end up with it in a form where we cannot do much with it.

Petrol is a very useful store of chemical energy. We use it in cars. It gives a car kinetic energy but, when the brakes are applied, that energy is turned to heat which escapes in the air. As the car is travelling along, it has to overcome the drag of the air. That also heats the air. The chemical energy of the petrol ends up as thermal energy in the air, which is not very useful.

In a barbecue, charcoal is burned to cook food. Explain how the energy stored in the charcoal ends up as thermal energy in the air.

You need to remember that:

- Energy can be stored in different ways.
- Useful stores of energy include chemical energy and thermal energy.
- Energy can be transferred in different ways.
- Useful forms of transferred energy include electrical energy, light energy and kinetic energy.
- Whenever a change occurs, the total amount of energy remains constant. This is the Principle of Conservation of Energy.
- Wasted energy does not disappear – it simply is not doing the job we want.

Next time »

Unit 17   A star is a giant ball of hot gas that gives out vast amounts of heat and light (page 307).

Previously »

| From Page 225 | The weight of an object is a force caused by the pull of the Earth's gravity. |
| From Page 281 | Light travels in straight lines at 300 000 000 m/s. |

Unit 17

The Solar System

How far into space have we travelled?

We all live on the Earth. It's unlikely that you will ever visit any other planet, but perhaps your children or grandchildren will.

A few lucky people have visited the Moon, but that was decades ago and it's unlikely that more people will land on the Moon in the near future.

You may have seen films making up stories about people visiting Mars. In fact, people have practised moving around in Mars-like environments by creating similar conditions on Earth. However, it will take a great effort if anyone is ever to go there in reality.

In this Unit, you will learn:

- ▶ about the Sun and planets;
- ▶ how planets orbit the Sun;
- ▶ how we know about the Solar System;
- ▶ how we know there are planets around other stars.

Key words

asteroids	gravity	planet
comets	mass	Solar System
ellipse	minor planets	star
exoplanets	orbit	telescopes

What is the Sun?

The Sun is at the centre of the **Solar System**. The word 'solar' means 'related to the Sun'.

The Sun is a **star**. It looks different from the other stars we see at night because it is much closer to us.

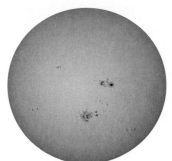

A star is a giant ball of hot gas that gives out vast amounts of heat and light. The Sun is hot:

- ▶ its surface temperature is about 5500 °C;
- ▶ inside, it's much hotter – about 15 000 000 °C!

The Sun rotates (spins) on its axis. Because it is made of gas, it doesn't all rotate at the same speed. The equator rotates faster than the poles.

Darker-looking sunspots are cooler patches on the Sun's surface. Their positions change from day to day, showing that the Sun rotates.

What does the Solar System contain?

The Earth is a **planet**. It orbits around the Sun. So do the other planets.

An **orbit** is the path of one object moving around another. The Earth's orbit around the Sun is almost circular.

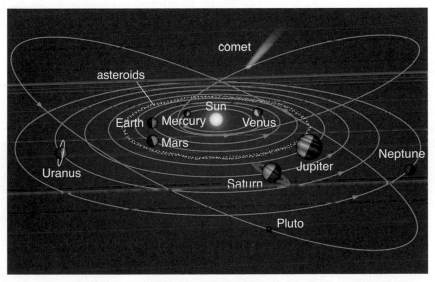

The Earth is the third planet from the Sun. The complete list of planets is:

Mercury, Venus, Earth, Mars, Jupiter, Saturn, Uranus, Neptune

Most of these planets have moons, and some have rings. Besides the planets, there are some other kinds of object that are also part of the Solar System:

- ▶ **minor planets** – too small to be 'true' planets and with unusual orbits; Pluto is a minor planet;
- ▶ **asteroids** – lumps of rock in orbit between Mars and Jupiter;
- ▶ **comets** – balls of frozen dust and gas that occasionally 'fall' towards the Sun from the cold outer edges of the Solar System.

 The biggest planet is fifth from the Sun. Name it.

What holds the Solar System together?

The Sun has a very large **mass**. This means that its **gravity** is very strong.

The Sun's gravity pulls on the Earth and everything else in the Solar System. This is what holds the Earth in its orbit. Without the Sun's gravitational pull, the Earth would fly off into the depths of space.

Now we can say what the Solar System is: it is everything that is held in orbit around the Sun by the pull of the Sun's gravity.

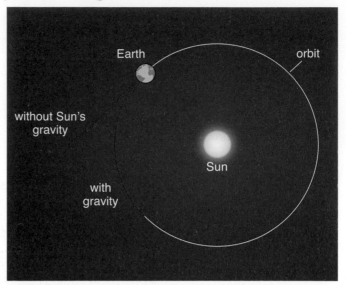

How do we know the Earth orbits the Sun?

Every day we see the Sun rise and set. It looks as though the Sun orbits the Earth. It took a long time for people to realise that the Earth orbits the Sun.

The evidence came from looking at the other stars. Each night, the pattern of the stars we see changes slightly. This is because, as the Earth orbits the Sun, we are facing in a different direction in space. This is why we see different stars in summer and winter.

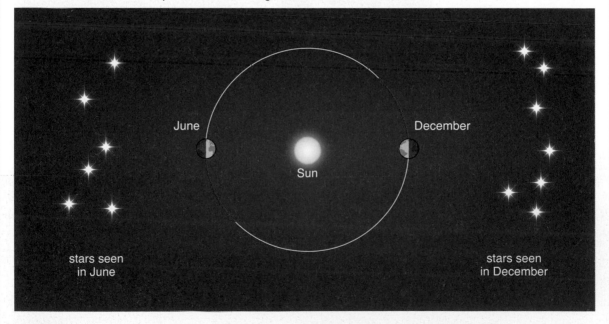

 Suggest another reason why we might see different stars at different times of year.

How do we know the other planets orbit the Sun?

The planets in the night sky look very similar to stars. However, their positions change gradually against the background pattern of the stars.

Thousands of years ago, people thought they were 'wandering stars' – the word *planet* means *wanderer*.

Like the Sun and stars, the planets seemed to be orbiting the Earth. However, Johannes Kepler showed that Mars orbits the Sun in an orbit shaped like an **ellipse** (a squashed circle). He guessed that all planets do this. He was right!

The orbits of planets are ellipses, almost circles. Comets have long, stretched elliptical orbits.

We have now taken so many detailed measurements of the planets and their moons that we can predict their orbits thousands of years into the future. We can aim spacecraft to arrive within metres of distance and seconds of time, after travelling for many years.

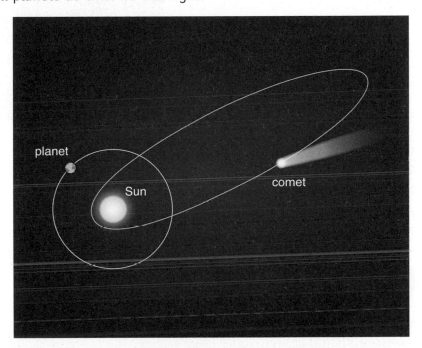

 The further a planet is from the Sun, the slower it moves. Which planet takes the longest time to orbit the Sun?

THINKING BEYOND...

Most people accept the scientific picture of the Solar System. However, it took very careful observations of the planet Mars and a lot of calculations to prove that the planets orbit the Sun, rather than the Earth.

It was a great achievement, but it took a long time for everyone to agree. For thousands of years, people had believed that the Earth must be at the centre of the Universe.

 Write a timeline of how people came to accept that the Earth and other planets orbited the Sun. You should include the scientists Ptolemy, Copernicus, Galileo, Kepler and Newton.

How do we explore the Solar System? @

Powerful **telescopes** based on the Earth or in orbiting spacecraft can give us a good look at the planets.

Better still, spacecraft have visited all of the planets and many of their larger moons.

The most distant planets are far out in space. Looking back, the Sun looks like a tiny dot in the dark sky, as if it was just another star.

Jupiter's moon Io looks like a giant pizza, due to volcanoes spewing out sulfur. Io has about 1/40th of the volume of Earth, yet some of its volcanoes are higher than Mount Everest!

 Astronomers are not the only people who use telescopes. Give two other examples of people who use them.

Are there other 'Solar Systems' out there?

Astronomers have discovered planets orbiting other stars. It seems that there may be many, many other stars with orbiting planets. Planets beyond the Solar System are called **exoplanets**.

How do astronomers make this sort of discovery? There are several ways – here are two.

▶ If a planet with a high mass orbits close to its star, the star will wobble slightly in space. With a sufficiently powerful telescope, we can detect those wobbles over time.

▶ If a planet orbits in front of its star, it will block the light. The star will go dim for a short time.

It's too early to say if there is life on any of these planets. Astronomers are hoping to detect oxygen in an exoplanet's atmosphere. That could mean there was some form of life there, doing the job that plants do for us on Earth.

You need to remember that:

▶ The Sun is a star at the centre of the Solar System.
▶ The Solar System is made up of everything that is in orbit around the Sun.
▶ The Sun's gravity holds the planets in their orbits.
▶ The orbits of planets are ellipses.
▶ There are many other stars that have planets in orbit around them.

Next time ≫

Unit 18 The Moon orbits the Earth while the Earth orbits the Sun (page 312).
Unit 18 A solar eclipse happens when the Moon blocks the face of the Sun from us (page 314).

Previously »

| From Page 287 | Refraction happens because light travels at different speeds in different materials. |
| From Page 308 | The Sun's gravity holds the planets in their orbits. |

Unit 18

Sun, Earth, Moon

Can we see the Moon during the day?

The Sun and Moon are the two most familiar objects in the sky. One is hot, the other is cold. One is gas, the other is solid.

We only see the Sun during the day – it's the Sun that gives us daylight.

Some people think that we only see the Moon at night, but that's not true. The Moon is often in the daytime sky but, if the sky is bright, the Moon may be too faint to see.

In this Unit, you will learn:

- ▶ why we have night and day;
- ▶ how we see the Moon;
- ▶ why the Moon shows phases;
- ▶ why we have seasons;
- ▶ why eclipses happen.

Key words

axis	phases
full Moon	reflects
lunar eclipse	seasons
new Moon	solar eclipse
orbit	total eclipse
partial eclipse	umbra
penumbra	

Why do we have night and day?

The Earth is a sphere. It rotates on its **axis**.

At any moment, only half of the Earth is in sunlight. Here, it is daytime. The other half is in darkness. It is night. As the Earth turns, parts that were in darkness move into the light. Night has become daytime.

We see the Sun rise in the East and set in the West. This is because the Earth turns from West to East.

It's surprisingly difficult to prove that the Earth turns. The first proof was Foucault's pendulum. Foucault set up a very long pendulum with a heavy mass on the end.

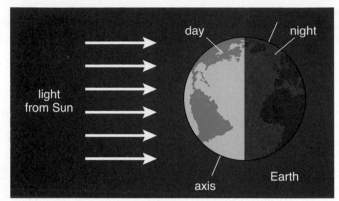

As time passed, he saw that it swung along a different line. This happens because the Earth turns beneath the pendulum.

 If the Earth turned in the opposite direction (from East to West), what difference would we notice?

Why do we have seasons? @

People living in the UK experience **seasons**.

▶ In summer, the Sun rises early and sets late. The midday Sun is high in the sky.

▶ In winter, the Sun rises late and sets early. The midday Sun is low in the sky.

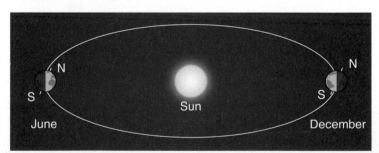

As a consequence, it is colder in winter than in summer.

The Earth orbits the Sun. It is tilted on its axis. The axis is at an angle to the plane of its **orbit**.

▶ In summer, the northern hemisphere is tilted *towards* the Sun. When the Sun appears higher in the sky, its rays are more concentrated on the ground. The days are also longer, so temperatures rise.

▶ In winter, the northern hemisphere is tilted *away from* the Sun. When the Sun is low in the sky, its rays are more spread out on the ground. The days are also shorter, so temperatures remain low.

How do we see the Moon?

The Moon is a cold, rocky sphere. Its diameter is about one quarter of the Earth's diameter. It is colder than the Earth, partly because it has no atmosphere to prevent heat escaping.

The Moon is not a source of light (unlike the Sun). We see the Moon because it **reflects** sunlight. There is more about sources of light and reflection in Unit 12: Light.

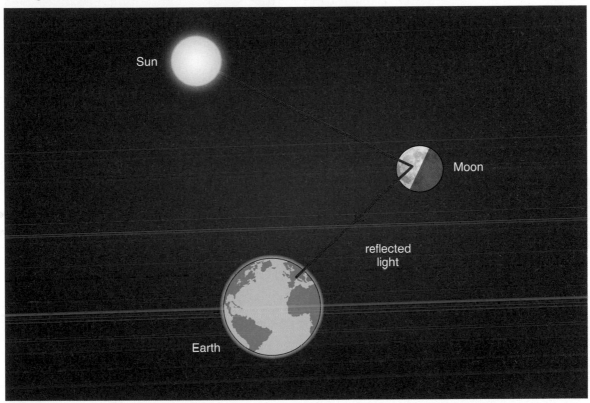

Sun

Moon

reflected light

Earth

 The Moon only reflects a small fraction of the sunlight that falls on it. What happens to the rest of the sunlight?

The full Moon can look very bright. However, the Moon's surface is actually very dark. It only reflects about 7% of the sunlight that falls on it. That's still enough to make it shine in the black night sky, because it is so much brighter than its surroundings.

We do sometimes see the Moon during the day. However, when the sky is bright, the Moon disappears from sight – its light is too faint to show up against the sky.

 In fact, the Moon is in the daytime sky just as often as it is in the night sky. Explain why this is.

Why does the Moon have phases?

Each month, the appearance of the Moon changes. It goes through a series of **phases**.

Half of the Moon is lit up by the Sun. Half is in darkness.

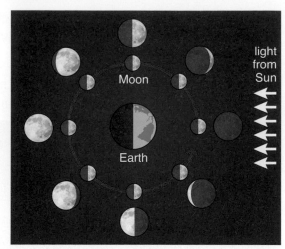

light from Sun

- ▶ When we look at the Moon, we may see all of the side that is lit up. Then we see a **full Moon**.
- ▶ We may see only half of the side that is lit up. This is a half Moon.
- ▶ We may see the side of the Moon that is in darkness. This is a **new Moon**.

What we see depends on where the Moon is in its orbit around the Earth.

- ▶ If the Moon is on the opposite side to the Sun, we see a full Moon.
- ▶ If it is on the same side as the Sun, we see a new Moon.

How does an eclipse of the Sun happen?

The Sun and Moon look as if they are the same size. However, the Sun is about 400 times bigger than the Moon, and 400 times further away.

Occasionally, the Moon's orbit places it directly between us and the Sun. It blocks the Sun's light. This is a **solar eclipse**.

- ▶ If you are on the right place on the Earth's surface, you will see the Sun completely blocked by the Moon. This is a **total eclipse**.
- ▶ Further away, the Sun's face will be only partly blocked. You will see a **partial eclipse**.

During a solar eclipse, there is a region of space where no sunlight reaches. It is in shadow. This is called the **umbra**.

The region of space that is only partly in shadow is called the **penumbra**.

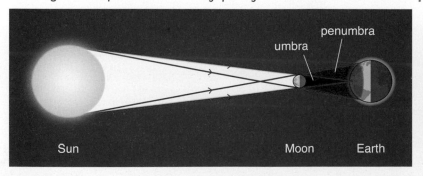

penumbra
umbra
Sun   Moon   Earth

During a solar eclipse, it may be possible to see the Sun's glowing corona (its atmosphere). This is cooler and darker than the main body of the Sun, but when the Moon blocks the brighter centre of the Sun, we can see the corona.

How does an eclipse of the Moon happen?

Occasionally, the Moon's orbit takes it behind the Earth, directly opposite from the Sun. The Earth blocks the Sun's light from reaching the Moon. This is a **lunar eclipse**.

If you are on the dark side of the Earth, you will see the Moon pass into darkness.

▶ At first, the Moon will only be partly in shadow. This is a partial eclipse.

▶ Then it moves in to full shadow. This is a total eclipse.

You are more likely to see an eclipse of the Moon than an eclipse of the Sun. This is because the Earth's shadow is much bigger than the surface of the Moon. Also, a lunar eclipse can be seen from half of the Earth's surface. Unlike a solar eclipse, you don't have to be in a precise spot to see a lunar eclipse from the Earth.

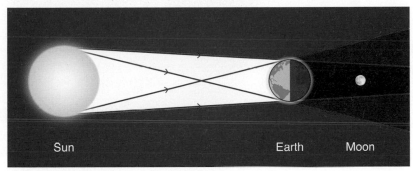
Sun   Earth   Moon

During a lunar eclipse, the Moon may appear dark red, as sunlight is refracted on to it by the Earth's atmosphere (see page 286).

 Draw a diagram to show that a lunar eclipse can be seen from half of the Earth's surface.

You need to remember that:

▶ We experience night and day because the Earth rotates on its axis.

▶ We experience seasons because the Earth is tilted on its axis.

▶ The Moon orbits the Earth while the Earth orbits the Sun.

▶ The phase of the Moon depends on where it is in its orbit around the Earth.

▶ A solar eclipse happens when the Moon blocks the face of the Sun from us.

▶ A lunar eclipse happens when the Moon moves into the Earth's shadow.

Next time ≫

Unit 19 Distances in space are measured in light-years (page 318).

Unit 19 Large numbers of stars cluster together to form a galaxy (page 318).

Previously ≫

From Page 281 — Light travels in straight lines at a speed of 300 000 000 m/s.

From Page 307 — The Solar System is everything that is held in orbit around the Sun by the pull of its gravity.

Unit 19

Astronomy

How many stars are there?

There are about 6000 stars that are bright enough to be visible to the naked eye. That's only a tiny fraction of the stars in the Universe. We think there are at least 300 000 000 000 000 000 000 000 stars in the Universe – that's 300 sextillion!

Some stars appear brighter in our sky than others, and they seem to make patterns. These patterns are called constellations. Astronomers use the constellations in order to explain which stars they are looking at – they might say, "I've observed a new comet in the region of the star Rigel in the constellation of Orion."

However, stars that seem close together in our sky may be vast distances apart in space.

In this Unit, you will learn:

- ▶ how we observe the Universe;
- ▶ about astronomical distances;
- ▶ how stars form galaxies;
- ▶ how the Universe is changing.

Key words

Big Bang	light-year	radiation
galaxy	optical telescope	radio telescope
gravity		

How do we observe the Universe? @

We can send spacecraft to explore the Solar System. To see further than this, we need to use telescopes.

Telescopes detect **radiation** coming from space. This includes the light we can see, and also infra-red radiation, X-rays, microwaves, radio waves and more.

● An **optical telescope** detects light. It uses mirrors and lenses to make a magnified image of distant stars.

● A **radio telescope** detects radio waves. These may be coming from stars or other objects in space.

On the surface of the Earth, telescopes have to look out through the atmosphere. This can distort their view. Also, the atmosphere absorbs some types of radiation.

There are two solutions to this:

● put telescopes on high mountains where the atmosphere is thin;

● put telescopes in space, above the atmosphere.

The Hubble Space Telescope orbits the Earth; it has provided clear images of many distant objects in space. Many telescopes are placed on high mountains; these are on Mauna Kea in Hawaii.

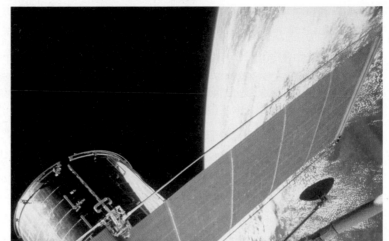

What is a light-year?

The distance from the Earth to the Sun is about 150 million kilometres. That's almost 4000 times the circumference of the Earth. There is a lot of empty space in the Solar System!

Light travels at 300 000 000 m/s. Nothing travels faster than light.

How long does it take light from the Sun ... ?
8 minutes to reach the Earth
about 4 hours to reach Neptune, the furthest planet in the Solar System
about 2 years to reach the furthest edge of the Solar System
about 4 years to reach the next star

It's easier to say that the next star is at a distance of 4 light-years. A **light-year** is the distance light travels in one year.

Take care! A light-year is a unit of *distance*, not time.

Roughly, 1 light-year = 10 000 000 000 000 km = 10 trillion km

 Can you guess what a 'light-second' is? How many kilometres will it be?

What is a galaxy?

The Solar System is held together by the Sun's **gravity**. Without gravity, the planets would drift away into space.

The Sun itself is attracted by the gravity of all the nearby stars. There are about 300 billion stars in our **galaxy**, held together by the gravitational pull of each star on all the others.

Galaxies come in different shapes and sizes. Our galaxy, the Milky Way, is a spiral galaxy. Our Solar System is part way out along one of the arms. On average, a galaxy contains between 100 billion and 1 trillion stars.

The picture shows an artist's impression of the Milky Way. As you can guess from its shape, the Milky Way slowly rotates.

There are many, many more galaxies in the Universe – about 500 billion of them. Some of them form clusters because they are attracted to each other by gravity.

That means there are vast numbers of stars in the Universe – about 300 000 000 000 000 000 000 000 stars in total.

It took a long time to work out the shape of our galaxy. After all, we can't get outside it to take a photograph.

Astronomers counted stars in every direction in space. They also estimated how far away they were. It is only recently that they have had enough data to produce a reliable picture proving that we live in a spiral galaxy.

This map of the Milky Way was made in 1784 by William Herschel. He didn't have enough data to draw an accurate map but you can see that he did realise that our galaxy has arms.

? The astronomer Edwin Hubble devised a way of cataloguing galaxies according to their shapes. Search the internet to find a chart of his classification system. Find photos of five different galaxies and classify them.

How is the Universe changing?

About a century ago, we made telescopes good enough to see many distant galaxies. Astronomers discovered that the galaxies are all spreading out in space. The most distant galaxies are moving fastest.

Astronomers deduced two things from this:

- the Universe is expanding;
- if you could rewind the expanding Universe in time, it must have appeared from a single point – the **Big Bang**.

Since then, more evidence has helped to support these ideas. We now think that the Universe is about 13.7 billion years old. That is the amount of time that has passed since the Big Bang.

And it seems as though the Universe is expanding faster and faster. Nobody quite knows why – watch this space!

? How old will the Universe be in 10 years' time?

You need to remember that:

- Astronomers use telescopes to gather radiation from space.
- Distances in space are measured in light-years.
- Large numbers of stars are drawn together by gravity to form a galaxy.
- The Universe has been expanding ever since the Big Bang.

Handling data

Why is handling data important?

One of the main reasons science works is that there are standard ways of communicating information. In science, we use tables, charts, graphs and diagrams to show how we do experiments. This means that any other scientist can understand what we have done and how we did it.

In this Unit, you will learn:
- ▶ how to present tables clearly;
- ▶ how to draw pie charts and bar charts;
- ▶ how to read graphs;
- ▶ what a formula tells us;
- ▶ how to draw graphs.

How can we present tables clearly?

A table is usually the best way to organise information where we want to compare properties or numbers.

- ▶ Organise the table with clear headings that say exactly what each column contains.

- ▶ Make sure you describe a quantity. Always put the units in the heading too, so you don't need to keep repeating the units each time you add a number.

- ▶ Usually, the names of things you need to compare go in the left-hand column, so that you can add columns of measurements to the right.

- ▶ Make sure you columns are wide enough to take the longest names – go onto two lines if needed.

- ▶ If you have numbers with decimal points, align them by the decimal points in a column. This way, you can see easily which are big and which are small numbers.

- ▶ If you are taking measurements in a table, start at the top with your first measurement. Write each measurement into the next row as soon as you get it.

Here, you can see easily that air is mostly made up from oxygen and nitrogen.

Gas	Percentage of the air (approx.) / %
nitrogen	78.1
oxygen	20.9
argon	0.95
carbon dioxide	0.04
other gases like helium, neon, methane, hydrogen	0.01

? What do the percentages of nitrogen and oxygen add up to?

How should we draw pie charts?

If you have data that can be shown as fractions or percentages, a pie chart is a good way to picture it. This pie chart uses data from the table on page 320.

Your teacher may give you a pie chart blank with dashed lines to help you.

▶ Remember always to start at the top position, at '12 o'clock', with the biggest piece. Then add each smaller piece in turn, clockwise.

▶ Draw straight lines to the centre of the circle; try to keep them thin.

▶ Label each segment with the name and value.

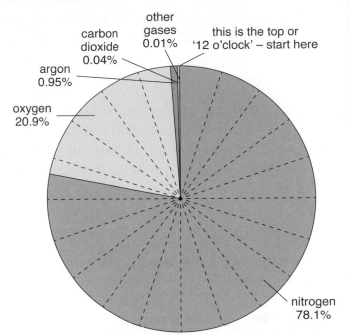

other gases 0.01%

carbon dioxide 0.04%

this is the top or '12 o'clock' – start here

argon 0.95%

oxygen 20.9%

nitrogen 78.1%

How should we draw bar charts?

Bar charts are good ways of comparing different numbers, where they are not fractions or percentages. This bar chart shows the densities of different materials (the table of data is on page 234).

If you draw a bar chart:

▶ Remember first to choose scales that mean you can fit every number onto your graph paper.

▶ Draw and label each axis carefully.

▶ Make the bars the same width and leave equal spaces between them.

▶ Keep the top of each bar straight.

▶ Label each bar with the name of what it shows.

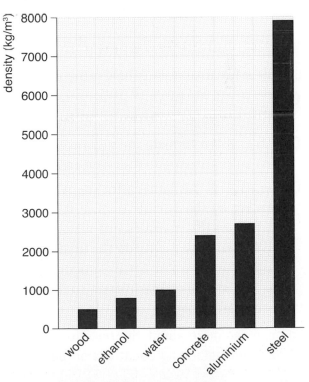

density (kg/m³)

wood, ethanol, water, concrete, aluminium, steel

Using the bar chart, roughly how many times more dense is steel than aluminium? Why don't we make planes from steel?

What do graphs tell us?

Graphs are used a lot in scientific experiments. They show us trends in values, and can be used to make predictions. This graph shows what happens to a flask of water as it is heated up.

When you read a graph:

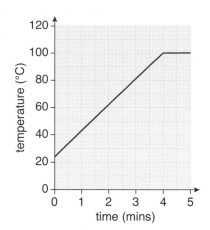

▶ Check the scale on each axis first to make sure you know what the big and little squares on the paper represent.

▶ Use a ruler to read off a value from the graph line to the axis – it's much quicker than doing it by eye alone!

▶ Always make sure you add in the units to your answer. Usually, the units are shown in brackets or after a '/' sign on the axis.

▶ The slope of the line is called the gradient. It tells you how fast something is changing.

1 Read off the temperature after 1.5 minutes.

2 What is happening between 4 minutes and 5 minutes?

What does a formula tell us?

Chemical formulas tell us how many atoms there are of each element in a molecule.

▶ H_2O is the formula for water. It tells us there are two atoms of hydrogen, and one atom of oxygen in every water molecule.

▶ H_2SO_4 is the formula for sulfuric acid. Each molecule contains two hydrogen atoms, one sulfur atom and four oxygen atoms.

▶ $Cu(NO_3)_2$ is the formula for copper nitrate. You need to multiply everything inside the bracket by the number outside it as follows:
  1. Nitrate NO_3 contains one nitrogen and three oxygen atoms.
  2. The number 2 outside the bracket in $Cu(NO_3)_2$ means there are two nitrates.
  3. So there are $2 \times 1 = 2$ nitrogen atoms and $2 \times 3 = 6$ oxygen atoms.
  4. This means copper nitrate contains one copper atom, two nitrogen atoms and six oxygen atoms.

You can see more about the rules for naming chemicals on page 159. You can also see more about balancing equations on page 163.

Work out how many atoms of each element are contained in the following molecules: O_2, HNO_3, $CuSO_4$, C_2H_6

How should we draw graphs?

If you need to draw a graph from some data, you will usually have a table of data to work with. It is important to plot the points on the graph carefully, and to draw a line of best fit that shows the pattern the points make. This is called a scatter graph. Here is a table of data from a ticker tape experiment to measure the distance a trolley travels in a particular time.

Time (s)	Distance (m)
0	0
0.2	0.14
0.4	0.30
0.6	0.46
0.8	0.59
1.0	0.60
1.2	0.60

If you draw a graph, remember these steps:

1. Draw the scales carefully and make sure they have enough room for all the values you need.
2. Label each axis with the name of what is being measured and its units.

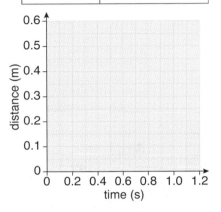

3. Plot each point, using a ruler to measure it out.
4. Draw each point using a '+' or a '⊙'.

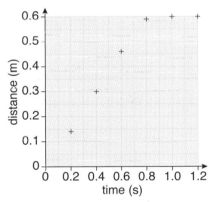

5. Draw a thin line of best fit through the points to connect them, using a sharp pencil.
   ▶ Sometimes it needs a straight line, so use a ruler.
   ▶ Sometimes it will be curved, so try to avoid any bumps in your curve.
   ▶ Sometimes, like this one, it will have a sharp kink in it.

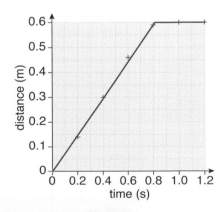

 What do you think is happening to the trolley between 0.8 and 1.2 seconds?

Glossary

abiotic factors the non-living things in the surroundings of an organism

absorb to take in, e.g. food molecules through the wall of the gut

absorber material that absorbs infra-red radiation

absorption process where food molecules cross the gut wall into the blood

accelerating speeding up; increasing speed

acid rain rain in which sulfur dioxide or nitrogen dioxide has been dissolved, making it acidic; causes chemical weathering

acids substances with a pH of less than 7; they neutralise alkalis

acne painful skin condition often suffered by adolescents

adapted how an organism is developed to fit with its environment

addictive describes drugs that people find almost impossible to stop taking

adjustable air hole controls amount of air supplied to Bunsen burner

adolescence stage of human development between childhood and adulthood

aerobic respiration process in which energy is released from food when oxygen is available

air resistance force of friction (drag) on an object when it moves through air

alcohol chemical produced by anaerobic respiration (fermentation) of sugars using yeast; used in many drinks as a legal recreational drug

alkalis substances with a pH greater than 7; they neutralise acids and are bases that will dissolve in water

alveoli air sacs in the lungs

ammeter instrument used for measuring electric current

amnion water-filled bag that protects the foetus inside the mother

amp (A) the unit of electric current; full name ampere

amplitude the greatest height of a vibration or wave

anaerobic respiration process in which energy is released from food when oxygen is not available

ancestor a living thing's parents, grandparents, great-grandparents, etc.

Angiosperms Phylum of flowering plants

angle of incidence angle between an incident light ray and the normal, used in refraction and reflection

angle of reflection angle between a reflected light ray and the normal

angle of refraction angle between a refracted ray of light and the normal

Animals Kingdom of worms, insects, birds, reptiles, fish, humans, etc.

antagonistic pair two muscles that work in opposite directions to each other to produce wide range of movement

anti-clockwise moment when the turning effect of a force tends to make a lever turn anticlockwise ↺

antibiotics chemicals used to kill disease-causing bacteria

antibodies chemicals made by the body to destroy bacteria or viruses

antigens chemicals on the surface of cells that antibodies recognise

arteries blood vessels that carry blood from the heart to the rest of the body

asexual reproduction process where a single individual creates copies of itself

aspirin medicine used to treat pains and fever; originally made from the bark and leaves of willow trees

assimilated describes the process in which food molecules are used in the body after digestion

asteroids small rocks orbiting the Sun between Mars and Jupiter

atmospheric pressure pressure on any object in or under the air, caused by the mass of air around it

atomic number number of protons in the nucleus of an atom

atoms individual particles of elements

attraction force that makes particles stay or move together

attracts what happens when an object exerts a force on another object, pulling it towards it; opposite electric charges or magnetic poles attract

auxin plant hormone with many different functions, including causing shoots and roots to bend

average sum of a set of values divided by the total number of values

average speed when an object's speed is changing, we can calculate: average speed = $\frac{\text{distance travelled}}{\text{time taken}}$

axis line through the centre of a planet about which it turns

bacteria single-celled organisms; some bacteria cause diseases

baking powder sodium bicarbonate, sodium hydrogen carbonate; often used in cooking, to make cakes rise

balance ability to stand upright and to move about without feeling dizzy

balanced where a chemical equation is written to show the Conservation of Mass, so that the number of atoms of each element is the same after the reaction as it was before the reaction

balanced diet sensible mix of different types of food that leads to healthy living

balanced forces two or more forces acting on an object with effects that cancel each other out

baleen plates of whalebone used by some whales to filter food from the sea

barometer instrument used for measuring atmospheric pressure

bases substances that neutralise acids; some bases dissolve in water to form alkalis

battery two or more cells joined together in series

biceps muscle that causes the arm to bend

Big Bang the event 13.7 billion years ago when the Universe came into being

binary fission	process where a single cell splits into two identical cells
bio-magnification	process in which small amounts of a harmful chemical add up to cause damage higher up a food chain
biodiesels	fuels made from animal or vegetable fats
biofuels	fuels that are made from materials made by living things
biological weathering	weathering caused by animals or plants
biomass	combined mass of all the living things of a particular type
biome	a large area of the Earth with similar conditions
biotic factors	the living things in the surroundings of an organism
birth rate	the number of animals born in a known time
blastula	stage in the development of a baby, formed when the fertilised egg divides
blood vessels	tubes that carry blood around the body
boiling point	temperature at which a liquid becomes a gas
boils	a liquid becoming a gas at a particular temperature, its boiling point
bonds	attraction (pulling together) between two atoms where their orbiting electrons have been shared or moved between them
bone	structure made from living and nonliving material that gives many animals their shape
bone marrow	living part in the centre of bones, which makes blood cells
brain size	volume of the brain of an animal; sometimes, but not always, related to its intelligence
breaking down	large objects reducing to many smaller objects
breathing	taking air into and pushing air out from the lungs
Bryophytes	Phylum of mosses, in the plant Kingdom
Bunsen burner	laboratory equipment fuelled by gas, used for heating
burner tube	upright tube in Bunsen burner
cancer	disease in which cells divide uncontrollably
cannabis	an illegal recreational drug
capillaries	small blood vessels that join arteries to veins; they allow substances from the blood to enter and leave body cells
carbohydrates	group of chemicals with molecules containing carbon, hydrogen and oxygen
carbon cycle	process of many stages in which the element carbon moves from non-living materials into living things and back again
carbon dioxide	colourless gas, formula CO_2, that is produced by respiration and used up in photosynthesis
carbon monoxide	substance with molecules containing one carbon atom and one oxygen atom; poisonous gas produced by incomplete combustion of hydrocarbons
carnivore	animal that eats other animals
carpels	female reproductive structures of flowering plants
cartilage	substance found in joints that makes their movements smooth
cell (1)	the basic unit of all life; contains many components that carry out life processes
cell (2)	device that produces an electrical voltage
cell wall	in plant cells and bacteria only, a rigid structure outside the membrane

cervix	opening at bottom of the uterus through which the baby passes during birth
chains	patterns into which thousands of atoms are arranged in DNA
chalk	type of sedimentary rock made from remains of microscopic marine plants and animals
changing state	a substance changing form: solid to liquid, liquid to solid, liquid to gas, gas to liquid, or solid to gas
characteristics	features of an organism
chemical changes	reactions in which the bonds between atoms in substances are rearranged to make new substances
chemical energy	energy stored in chemical substances, released in a chemical reaction
chemical equation	shows the reactants and products of a chemical reaction by using chemical formulas
chemical reactions	irreversible changes in a substance to form new substances, which involve chemical bonding
chemical weathering	weathering caused by the reaction of acids with rock
chloride	substance that contains chlorine ions bonded to metal ions
chlorophyll	green chemical found in plants, which collects light energy for photosynthesis
chloroplasts	structures in plant cells where photosynthesis happens
Chordates	Phylum of animals with a backbone
chromatography	process in which different coloured chemicals are separated from a mixture as it rises up filter paper
circuit symbol	standard symbol used to represent a component in an electrical circuit diagram
Class (plural Classes)	level of classification for living things, below Phylum and above Order
climate	average of weather conditions across a large area, over a long period of time
climate change	effects on the climate of rising average temperatures, such as changing the flow of ocean currents
clockwise moment	when the turning effect of a force tends to make a lever turn clockwise (↻)
clot	to make blood solid, e.g. in forming a scab over a cut
collar	metal ring on Bunsen burner that contains adjustable air hole
colorimetry	process in which the amounts of substances in solutions are worked out by measuring the intensity of their colours
colour addition	process in which two or more colours of light are combined to produce a new colour
colour change	a sign a chemical reaction has taken place, where the products are differently coloured to the reactants
colour subtraction	process in which some colours are removed from a mixture of colours of light, e.g. when passed through a filter
combustion	reaction in which a substance burns with oxygen from the air
comets	lumps of ice and dust in orbit around the Sun
communicate	to transfer information from one thing to another
communities	all the populations of all the different species found in an area

compass	device that uses a permanent magnet to indicate direction by pointing north
competition	occurs when animals or plants need the same resource, which is in short supply
component	any device connected in an electric circuit
compound	any substance made chemically from two or more different elements
compressed	substance squeezed into a smaller volume by increasing pressure
compression	process where something is squeezed, e.g. layers of sediment at the bottom of an ocean are compressed by the weight of the layers of rock and water above
condensation	process in which a gas cools to form liquid
condense	when a gas cools to form liquid
conduction	process in which heat energy or electricity passes through a solid material
conductors	materials that allow heat energy or electricity to pass through
cones	cells in the retina that allow humans to see in colour
Coniferophytes	Phylum of fir trees and pine trees, in the plant Kingdom
conservation of mass	science law that means the number of atoms after a reaction must be the same as before the reaction
conservation status	how rare and threatened a species is thought to be
constituent part	basic components of a material, e.g. solute and solvent are constituent parts of a solution
contact force	force one object exerts on another when they touch
contraception	process in which a man and a woman choose to prevent sperm from fertilising an egg; several methods exist
contracts	process in which a substance reduces in volume
convection current	process in which a fluid flows, carrying heat energy with it
core	piece of magnetic material placed inside an electromagnet coil to increase its strength
corrode (*noun* **corrosion**)	process in which a compound is worn away by chemical reactions, e.g. iron rusting in water and air
covalent compound	type of compound made from molecules in which two atoms 'share' electrons
cream of tartar	sodium aluminium sulfate; sometimes used in cooking with sodium bicarbonate to make cakes rise
crystallisation	process in which a solid forms when a solution is left to evaporate
crystals	solid substances with the atoms arranged in repeating patterns
data logger	device that records the output from a sensor
death rate	the number of animals dying in a known time
decomposition	process in which dead living things decay and release their chemicals back into the environment
dendrochronology	science of using tree growth rings to work out age and weather
density	measure of the concentration of mass in an object or material, calculated using $\text{density} = \frac{\text{mass}}{\text{volume}}$
deposited	laid down
descendants	a living thing's offspring; in humans, children, grandchildren, etc.

diaphragm	the floor of the thorax, used in breathing
diffusion	process in which a gas or liquid spreads more widely, often through another gas or liquid
digestion	process where food is broken down into small molecules
dilute	to add water to an acid or an alkali to reduce the number of acid or alkali molecules in a particular volume
diseases	illnesses, which can be caused by a number of different things, including bacteria and viruses
dispersion	process in which white light is separated into the spectrum of colours
displacement reaction	reaction in which a more reactive element 'pushes out' a less reactive element from a compound, to form a new compound
dissolve	to combine a solid substance with a liquid such as water to make a solution
distance	how far an object has moved
distance–time graph	graph showing how the distance an object has moved changes at different times
diurnal	active during the day
diversity	measure of how varied the species are in an area
DNA	chemical from which genes are made
drag	force of friction on an object when it moves through a liquid or gas
ear canal	tube in the ear connecting the outside part of the ear to the eardrum
eardrum	structure that vibrates when sound waves enter the ear
ecosystem	all the living and non-living things in an area
effort	force applied to a lever or other machine in order to move a load
egestion	process in which undigested food passes out of the body
eggs	female sex cells
elastic energy	energy stored when a material is stretched or squashed
electric charge	property of some particles that causes forces between them
electric current	movement or flow of electric charge; measured in amps (A)
electrical energy	energy transferred when an electric current flows
electromagnet	magnet that operates when electric current flows through it; it loses its magnetism when it is switched off
electron microscope	instrument used to magnify small things using a beam of electrons
electrons	particles that surround an atom, with a negative electric charge; they also carry current in electric circuits
elements	substances made up of only one type of atom
ellipse	path of a planet's orbit, shaped like an elongated circle
embryo	stage in the development of a baby, formed after the fertilised egg has divided several times
emitter	material that gives out infra-red radiation
emphysema	disease where the walls of the alveoli are destroyed; can be caused by smoking
endothermic	describes any reaction that takes in heat energy
energy	measure of the ability of something to carry out processes, e.g. of a battery to push a current round a circuit; energy exists in many different forms (electrical, kinetic, heat, etc.) and can be transformed between them

energy flow	movement of energy between levels in a food chain
energy resource	anything from which humans can obtain a supply of energy
engineer	person who uses scientific ideas to devise new machines, structures and methods for performing useful tasks
environment	the surroundings of an organism
environmental	describes variation between individuals of the same Species, caused by the conditions in which they live
enzymes	proteins that speed up some of the chemical reactions of life
erosion	process in which pieces of rock are moved by wind, water or ice
evaporates (1) (*verb*)	where molecules on the surface of a liquid are taken into the air as vapour
evaporates (2) (*noun*)	sedimentary rock formed when water evaporates and leaves dissolved salts behind, e.g. rock salt
evaporation	process in which molecules on the surface of a liquid are taken into the air as vapour; not the same as boiling
evidence	measurements used in experiments to answer a question, support a hypothesis or reach a conclusion
evolve (*noun* evolution)	to change the genetic make-up of a population over time; usually caused by natural selection
excrete	to pass waste from chemical reactions out of the body
exoplanets	planets that orbit around a star other than the Sun
exothermic	describes any reaction that gives out heat energy
expand	to increase in volume
experiment	scientific process designed to record evidence, test a hypothesis or demonstrate a fact
expose	to gather light on the retina (in the eye) or on a sensor (in a camera), to form an image
extinct	describes a species with no living individuals left on Earth
extract	to take metal from naturally occurring materials, e.g. gold is separated from a mixture, and iron is reacted to take it out of its natural oxide ores
faeces	undigested food that is passed out of the body
Family (*plural* Families)	level of classification for living things, below Order and above Genus
farmed	describes process in which humans gather animals into herds to produce milk or meat
females	individuals that make female sex cells
fermentation	type of reaction (anaerobic respiration) in which sugars are converted to either gases (to make bread rise) or alcohol (to make alcoholic drinks)
fertilisation	process where a male sex cell joins with a female sex cell
filter	transparent material that allows only some colours of light to pass through
filtration	process of separating a solid from a liquid by passing it through filter paper
fireworks	devices bright in colour, loud in noise and short in duration, which contain metallic substances that burn with different colours
five senses	sight, smell, touch, taste and hearing
fizzing	forming of bubbles of gas, e.g. in a liquid; a sign that a chemical reaction has taken place
flame test	method for identifying some metals, which burn with different colour flames
fluids	any materials that can flow; all liquids and gases are fluids
fluorescent	describes a substance that gives out light energy
focus	point at which parallel rays of light meet after passing through a lens
focused	when an image looks sharp not blurred
foetus	a developing baby
follicle	structure that forms an egg inside the ovary
food	substances eaten to provide a supply of energy and materials
food chain	chain of eater and eaten found in an ecosystem
food web	combined food chains in an ecosystem
force	interaction between two objects that results in each exerting a push or a pull on the other
forcemeter	device used to measure forces; also called a newtonmeter
forces of attraction	forces (pulls) between objects that interact, e.g. the bonds between positively charged and negatively charged ions in a molecule
formula	code for a compound that shows how many atoms of different elements it contains
fossil fuels	sources of energy from organisms that died millions of years ago
fractional distillation	process in which chemicals are heated and separated from a mixture because they have different boiling points
freeze-thaw weathering	weathering caused by water inside a crack freezing and expanding
freezes	a liquid becoming a solid at a particular temperature, its freezing point
frequency	the number of vibrations each second, measured in hertz (Hz)
friction	force caused when one surface rubs against another
fruit	structure produced by many plants to contain seeds and encourage distribution, e.g. eating by animals
fuels	substances that can be burned to release heat energy
fulcrum	another name for pivot; the point about which a lever turns
full Moon	when the fully lit face of the Moon is turned towards the Earth
Fungi	Kingdom of mushrooms, toadstools and moulds
galaxy	collection of billions of stars, held together by gravity
galvanisation	process in which iron is coated with zinc to prevent corrosion
gametes	sex cells, e.g. sperm, eggs
gas exchange	movement of oxygen into the blood and carbon dioxide out of it in the alveoli
gas pipe	tube that connects Bunsen burner to gas supply
gas tap	controls amount of gas supplied to Bunsen burner
gases	substances in a state with no fixed shape or volume
gauge	sensitive instrument used to measure physical changes
gene	large molecule (a section of DNA) that is a 'code' specifying a characteristic of a living thing
genetic	describing anything involving genes

Glossary

genetic engineering (GE)
humans changing genes in animals or plants to produce new characteristics

genetic modification (GM)
process in which living things are genetically engineered

Genus (*plural* Genera)
level of classification for living things, below Family and above Species

germinate
a seed starting to grow into a new plant

girth
total distance round a large object such as a tree

global warming
process in which the atmosphere is heating up over time, probably because of gases produced by human activities

glucose
sugar made by plants in photosynthesis and used as 'fuel' by many living things

gradient
slope of a graph

granular cytoplasm
jelly-like substance inside a cell, outside the nucleus; the granules carry out a number of different functions

gravitational field
the region around an object where other objects feel the pull of its gravity; anywhere where an object has weight

gravitational potential energy (GPE)
energy stored when an object is lifted upwards

gravity
force between two objects caused by their masses

greenhouse effect
process of warming caused by certain gases in the Earth's atmosphere, such as carbon dioxide

greenhouse gases
gases in the atmosphere that reflect heat back to the Earth's surface, e.g. carbon dioxide

Group
column of the Periodic Table; elements in the same Group tend to have similar properties

gut
tube along which food passes during digestion

habitat destruction
human actions causing loss of areas where organisms live

habitats
areas in which living things find all their needs

haemoglobin
chemical in red blood cells that carries oxygen

harmful
describes a substance that is dangerous to life

hazard symbols
labels on chemical containers, usually in red triangles, warning about the ways in which a chemical can be dangerous

hearing
sense that allows animals to detect sounds

heart
pump that sends blood around the body

heartbeat
vibration caused by the heart pumping

heat *or* heat energy
energy moving from a hotter place to a colder place

heatproof mat
tile used to protect surfaces from heat

'heavy' touch
sense of pushing; detected by cells in the skin

herbicides
pesticides that kill plants

herbivore
animal that eats plants

hertz (Hz)
the unit of frequency; 1 Hz = 1 per second

hibernate
when some animals rest in a warm place during the winter months

hormones
chemicals that pass information between parts of the body

humus
decaying plant and animal materials in soil

hydraulic machine
machine that uses a fluid to transmit pressure from place to place

hydrocarbons
compounds with molecules that contain only hydrogen and carbon atoms

hydrochloric acid
strong acid, formula HCl, with molecules containing hydrogen and chlorine ions

hydrogen
first element in the Periodic Table, usually found as a colourless gas that burns with a 'squeaky pop'

hydroxides
compounds formed from a metal, hydrogen and oxygen

igneous rock
rock made when molten lava or magma cools

illegal drugs
any drugs that are banned

image
representation of an object formed by light

imitate
to copy without understanding

immune
protected from a disease

immune response
process with many stages in which specialised cells and chemicals work together in the body to kill off organisms that cause infections

immunisation
general name for the process in which people are protected against diseases, e.g. by being injected with antigens

implants
process in which a fertilised egg attaches to the lining of the uterus

in parallel
describes components connected side-by-side in a circuit

in series
describes components connected end-to-end in a circuit

incident ray
ray of light striking a surface, before it is reflected or refracted

incomplete combustion
reaction in which a fuel is burnt with only limited amounts of oxygen

indicator
chemicals that change colour depending on the pH

infection
process in which bacteria or viruses get into the blood and cause illness

infra-red radiation
heat energy spreading out from a hot object, similar to light

infrasound
sounds with frequencies that are too low for humans to hear

inherited
where a characteristic has been passed down from a living thing's parents

insoluble
a solid that will not dissolve

insulation
material that prevents sound or heat from passing through

insulators
materials that do not allow heat energy or electricity to pass through

insulin
hormone that helps to control levels of sugar in blood

intelligence
ability to acquire knowledge and apply skills

interact
to affect each other, e.g. two particles or two objects

ionic compound
type of compound made from molecules in which one atom 'gives away' an electron to another atom, leaving both atoms with electrical charges

ions
atoms that have gained or lost electrons, so they have an electrical charge

iris
structure at the front of the eye that controls the amount of light entering

irreversible
describes any process that cannot easily be changed back again, e.g. in a chemical reaction such as iron corroding to make iron oxide

joint
structure where two bones meet

joules (J)
the SI unit of energy

keys
series of questions that help us to work out the species of a living thing

kinetic energy (KE)
energy of a moving object

Kingdoms
highest level of classification for living things, e.g. Animals or Plants

krill
small, shrimplike creatures that are the main food of some whales

labour
process of giving birth

lactic acid	chemical produced by anaerobic respiration in muscles, causes cramp
landfill gas	gas produced by decomposing waste; contains methane which can be used as a fuel
larynx	organ in a human that produces sounds; the voice box
lava	magma after it reaches the surface of the Earth when a volcano erupts
Law of Reflection	law that relates the angles of incidence and reflection, so that we can predict where a reflected light ray will go
layers	formed in rock where different sediments have settled at different times
lens	piece of material (e.g. glass) shaped so that it will bend rays of light towards a focus; eyes contain flexible lenses
levers	simple machines; rods that turn about pivots when a force is applied to them
light energy	energy transferred by light
light gate	device that starts or stops a timer when an object passes
light microscope	instrument used to magnify small things using light
'light' touch	sense of stroking; detected by cells in the skin
light-year	the distance light travels through empty space in a year
lighted splint	long stick that burns slowly; safer way to light Bunsen burner
lightning	electric current between a thundercloud and the ground
limewater	solution of calcium hydroxide that goes white when carbon dioxide passes through it
Lincoln Index	a way of estimating the population of moving animals
liquids	substances in a state with a fixed volume, but no fixed shape
lithification	process in which layers of rock are compressed and all the water is squeezed out
litmus paper	coloured paper that changes colour in acid or alkali
load	force (often an object's weight) that is moved using a lever or other machine
loudness	how loud a note sounds to human ears
lubrication	reduction of friction, often using a thick liquid, e.g. oil
lunar eclipse	event when the Earth passes between the Sun and the Moon, blocking the Sun's light from the Moon
machine	any device that assists in performing a task involving forces
macro-decomposers	large organisms that take part in decomposition
magma	hot, liquid rock found deep underground
magnet	piece of metal that attracts another piece of metal with a magnetic force
magnetic field	region where a magnetic force acts on a magnetic material
magnetic field lines	lines drawn to show the direction and strength of a magnetic field
magnetic material	any material that can be attracted by a magnet
magnetic pole	point in a magnet where its magnetic force is most concentrated; every magnet has two poles
males	individuals that make male sex cells
malnutrition	where a person is eating too much or too little of some types of food and grows ill

marble	metamorphic rock formed when limestone is subjected to high heat and pressure
Marchantiophytes	Phylum of liverworts, in the plant Kingdom
mass	amount of matter in an object, measured in kilograms (kg)
matter	general name for the 'stuff' from which all substances are made
medium	any material through which sound or light passes
melting point	temperature at which a solid becomes a liquid
melts	a solid becoming a liquid at a particular temperature, its melting point
membrane	outer barrier between a cell and its surroundings
memory cells	specialised cells developed by the body to 'remember' antigens on a bacterium or virus, so people become immune to a disease they have had once
menstrual cycle	monthly cycle of egg production in women
menstruation	monthly process in which the uterus lining is lost if a woman is not pregnant
meristems	growth regions in a plant
metabolic pathway	many different metabolic reactions joined together in order, so the products of one reaction are used as reactants in the next
metabolic reactions	many different reactions in living things that enable living things to grow, reproduce, maintain organs and respond to their environment
metabolism	processes in living things that involve the breaking down of substances to release energy or the making of new substances; collective name for metabolic reactions
metals	materials that conduct electricity and heat well, and which are often shiny and hard
metamorphic rock	rock produced when other rocks change structure due to high temperature and pressure
micro-decomposers	small organisms that take part in decomposition
migrating	travelling long distances each year to avoid harsh winter conditions
minerals (1)	non-living substances used by plants and animals to live and grow, e.g. iron
minerals (2)	naturally occurring substances with a crystal structure that make up rocks
minor planets	objects in orbit around the Sun, too small to be classed as planets
mirror image	image seen in a mirror, which looks reversed
mitosis	process where cells divide
mixture	different substances combined physically but not chemically, which can be separated
molecules	particles made up of two or more atoms joined together by chemical bonds
moment	a measure of the turning effect of a force; moment = force × distance of force from pivot, measured in newton metre (N m)
monomers	molecules that can be joined together in long chains as building blocks for polymers, e.g. nylon, plastics
MRSA	methicillin-resistant *Staphyloccus aureus*, a species of bacterium that has evolved so it cannot be killed by antibiotics
mucus	sticky substance in some parts of the body, e.g. the nose, which traps viruses and bacteria
multicells	living things made of many cells, for example an oak tree
muscles	body tissue that can contract; muscles enable animals to move

mutations	changes in the genes of a living thing
natural selection	process by which individuals more suited to their environment reproduce more successfully and dominate a species
nature reserves	areas of habitat managed by people to help a wide variety of living things to survive
negative charge	one type of electric charge; the opposite of positive charge
nerve impulses	electrical signals that pass from sense organs to the brain, and from the brain to muscles and organs
neutral (1)	describes a solution with a pH of 7
neutral (2)	uncharged; having no electric charge
neutralise (*noun* neutralisation)	to react an acid and an alkali to produce a neutral solution containing a salt
neutrons	particles found in the nucleus of an atom, with no electric charge
new Moon	when the unlit side of the Moon is turned towards the Earth
newton (N)	the SI unit of force
newton metres (N m)	the unit of moment of a turning force
newtonmeter	device used to measure a force; also called a forcemeter
nitrate	substance formed when nitric acid reacts with a metal
nitric acid	strong acid, formula HNO_3, with molecules containing hydrogen, nitrogen and oxygen atoms
nocturnal	active only at night
noise	unwanted sound
non-metals	elements that do not conduct heat or electricity well, and which are either gases at room temperature or dull, brittle solids
non-porous rocks	rocks that do not let water flow through
non-renewable	anything that cannot be replaced naturally once it is used up
non-renewable resources	any material resources that are not naturally replaced after we have used them, e.g. fossil fuels
normal	line drawn at right angles (90°) to a surface at a point
north pole	one pole of a magnet, which is attracted towards the Earth's North Pole
nuclear energy	energy stored in the nucleus of every atom, released in a nuclear reaction
nuclear fuels	elements from which we can obtain energy using nuclear reactions
nucleus (1)	dense centre of an atom, containing protons and neutrons
nucleus (2)	part of cell containing instructions for growth and life of the cell
oestrogen	hormone that causes uterus lining to thicken
olfaction	act of smelling something
olfactory cells	cells in the nose that can detect chemicals from the air
onion-skin weathering	weathering caused over time by large changes in temperature between daytime and night-time
opaque	describes a material that does not let light pass through
optical telescope	telescope that uses light to see distant objects
orbit	path of an object around another, e.g. a planet round the Sun
Order (*plural* Orders)	level of classification for living things, below Class and above Families

organ	collection of different tissues that work together
organic materials	compounds containing carbon atoms; most organic materials are part of, or made by living things
ovaries	organs in female mammals that make eggs
over-the-counter drugs	medicines that can be bought from a pharmacy to treat illnesses
ovulation	process where ovary releases an egg
ovules	structures in plants that contain eggs
oxidation	reaction where oxygen is added to a substance
oxides	compounds formed from a metal and oxygen only
Pacinian corpuscle	structure in the skin that detects touch
parallel	describes two lines separated by a constant distance so they never cross or grow further apart
partial eclipse	event when part of the Sun's face is blocked from view by the Moon, or part of the Moon is in the Earth's shadow
Particle Theory	description of how particles behave in solids, liquids and gases
particles	small pieces such as atoms or molecules that make up a substance
pascal (Pa)	the unit of pressure, equal to 1 N/m^2
pathogens	living things that cause diseases
patterns	similarities or trends in measurements or properties
penis	organ in male mammals through which urine and semen pass
penumbra	region of partial shadow, during an eclipse
Period	row of the Periodic Table; elements in the same Period show changing trends in their properties
Periodic Table	table that shows all the known elements listed in order of their atomic number
permanent magnet	magnet that keeps its magnetism for a long time
pesticides	chemicals that destroy plants or animals which cause damage to other living things
pH	scale used to measure the strength of acids and alkalis
phagocytosis	process in which white blood cells wrap themselves around bacteria or viruses to kill them
phases	the different shapes of the lit part of the Moon seen from Earth
photosynthesis	process in which plants use light energy, carbon dioxide and water to make glucose
Phylum (*plural* Phyla)	level of classification for living things, below Kingdom and above Class
physical changes	reversible changes in a substance that do not involve chemical bonding, e.g. change from a liquid to a gas
physical state	describes whether a substance is a solid, liquid or gas
physical weathering	weathering caused by physical changes, e.g. freezing and melting of water inside rocks
piston	component that moves inside a cylinder when a fluid presses on it, or when it presses on a fluid
pitch	how high a note sounds to human ears
pivot	the point about which a lever turns
placenta	structure that passes food, waste and gases between mother and foetus
planet	very large, rounded object spinning on its axis and orbiting the Sun

Plants	Kingdom of non-flowering plants like mosses and ferns, and flowering plants like dandelions and daisies
plasma	watery part of the blood
platelets	small particles in the blood, which help in clotting
pollination	movement of pollen from one flower to another
pollutants	chemicals produced by human activities that damage the environment
polymers	materials containing long chains of repeated molecules (monomers); they are easily made and often have many uses, e.g. nylon, plastics
pop test	test for hydrogen, in which a glowing splint makes the gas burn with a squeaky pop
populations	all the individuals of single species found in an area
porous rocks	rocks containing lots of small holes that let water flow through
positive charge	one type of electric charge; the opposite of negative charge
potential difference	another name for voltage
potential energy	energy stored in an object because of its position
precipitate	a solid formed in a solution; a sign that a chemical reaction has taken place
precipitation	process in which rain or snow falls
precipitation reaction	type of reaction between two solutions that produces a solid – a precipitate
predator–prey cycle	natural process in which predator numbers go up and down as prey numbers go up and down
predators	animals that hunt other live animals
predict	to use patterns to work out what will happen in an experiment
prescription drugs	medicines that are controlled for safety, but which a doctor can give people to treat illnesses
preserved	dead living material that is prevented from decomposing
pressure	measure of the concentration of a force on an area, calculated using pressure = $\frac{force}{area}$
pressure gradient	difference in pressure between one place and another, leading to movement of air or liquid
prey	animals that are hunted by predators
primary colours of light	red, green and blue; other colours can be made by combining these
Principle of Conservation of Energy	law that energy is never used up; the total amount stays the same as it changes from one form to another
Principle of Moments	when an object is balanced, clockwise moment = anticlockwise moment
probes	sensors attached to a wire
products	the substances that are present after a chemical reaction has finished
Prokaryotes (Monera)	Kingdom of bacteria and some algae
properties	qualities of a substance that can be measured and compared with other substances, e.g. iron is a magnetic metal but aluminium is a non-magnetic metal
proteins	chemicals made from amino acids that carry out many important life processes
Protoctista	Kingdom of single-celled organisms such as *Amoeba* and seaweeds
protons	particles found in the nucleus of an atom, with a positive electric charge
Pteridophytes	Phylum of ferns, in the plant Kingdom
puberty	stage in human development where sex organs start to function
pyramid of numbers	the total numbers of organisms at each level in a food chain
radiation	energy that comes from a source and that travels through space or a medium; light and sound energy are examples
radio telescope	telescope that detects radio waves coming from distant objects
random sampling	a way of sampling that avoids any choice by the sampler
raw materials	naturally-occurring substances that are used to make new materials
ray	line showing the path followed by light
reactants	the substances that are present at the start of a chemical reaction
reactivity	measure of how easily a substance will take part in reactions
reactivity series	list of substances, often metals, in order of their reactivity
recreational drugs	drugs that are not medicines, which can be used to relax or change people's mood; they can all be dangerous
recycling	taking old manufactured items, breaking them down into chemicals and making new materials from them to prevent waste
red blood cells	blood cells that carry oxygen
redox	reaction where REDuction and OXidation take place at the same time
reduces (*noun* reduction)	where one substance takes oxygen atoms away from another substance
reflected ray	ray of light that has been reflected by a surface, e.g. a mirror
reflects (*noun* reflection)	bounces off a surface; usually describes light or sound
refracted ray	ray of light that changes speed and 'bends' when it passes from one medium into another
refract (*noun* refraction)	change speed and direction, e.g. when light rays pass from one medium into another
relative atomic mass	average mass of an atom of one element
relieve	make someone feel better by easing symptoms of illness, but not curing them
renewable	anything that can be replaced naturally after it has been used
renewable energy	any energy resource that is naturally replaced after we have used it
renewable resources	any material resources that are naturally replaced after we have used them
repel	push away; like electric charges or magnetic poles repel
resistance	the tendency of a component in a circuit to reduce the current in it
resistant	describes an individual that develops the ability to survive something which may kill other individuals, e.g bacteria may become resistant to antibiotics
resources	supplies of raw materials that can be used to make new materials
respiration	process in which living things release energy from food; it can be aerobic or anaerobic
results	observations or measurements made during an experiment
retina	light-sensitive structure at the back of the eye

reuse	to take old manufactured items and use them again; often better than recycling because no energy is needed to break the objects down and make new ones
reversible changes	changes in substances that can be changed back again, e.g. a solid can be melted, and the liquid formed can be made solid again
ribs	the movable bones at the front of the chest cavity
rock cycle	process in which rocks form, break down, re-form into different types and eventually return to the start of the process
rods	cells in the retina that allow humans to see in black and white
roots	parts of a plant below ground
safety goggles	eye protection when doing any experiment
salt (1)	generally, an ionic compound containing metal and non-metal elements, produced by the reaction of an acid with an alkali
salt (2)	the particular compound called sodium chloride is often referred to as 'salt'
sampling	observing and recording part of an ecosystem
Sankey diagram	diagram showing how much energy is changed to different forms in a process
saturated solution	a solution in which no more solid can be dissolved
scab	dried blood clot on the skin
scatter	to reflect light or sound in all directions
seasons	parts of the year with different lengths of day and night, caused by the orbit of the tilted Earth round the Sun
sediment	small pieces of material that are carried by oceans, rivers, glaciers or the wind to settle and form layers
sedimentary rock	rock produced by layers of materials that build up over time, e.g. sandstone
seed	structure produced during plant reproduction; contains an embryo, a food store and a protective coat
selective breeding	humans choosing which individual animals or plants will reproduce
sense organ	organ that converts a stimulus, e.g. light falling on the eye, into nerve impulses to the brain
sensors	devices that detect changes in the environment, e.g. light, humidity, etc.
separate	to get back the original chemicals from a mixture, e.g. by filtering sand from water
sexual intercourse	process where a male and a female join together, so that sperm is passed into the female for fertilisation
sexual reproduction	process where two individuals (one male, one female) join to create new individuals
shadow	area or space where no light falls
shoots	parts of a plant above ground
SI units	the International System of units, used in scientific measurements
sight	sense that allows animals to detect light
skeleton	arrangement of bones and joints to which muscles are attached, and which gives many animals a shape
skin	tough barrier around the body containing many layers of cells and sense organs, which helps prevent infections
slate	metamorphic rock formed when clay is subjected to high pressure; it forms thin layers and is sometimes used on roofs of buildings
smell	sense that allows animals to detect chemicals in the air
smoking	breathing tobacco smoke into the lungs
solar cells	devices used to convert the energy of sunlight into electrical energy
solar eclipse	when the Moon passes in front of the Sun, blocking its light from view at places on Earth
Solar System	the Sun and everything that is held in orbit around the Sun by the pull of its gravity
solenoid	coil of wire; it becomes an electromagnet when a current flows in it
solids	substances in a state with a fixed shape and volume
solubility	measure of how much substance will dissolve in a liquid
soluble	describes a solid substance that will dissolve in a liquid
solute	the solid that dissolves in a liquid to make a solution
solution	liquid containing dissolved solid
solvent	the liquid in which a solid is dissolved to make a solution
sound energy	energy transferred by sound
sound wave	vibrations of a medium as a sound passes through it
sour taste	taste caused by acids
sources of light	things that produces their own light
south pole	one pole of a magnet, which is attracted towards the Earth's South Pole
specialised cells	cells that carry out a particular function
Species (*plural* **Species**)	level of classification for living things, below Genus
spectrum	different colours of light, spread out
speed	the rate at which an object moves: $\text{speed} = \frac{\text{distance}}{\text{time}}$
sperm	male sex cell
stamens	male reproductive structures of flowering plants
star	very hot ball of gas that is held together by gravity and gives off light
static electricity	effects produced by electric charges when they are not moving
stigma	part of carpel on which pollen grains land
stimulus	event that a sense organ can detect, e.g. a sound wave arriving at the ear
stomata	small holes on the underside of leaves that allow gases to move in and out
strata	layers, e.g. of sediment that build up to form sedimentary rocks
sublimes	a solid changing straight to a gas
sulfate	substance formed when sulfuric acid reacts with a metal
sulfuric acid	strong acid, formula H_2SO_4, with molecules containing hydrogen, sulfur and oxygen atoms
surface area (SA)	sum of all the areas of each face of an object, measured in m^2
surface area to volume ratio (SA/V)	an object's total surface area divided by its volume
suspension	solid that will not dissolve but does mix with a liquid, e.g. milk

sustainable development	approach to human life and activities that means enough resources are left for future use
switch	component in an electrical circuit that can open or close to break or complete the circuit
symbol	one- or two-letter code for an element
symptoms	effects of an infection, such as a fever or cough
synovial fluid	liquid in joints that reduces friction between moving bones
synovial joints	joints that contain synovial fluid
synthesise	to make new materials from raw materials
synthetic medicines	medicines made by chemical reactions in factories
syrinx	organ in a bird that produces sounds
system	collection of different organs that work together
tarnish	forming a layer of oxide on the surface of a metal; this can make the shiny metal look dull
taste	sense that allows animals to detect chemicals in food
taste buds	structures on the tongue that can detect chemicals
telescopes	devices used to produce enlarged images of distant objects such as stars and planets
temperature	measure of the hotness of an object
temperature changes	changes in which a substance becomes hotter or colder
terminal	one end of an electrical component, which allows it to be connected to another component as part of a circuit
testes	organs in male mammals that make sperm
testosterone	hormone that causes male sex organs to function
thermal energy	energy stored in a hot object
thermometer	instrument used to measure changes in temperature
thorax	the chest cavity
thought experiment	experiment carried out only in the mind
time	something through which the Doctor travels; difficult to define, but measured in seconds (s)
tissues	collections of cells of the same kind that carry out a particular function
total eclipse	event when the whole of the Sun's face is blocked from view by the Moon, or the whole of the Moon is in the Earth's shadow
touch	sense that allows animals to detect pushes and pulls
transducers	structures inside sense organs that convert a stimulus into an electrical signal
transfer	to move something (e.g. energy) from place to place
translucent	describes a material that lets light pass through, but which scatters the light so that you cannot see through clearly
transparent	describes a material that lets light pass through
transpiration	process in which plants lose water from the surface of the leaves
transported	rock that has been moved by wind, water or ice
triceps	muscle that causes the arm to straighten
turning effect	effect of a force, acting on a lever, causing it to turn
ultrasound	sounds with frequencies that are too high for humans to hear
umbilical cord	tube connecting foetus to placenta
umbra	region of full shadow, during an eclipse

unbalanced forces	two or more forces acting on an object with effects that do not cancel out
unicell	living thing made of only one cell, e.g. an amoeba
Universal indicator	a mixture of different dyes that changes colour depending upon pH
upthrust	upward force on a solid object when it is in a liquid or gas
uterus	organ in female mammals in which a foetus grows
vaccinated	describes someone who has been made immune to a dangerous disease by being injected with a related, but less dangerous disease
vacuole	water-filled 'bubble' inside a plant cell
vacuum	empty space; space from which all matter has been removed
vagina	organ in female mammals into which the penis is inserted during sexual intercourse, and through which a baby passes during birth
valves	structures that allow blood to move in only one direction
vaporises	a liquid changing into a gas
variation	range of different types of individuals within a species
veins	blood vessels that carry blood from the body back to the heart
vibration	regular back-and-forth movement
villi	small folds inside the gut that help food to be digested
virtual image	image that appears to be at a point, even though no light comes from that point
viruses	organisms, smaller than bacteria, which reproduce inside cells and cause diseases
vocal folds	parts of the larynx that vibrate to produce sounds; sometimes known as the vocal cords
volt (V)	the unit of electrical voltage or potential difference
voltage	a measure of the energy a cell or battery gives to electric charges to move them round a circuit; also called potential difference and measured in volts (V)
voltmeter	instrument used for measuring electrical voltage
volume	amount of space taken up by an object, measured in m^3, cm^3, litres
waggle dance	pattern followed by honeybees to communicate where flowers with nectar can be found
water cycle	process of many stages in which water moves around the environment; stages include evaporation, condensation, precipitation and transpiration
weather	conditions in the atmosphere such as rainfall, temperature and sunshine in one place at one time; different from climate
weathering	process in which rocks are worn away
weigh	to measure an object's mass, often by using a balance
weight	the pull of gravity on an object; a force, measured in newtons (N)
Welwitschia	very unusual plant that grows up to 2 m long with two huge leaves, and can live for 2000 years
white blood cells	blood cells that protect us against disease
yeast	fungus needed for fermentation
zygote	cell formed when a male sex cell and a female sex cell join together

Useful data

Reactions

Photosynthesis	carbon dioxide + water $\xrightarrow[\text{light energy}]{\text{chlorophyll}}$ glucose + oxygen
Aerobic respiration	glucose + oxygen $\rightarrow$ carbon dioxide + water + energy
Neutralisation	acid + alkali $\rightarrow$ salt + water
Burning of fuels	fossil fuel + oxygen $\rightarrow$ carbon dioxide + water + energy released

Formulas

Surface area to volume ratio	$\dfrac{SA}{V}$
Speed	speed (m/s) = $\dfrac{\text{distance travelled (m)}}{\text{time taken (s)}}$
Force	force is measured in newtons (N)
Weight	on the Earth's surface: weight (N) = 10 × mass (kg)
Moment	moment (Nm) = force (N) × distance from pivot (m)
Density	density (kg/m³) = $\dfrac{\text{mass (kg)}}{\text{volume (m}^3\text{)}}$
Pressure	pressure (Pa) = $\dfrac{\text{force (N)}}{\text{area (m}^2\text{)}}$

Diagrams and quantities

Series circuit   Parallel circuit

Speed of sound in air	330 m/s
Speed of light in space	300 000 000 m/s

Principles and Laws

Moments	for a balanced lever: clockwise moment = anticlockwise moment
Conservation of energy	total energy before = total energy after
Conservation of mass	total mass before = total mass after
Magnets	like poles repel, unlike poles attract
Static electricity	like charges repel, unlike charges attract
Reflection	angle of incidence = angle of reflection
Refraction	Light bends *towards* the normal as it slows down (e.g. when moving from air to glass) Light bends *away from* the normal as it speeds up (e.g. when moving from glass to air)

Characteristics of life in the five Kingdoms of living things

	Plants	Animals	Fungi	Protoctista	Prokaryotes (bacteria)
Cells (mainly Biology Unit 1)	basic cell structure with a wall; some have chloroplasts and a large vacuole; a few different types	basic cell structure (with no wall); many different types and specialised cells	basic cell structure with addition of a wall; only a few different types	basic cell structure with a wall; some have chloroplasts; a few different types	very different cells from the other four Kingdoms; capsule containing DNA with flagellum and pili outside
Life processes					
Nutrition (mainly Biology Unit 6)	make their own food from water and carbon dioxide, and use light energy	eat plants and other animals	generally get food from dead animals and plants, but some get it from living things	some make their own food like plants, some feed like animals	some make their own food like plants, some feed like animals and fungi
Respiration (mainly Biology Unit 7)	mostly use oxygen to produce energy, with water and carbon dioxide as wastes; some parts can respire without oxygen, producing alcohol, carbon dioxide and less energy	mostly use oxygen to produce energy, with water and carbon dioxide as wastes; some parts can respire without oxygen, producing lactic acid, carbon dioxide and less energy	mostly use oxygen to produce energy, with water and carbon dioxide as wastes; some parts can respire without oxygen, producing alcohol, carbon dioxide and less energy	mostly use oxygen to produce energy, with water and carbon dioxide as wastes; some respire without oxygen, producing alcohol, carbon dioxide and less energy
Excretion (mainly Biology Units 6 and 7)	pass wastes into soil and air, sometimes into leaves that fall – this causes the autumn colours in tree leaves	small water-living animals pass wastes directly into surrounding water; bigger animals and those that live on land have special organs to remove waste before it is excreted (e.g. kidney in mammals)	pass wastes into soil and air	pass wastes into soil and air	pass wastes into soil (or whatever they are growing on) and air
Movement (mainly Biology Unit 9)	make small movements inside cells; move whole organism by growing; some have fast movements (e.g. the sensitive plant)	make small movements inside cells; many have some form of skeleton, either outside or inside the body, which they can pull on with muscles to cause movement	make small movements inside cells; some can creep across a surface	make small movements inside cells; various kinds of swimming and creeping movements	make small movements inside cells; some cannot move and some swim in various ways
Reproduction (mainly Biology Unit 10)	most reproduce sexually; in flowering plants the flower is the sex organ; some reproduce asexually	most reproduce sexually but some reproduce asexually	most reproduce sexually but some reproduce asexually	most reproduce sexually but some reproduce asexually	most reproduce asexually, but some use a primitive form of sexual reproduction
Growth (mainly Biology Unit 11)	increase number and size of cells	increase number of cells	increase number and size of cells	each cell increases in size; numbers of cells in a group increase	each cell increases in size; numbers of cells in a group increase
Sensitivity (mainly Biology Unit 12)	can sense light, gravity, water, and can grow toward or away from them; some can sense touch and heat, and respond quickly	most can sense light, sound, chemicals (taste and smell), touch and respond in many ways, including movement	have basic senses like plants	most can sense light, sound, chemicals (taste and smell), and respond in many ways, including movement	varied, from very basic to animal-like responses

Periodic Table

Group — 1, 2, TRANSITION METALS (3, 4, 5, 6, 7, 8, 9, 10, 11, 12), 3, 4, 5, 6, 7, 0

Period — 1–7

metals ← → non-metals

Period	Element data
1	**H** Hydrogen 1, 1.00794 — **He** Helium 2, 4.0026
2	**Li** Lithium 3, 6.941 — **Be** Beryllium 4, 9.0122 — **B** Boron 5, 10.811 — **C** Carbon 6, 12.011 — **N** Nitrogen 7, 14.0067 — **O** Oxygen 8, 15.9994 — **F** Fluorine 9, 18.9984 — **Ne** Neon 10, 20.183
3	**Na** Sodium 11, 22.9898 — **Mg** Magnesium 12, 24.305 — **Al** Aluminium 13, 26.9815 — **Si** Silicon 14, 28.086 — **P** Phosphorus 15, 30.9738 — **S** Sulfur 16, 32.066 — **Cl** Chlorine 17, 35.453 — **Ar** Argon 18, 39.948
4	**K** Potassium 19, 39.098 — **Ca** Calcium 20, 40.08 — **Sc** Scandium 21, 44.956 — **Ti** Titanium 22, 47.87 — **V** Vanadium 23, 50.942 — **Cr** Chromium 24, 51.996 — **Mn** Manganese 25, 54.9380 — **Fe** Iron 26, 55.845 — **Co** Cobalt 27, 58.9332 — **Ni** Nickel 28, 58.69 — **Cu** Copper 29, 63.546 — **Zn** Zinc 30, 65.39 — **Ga** Gallium 31, 69.72 — **Ge** Germanium 32, 72.61 — **As** Arsenic 33, 74.9216 — **Se** Selenium 34, 78.96 — **Br** Bromine 35, 79.904 — **Kr** Krypton 36, 83.80
5	**Rb** Rubidium 37, 85.47 — **Sr** Strontium 38, 87.62 — **Y** Yttrium 39, 88.906 — **Zr** Zirconium 40, 91.22 — **Nb** Niobium 41, 92.906 — **Mo** Molybdenum 42, 95.94 — **Tc** Technetium 43, (98) — **Ru** Ruthenium 44, 101.07 — **Rh** Rhodium 45, 102.905 — **Pd** Palladium 46, 106.4 — **Ag** Silver 47, 107.868 — **Cd** Cadmium 48, 112.41 — **In** Indium 49, 114.82 — **Sn** Tin 50, 118.71 — **Sb** Antimony 51, 121.76 — **Te** Tellurium 52, 127.60 — **I** Iodine 53, 126.9045 — **Xe** Xenon 54, 131.29
6	**Cs** Caesium 55, 132.905 — **Ba** Barium 56, 137.33 — **Hf** Hafnium 72, 178.49 — **Ta** Tantalum 73, 180.948 — **W** Tungsten 74, 183.84 — **Re** Rhenium 75, 186.2 — **Os** Osmium 76, 190.2 — **Ir** Iridium 77, 192.2 — **Pt** Platinum 78, 195.08 — **Au** Gold 79, 196.967 — **Hg** Mercury 80, 200.59 — **Tl** Thallium 81, 204.38 — **Pb** Lead 82, 207.2 — **Bi** Bismuth 83, 208.98 — **Po** Polonium 84, (210) — **At** Astatine 85, (210) — **Rn** Radon 86, (222)
7	**Fr** Francium 87, (223) — **Ra** Radium 88, (226) — **Rf** Rutherfordium 104, (261) — **Db** Dubnium 105, (262) — **Sg** Seaborgium 106, (266) — **Bh** Bohrium 107, (264) — **Hs** Hassium 108, (265) — **Mt** Meitnerium 109, (268) — **Ds** Darmstadtium 110, (281) — **Rg** Roentgenium 111, (280) — **Cn** Copernicium 112, (280) — **Uut** Ununtrium 113, (284) — **Fl** Flerovium 114, (289) — **Uup** Ununpentium 115, (288) — **Lv** Livermorium 116, (292) — **Uus** Ununseptium 117, (294) — **Uuo** Ununoctium 118, (294)

Lanthanides

La Lanthanum 57, 138.91 — **Ce** Cerium 58, 140.12 — **Pr** Praseodymium 59, 140.908 — **Nd** Neodymium 60, 144.24 — **Pm** Promethium 61, (145) — **Sm** Samarium 62, 150.36 — **Eu** Europium 63, 151.96 — **Gd** Gadolinium 64, 157.25 — **Tb** Terbium 65, 158.925 — **Dy** Dysprosium 66, 162.50 — **Ho** Holmium 67, 164.930 — **Er** Erbium 68, 167.26 — **Tm** Thulium 69, 168.934 — **Yb** Ytterbium 70, 173.04 — **Lu** Lutetium 71, 174.97

Actinides

Ac Actinium 89, (227) — **Th** Thorium 90, 232.038 — **Pa** Protactinium 91, 231.036 — **U** Uranium 92, 238.03 — **Np** Neptunium 93, (237) — **Pu** Plutonium 94, (244) — **Am** Americium 95, (243) — **Cm** Curium 96, (247) — **Bk** Berkelium 97, (247) — **Cf** Californium 98, (251) — **Es** Einsteinium 99, (252) — **Fm** Fermium 100, (257) — **Md** Mendelevium 101, (258) — **No** Nobelium 102, (259) — **Lr** Lawrencium 103, (262)